Praise for *The Corbyn Effect*

'It appears likely that Jeremy Corbyn will one day inhabit 10 Downing Street. More than a destination however, *The Corbyn Effect* takes that as a starting point. This is a must-read for understanding not only how we got here, but where we are going. Read it to inform yourself about a historical moment whose consequences will be felt for a lifetime.'

— **Aaron Bastani, Co-Founder of Novara Media**

'Far from being a ship in the night, as most political commentators and actors on the left and right dismissed him, Jeremy Corbyn is here to stay. He was a revelation in the 2017 general election campaign and did what no Labour leader has succeeded in doing since 1979, namely undermined the dominance of neoliberalism. Understanding Corbyn, his significance and his potential, is a key task. This book will surely make an important contribution.'

— **Martin Jacques, Former Editor *Marxism Today***

'The Corbyn phenomenon is the biggest turnaround for the left in Europe in decades – nothing short of a post-Blairite resurrection. Understanding it, learning from it, completing it and repeating it is vital. *The Corbyn Effect* rises to the challenge.'

— **Jon Lansman, Chair of Momentum**

'Love or loathe Jeremy Corbyn, Labour is never going back to a pre-Corbyn era, so we'd better understand why Pasokification happened within and not without Labour, and what it means for the future of the left – for good and bad. *The Corbyn Effect* is a brilliant collection of essays that helps us think through the possibilities of the revolution that is sweeping th͏   ͏.abour and possibly the country.'

Compass

'Jeremy Corbyn has re-packaged socialism into something progressive and essential, something that isn't archaic as we've been told it is for so long. Striving for justice and fairness isn't a sign of our weakness but the sign of our great strength. That's the Corbyn effect and this book explains why.'

– Maxine Peake

'Jeremy Corbyn's Labour has breathed life into the fading hopes of many party members and hordes of others who stayed outside a timid, neoliberal machine, offering little hope and even fewer dreams. Party members have again found their place in a dynamic, revitalised democratic party, which they have done so much to shape and place on the verge of power. This book tells us that story.'

– Heather Wakefield, Head of Local Government, Police and Justice, UNISON

The Corbyn Effect

For Edgar, Moulsecoomb Get out the Vote, 8 June 2017

The Corbyn Effect

Edited by Mark Perryman

Lawrence & Wishart
London 2017

Lawrence and Wishart Limited
Central Books Building
Freshwater Road
Chadwell Heath
RM8 1RX

ISBN 9781612064687

British Library Cataloguing in Publication Data.
A catalogue record for this book is available from the British Library

Typesetting: e-type
Cover design: Matter / matter@pobox.com
Front cover photograph copyright © Jason Bye
Back cover photograph copyright © Geoff Dexter

Contents

Preparing for Power

Afterwords

What is the Corbyn effect?

Paul Mason

The period since the 2017 general election has proved the power and the potential of the Corbyn effect. Suddenly, we have a Labour Party that could genuinely represent us in an entirely new phase of politics and economics.

The cause of Labour's sudden radicalisation is clear. Neoliberalism no longer works. It has suppressed wages for decades, forced working poor families to depend on credit, edged an entire generation of young workers out of the property market and saddled them with unpayable debts.

If the original promise of neoliberalism was 'like this but forever', after 2008 it became 'like this forever, only worse'.

It took several years and a few wrong turns for the discontent, triggered by the 2008 banking crisis and subsequent austerity, to find its way into the Labour Party. How it did so, and the consequences of this, are outlined in the contributions to this book.

What matters now is understanding the scale of the challenge that Corbynism poses for the political and social elite that runs Britain. And this book seeks to understand exactly that. I am not talking about the factory owners, nor the millions of small business owners, nor even the managers at major firms. The British elite is dangerously divorced from all of them: it manages other people's money and enforces the will of global capital onto the UK population.

The challenge arises from the fact that, in a globalised world, where the exploitation of ordinary people takes place through the consumer market, the internet and the credit system, we cannot go backwards. There is no return to a world where we work for the same employer all of our lives, where our townscapes remain familiar and predictable, where our social networks are not constantly changing.

We have to go forward – and that means executing a set of changes just as radical and, in their own way, just as ruthless as the ones Thatcher unleashed after 1979.

In the long term, that means, as some of the authors writing in *The Corbyn Effect* suggest, a focus on post-market forms of economics: introducing universal basic income and seizing collective ownership of information – such as that generated by the healthcare system or the smart city.

But in the short term, it means eroding the economic power of the neoliberal elite, and the stranglehold over democratic institutions that it has created.

As the process of change unfolds, everybody in this project needs to understand what the stakes are: the need to combine sophisticated politics in parliament, national assemblies, mayorships and local councils with an equally sophisticated take on where social movements fit in.

The kit of parts assembled by Corbyn's leadership, even amid months of sabotage and non-compliance by Labour MPs, is a valid starting point when it comes to policy.

The critical commitment will be to borrow £250 billion in order to fund a national investment bank, with regional branches. This plan – never before contemplated in a country like the UK – would give a very diverse set of people an essential stake in the positive outcome of the project.

Towns would be financed to become communities again, instead of the deserted edge-places that neoliberalism created. Major infrastructure projects, delayed or cancelled by the cash-strapped Tories, could be implemented immediately – bringing jobs, training, green energy and hi-tech industries to all parts of the UK. Even the City would have something to gain – with the long-term money wrapped up in pension and investment funds attracted by the implicit government guarantee that a national investment plan involves.

With the National Investment Bank as the strategic policy, the tough measures Labour needs to take – taxing the rich and large corporations to the tune of £40-50 billion to reverse public service cuts and provide free university tuition – might become palatable enough to the 0.1 per cent that their urge towards sabotage, tax evasion and capital flight might be balanced by a deeper urge to take part in a massively popular national renewal.

Or they might not.

If not, we can write the script easily enough: in the run up to the next election, a segment of the Parliamentary Labour Party would defect, forming a new party, whose aim is the sabotage of Labour and the creation of a centrist power-broker group to create, once again, a Tory-Liberal coalition.

If the price for that coalition is to reduce austerity and delay or cancel Brexit, do not be surprised. Austerity and Brexit were never projects pursued for their own sake, but to enhance the power of the rich over the poor in Britain.

In contrast, we can be certain that if Jeremy Corbyn becomes prime minister, the power of the rich over the poor will not be enhanced.

And the stakes are not just economic. If Corbyn becomes prime minister, even if Britain were to maintain all its essential geopolitical relationships – with Israel, Saudi Arabia, NATO, China and the Hindu nationalist government in Delhi – all the secret deals could become known. And of course, this will change those relationships, or bring them under scrutiny and democratic control.

So it is not just the British 0.1 per cent we have to fear resorting to political and economic sabotage in the face of a Labour victory, but others too.

If the neoliberal wing of Labour is the last line of defence for the current system, it also has other lines of defence: the judiciary, the intelligence services and the military. In a democracy signed up to global human rights treaties, and with a supreme court, the checks on anti-democratic sabotage by rogue elements are greater. But it is still wise to expect disruption.

Market panic was what forced the last attempt by a major country to defy neoliberalism to end: François Mitterrand was in 1983 forced to choose between social justice and the European exchange rate mechanism. By the time Greece attempted its break from neoliberal austerity in 2015, it was so completely at the mercy of markets, and the institutions of the IMF and ECB, that resistance became impossible. In the three decades that separate the French and Greek debacles, the extra-parliamentary power of the elite has become far more focused on markets than what the left used to fear: 'rogue' elements in the civil service, security service or the judiciary.

In the face of this there is one lesson we should learn above all others from Syriza in Greece – and it is not a palatable one for politicians like Corbyn, whose specialist subject has been opposition to militarism and imperialism. If we are going to dismantle the economic power of the elite, we cannot simultaneously try to disrupt their institutional, diplomatic and geostrategic certainties. In fact, the Greek experience shows that – in order to effect strategic economic change – the left has to align itself with parts of the 'national story' and take parts of that apparatus with it.

In a country like Greece, where the left led the defeat of fascism, that alignment is easier than in a country like the UK, whose story has become fragmented into separate nationalisms, and where the old left operated a knee-jerk anti-imperialism. That makes it even more important for Labour to seek allies on the basis of economic change combined with the promise of relative geo-strategic stability.

Corbynism is the promise of a Nordic welfare state in a neoliberal economy. That's why it feels revolutionary to many people: because all the structures and norms of the economy are geared towards recreating selfish, nationalist, acquisitive attitudes.

As the neoliberal story has fallen apart, we are left with a system that can no longer justify itself on principle: its justification resides only in force and routine. So a movement that has concentrated on winning arguments – from the university to the council estate – has to become expert at executing solutions. It needs to phase those solutions, to mould them around a global finance and trade system that will be initially hostile, and to build an international alliance of social democrats, radical leftists and greens to extend and defend the first move against neoliberalism, if it is taken in the UK.

This means, alongside opposing the privatisation, estate clearances and wage cuts of the end of Toryism, we have to engage in a rapid offensive to convince key segments of what is now called 'centrism' that the Labour project can deliver some of what they also want. We have to find channels through which the energies of centrism, liberalism and the left wing of the ruling elite can flow alongside our own energies.

That means, as long as there is a mandate for Brexit, we need to execute it in a constructive, multilateral way, seeking maximum continuity and engagement with the EU. It also means, should Brexit's popular mandate evaporate, we need to be prepared to see the decision reversed.

These are daunting tasks for any left social democratic party, let alone one faced with the internal resistance Corbyn faces.

But the fact remains: one Thursday, in the next two to five years, there will be an election, the outcome of which could be the end of neoliberalism in Britain by the following Friday morning.

Understanding what we will do on that Friday, and all the tortuous days that follow, is the task of the left and our fellow progressives in Britain today.

INTRODUCTION

The Corbyn Effect

As a collection, *The Corbyn Effect* ranges far, wide and deep to provide an understanding of Corbynism, an explanation of how it has been 'framed', a critical examination of its limitations and a hopeful forecast of its potential. The book is not an account of Jeremy Corbyn's rise to become leader of the Labour Party, this is best provided by *The Candidate: Jeremy Corbyn's Improbable Path to Power* by Alex Nunns. Nor is the collection written according to a single unified viewpoint; the best interpretation of this kind, from the left of Corbynism, is provided by Richard Seymour's *Corbyn: The Strange Rebirth of Radical Politics*. Rather, this book combines a thematic approach with a variety of viewpoints, which all have varying degrees of agreement and disagreement with Corbynism.

Mark Perryman's keynote essay, *The Great Moving Left Show*, traces the emergence of Corbynism via Labour's adoption of one single model of modernisation, the Blairist-Brownite version. Perryman counters this by uncovering alternative, radical models of left modernity, which now have the potential to re-emerge as the Corbyn moment continues to take shape.

The Corbyn Effect seeks to understand Corbynism in the context of the changing terrain of politics, economics and society characterised by some as 'New Times'. Jeremy Gilbert powerfully illustrates this in his opening chapter to the book. A companion piece by Andrew Gamble relates such an analysis to the specificities of the 2017 general election, and in particular the rise and fall of Theresa May.

Jeremy Corbyn's election and re-election as Labour leader against all apparent odds was largely due to changes in the party's previously arcane method of voting in these elections. One member one vote, combined with an audacious registered supporters' scheme, threatens to transform Labour's organisational and campaigning culture. Jessica Garland puts this dramatic change in the context of what being in the Labour Party now means for its hundreds of thousands of new members.

Scotland was a key battleground for the 2017 general election, and it will most certainly be just as important for the next, whenever it is called. Gerry Hassan accounts for 2017's dents in support for the SNP and the cause of independence, while describing the emergence of a Caledonian version of Corbynism that before the election barely seemed to exist.

No recent party leader has had to suffer the kind of media-trashing *The Sun* and the *Daily Mail* have dished out against Jeremy Corbyn, ever since his election as Labour leader, which became most sharp of all as the 8 June polling day approached. Yet as the votes were counted and the story of Labour's 'blue murder' was replaced by a historic shift in the party's share of the vote and new seats won, the idea that it is 'the media wot wins it' for the right took a knocking, alongside the more simplistic critiques of inevitable 'mainstream media' bias. Des Freedman's chapter combines a theory of how the 'framing' of Jeremy Corbyn was constructed via the press and TV, with a strategy to challenge media power from the left.

One of the main themes of any coverage of Corbyn's Labour has of course been the vivid reality of a party divided. How is such a division explained? Hilary Wainwright gets behind the parliamentarianism of most theories on offer, to revisit the meaning of 'Labourism' as an obstacle to Labour's radical potential. She suggests how Corbyn has become the vehicle for such a dramatic change in direction: to the left. Corbyn as a serial backbench rebel since the 1980s of course has long personified this, but this has always been from the margins; he has never before had anything remotely near this level of influence within Labour. It is that long and principled journey which provides Jeremy Corbyn with what Eliane Glaser in her chapter calls 'authenticity'. It is this that has helped spark unprecedented support for Labour amongst young people. One of the most surprising events in the 2017 campaign was the way #Grime4Corbyn took off, but Monique Charles cautions readers not to be so surprised. Corbyn's youthful, and musical, support originates in the alienation of young people from pre-Corbyn politicians' conduct of themselves. For many, this connects to a musical culture, grime, which is embedded in the values of the collective, and is quite different to the celebrity-driven individualism with which popular music is commonly associated.

The combined vote share of Labour, the SNP, Plaid Cymru, the Greens and Lib-Dems would amount to a rainbow coalition of a government rather than the Tory-DUP coalition of chaos. Of course, our anything-but-proportional electoral system prevented this outcome. Now, Labour's eyes are on the sixty-six target seats that if won, along with holding the nineteen key defences, would deliver a majority Labour government the next time round. Sue Goss urges that any such ambition mustn't be allowed to crowd out pluralism and co-operation amongst progressives who share so much in common. In practical terms, Labour still needs the votes from supporters of these other parties to win, and save, the required numbers of seats. And politically, it needs to open out to a radicalism that is broader than what party membership card we have, or don't have. 2017 was a snap general election, Labour fought a hugely effective, if rather last-minute, campaign on a manifesto that clearly caught the popular imagination. But politics doesn't stand still, there are fundamental socio-economic and cultural changes underway that, as Phil Burton-Cartledge's argument in his chapter goes, impact on a class politics. That class politics is key to – but doesn't leave unchanged – any Labour politics worth its name. The party is only just catching up with the meaning of this, and needs to construct a politics not simply of the present but for the future too.

Migration remains central to many of these changes, and is an issue that Labour continues to have problems getting to grips with, veering from reaction to rhetoric and nothing very much in between. Talking about migration has become an unseemly 'race to the bottom', as Maya Goodfellow puts it in her chapter, from which Corbyn's Labour has not been immune. To avoid the ugly consequences of such a descent, Corbynism itself remains in urgent need of change on race and migration. Any failure to develop a wider coalition of support, to engage with changing class relations, to cherish a multiple society as a product of modern migration, would contribute to the defeat of any future Corbyn Labour government. Indeed, the portents of a radical left government under siege and in retreat are obvious enough in Syriza's Greece. Marina Prentoulis urges Labour to learn these Greek lessons, not to write off either all that Syriza, in the most difficult of conditions, has achieved, nor to erase Labour's possibilities to make a difference either. Rather we should learn from Greece to help us ensure that the worst possible outcomes are avoided.

Our best hope remains, of course, that a Corbyn-led Labour victory leads to a Labour government of the sort we could only ever dream of before. Key to this, will be reversing inequality by abandoning the myth of meritocracy which limits thinking and policy from the liberal wing of British conservatism across to Labour's centre-right. Jo Littler provides ideas on how to dismantle the myth and replace it with policies for social change.

James Doran originated the thesis of 'pasokification' to describe a sorry outcome for Labour if it continued with a politics that failed to oppose austerity and break with the cross-party neoliberal consensus. It is a fate that has afflicted social-democratic parties across Europe and the Democrats in the US too. Here, Doran describes how Corbyn has led Labour to buck that trend of dismal decline and what it will take to continue doing so.

'Oh Jeremy Corbyn' became the unofficial soundtrack of a post-election summer, testament to Corbyn's huge personal popularity. James Kellam details the perils and the potential of such a moment, and suggests what is needed to translate this into an enduring popular left politics and support. But none of this will amount to very much unless Labour can win, rather than come a good second. Paula Surridge's concluding chapter helps focus us on this salient fact, with her detailed analysis of the demographics and voter attitudes in Labour's sixty-six target seats. This is the electoral terrain for the next five years, hopefully for a shorter period if another early general election is called or forced to be called, on which the 'Corbyn effect' has the potential to amount to something substantial.

And as afterwords, in this volume there are two useful tools to aid the process of preparing for power. Firstly, there is a seat-by-seat profile of Labour's target seats and key defences with the 2017 general election results, and contact details for local groups, to help readers to get involved with Labour's 'permanent election' campaigning. Secondly, for those inspired to find out more about the various ideas and critiques raised in this book, there is a further reading list with other resources including campaigns, websites, blogs and twitter feeds.

'Books are weapons' in the battle of ideas, and this one aims to challenge the assumption – prevalent over the last couple of years – that daring to dream has no place in politics.

The Great Moving Left Show

Mark Perryman

Whether it loses 30, 50 or 70 seats, the Labour Party is heading for a shattering defeat under Jeremy Corbyn.

Jason Cowley, *New Statesman*[1]

We're all allowed to get things wrong. And there were many on the left who weren't feeling particularly chippy in the week before polling day in June 2017 when Cowley's confidently dire prediction was published. Many of us had allowed pessimism of the intellect to overwhelm optimism of the will as the election approached. But perhaps a decent period of reflection is now in order on the part of the left-leaning commentariat that so misunderstood and so misrepresented the Corbyn effect for such a long time.

For the best part of two years – in fact until the exit poll at 10pm on election night in 2017 – it has been hard to endure being told, day in day out, by writers I otherwise respect (and not just in the *Statesman*), that my support for Corbyn meant I'd become delusional, had signed up to a personality cult rather joined a political movement, had been manipulated by entryists, colluded with anti-Semites, and, of course, had backed the losing side.[2] With all that being thrown at us, even the most convinced Corbyn supporter was likely to sometimes feel doubts.

This inability to recognise the change that Corbyn represented is less surprising, however, when considered alongside the long history of failure on the left since the advent of Thatcherism in 1979. For, although New Labour seemed to represent a winning streak after 1997, their success was only achieved through the abandonment of many cherished tenets of the left. The common sense view for the last thirty years and more has been that anything representing socialist politics has had no chance of success. The overturning of this deep pessimism is therefore one of Jeremy Corbyn's greatest successes.

The party's turn to the right stopped delivering Labour election victories long ago: the Labour Party had been in crisis for a considerable time before Corbyn won the leadership election. Writing in 2015, John Harris combined a healthy scepticism for what Corbyn might be able to achieve with an acute sense of the depth of the crisis he had inherited. Here he describes the context of Corbyn's stunning win in the 2015 Labour leadership election:

> Centre-left politics all over Europe remain locked in deep crisis, sidelined by the dominance of the centre-right, and further unsettled by the rise of new populist and nationalist parties from both ends of the political spectrum. In the delirium of Corbynmania and the arrival of tens of thousands of new members, the cold reality of Labour's predicament has been somewhat forgotten. At the last election (2015), it won its second-lowest share of the vote since 1983.[3]

This was the wreckage from which Corbyn was expected to climb with the party in tow. Nobody, including many committed supporters, believed he could achieve that if the Tories set the trap of an early general election. What in those circumstances could possibly go right?

And, lest we forget, despite the shock and awe, Labour didn't actually win a majority in the 2017 election, and under the UK's first-past-the-post electoral system that is pretty much all that matters. It's just that Corbyn did so much better than almost everybody expected: he didn't do enough to change that losing streak, but he got Labour close and might yet turn defeat into victory.

The fate that was staring the Labour Party in the face before the election of Corbyn to the leadership – along with many other European social-democratic parties – was 'Pasokification', a process named after the virtual elimination of Pasok in Greece.[4] Pasok, once a successful social democratic party, lost nearly all its support when it signed up to neoliberal policies and ceased to represent the people who had once elected it. It was effectively replaced by Syriza, a party of the left. Corbyn has been able to partly avert this prospect by shifting the Labour Party back towards some of its traditional positions. The party's manifesto, welcomed by previous regular Corbyn critic Polly

Toynbee as 'a cornucopia of delights', created a platform for the left populism that Corbyn had promised to deliver.[5]

The manifesto was notable in that it represented the first clear break from New Labour's neoliberal legacy. When it was published, a *Guardian* leader broadly welcomed it: 'its achievement is to expand the limits of the thinkable in British politics' (though it reserved judgement on its likely effectiveness in terms of Labour's appeal, declaring that it was rooted in 'Mr Corbyn's preference for energising his own support rather than persuading those outside it').[6] The reservation wasn't entirely misplaced, as every day that we endure under a minority Tory government should convince us, but the spectacular expansion of Labour's previous base of support is enough to suggest that the direction of travel mapped out – 'For the many not the few' – is decisively the correct one.

Michael Rustin also situated Corbynism's potential as a break, though somewhat more unreservedly:

> Jeremy Corbyn's election campaign, and its outcome, is without doubt the most positive development that has taken place in British politics for more than twenty-five years – since Tony Blair became leader of the Labour Party. The reason for this is that it is the first substantial challenge to neoliberalism from Labour in all those years. Corbyn's campaign has now demonstrated that a politics based on the rejection of neoliberalism – the contemporary version of 'full capitalism' – and the development of an alternative to it – is capable of success.[7]

This is borne out by my experience in the election campaign. Peter Kyle, one of the local MPs for whom I campaigned in Hove and Portslade, was defending a slender 1274 vote majority over the Tories, and we thought he was doomed. But if Labour was to survive 2017, this seat was one of the ones we needed to save. Kyle had been quoted in the eve-of-election *New Statesman* piece predicting Labour's worst defeat ever, and, perhaps minded not to rock the boat too much at this delicate time, he had chosen his words carefully: 'If we aspire to govern, we should listen to what the electorate is about to say on 8 June; we should listen to what will be the unvarnished truth'.[8] In the early hours of 9 June the unvarnished truth was that Peter Kyle's seat had switched from being a Labour marginal to one with a whopping 18,757 Labour majority. Kyle's election publicity had been very much focused on his own performance as an MP rather than Labour's leader. Jeremy Corbyn didn't get a look-in. And it was a good and hard-fought local campaign. But those 18,000-plus extra votes were not won by local factors: the truth is that Corbyn as leader, with a manifesto that sought to break with an austerity-driven neoliberal consensus, had reached voters in a way in which no individual candidate, however good, could emulate. This was the Corbyn effect many of us had been waiting for.

MAKING THE SPACE FOR A NEW POLITICS

The crucial difference in the 2015 leadership election, which enabled all these subsequent changes to happen, was the Labour Party electorate. Voting rights were extended from 'one member one vote' to include 'registered supporters', who could simply sign up for just £3 to get a vote. This at last gave a chance for a vast range of people to express their desire for change in and through the Labour Party; and the momentum that was generated during Corbyn's leadership campaign has since then continued and grown: it is this that has made the political sea-change possible.

I had never been a member of the Labour Party before, but when the opportunity came to vote for a Labour leader I could actually believe in and share some ideals with, one who could make a difference to the mish-mash of honourable defeat and shoddy compromise I'd witnessed for most of my adult life, I duly signed up to the rather surprising notion that I was entitled to have this vote.

The registered supporter scheme has the potential to entirely reinvent what a political party looks like. It banishes the 'strong-power' barriers to entry – the party card, the closed ideological identification, the need to subscribe to all manner of policy positions, a one-size-fits-all model of activism, the endless rounds of meetings, committees and conferences, a bewildering rule book, and the expectation that one would be Labour to the exclusion of any kind of affection for any other party. It was not just because of political direction that until 2015 Labour's membership had been experiencing a headlong decline in numbers.

Now the party has at least the beginnings of becoming a soft power organisation. In my case the identification was simple – with a guy called Jeremy Corbyn and the hopes I projected upon him. I shelled out my £3. But at that point my loyalty to Labour didn't involve much more than that. I certainly didn't assume I was signing up for life. Shallow and inconsequential, opportunistic even? Yes, I suppose so, but my guy won and now I had my toe in the party, I was willing to give more, to see if this could be made to work, shifting Labour to the left – me and several hundred thousand more. British politics, the Labour Party, had never seen anything quite like it before.

As Gary Younge commented, those yearning for 'the Corbyn effect' to represent meaningful, radical change, including those who fondly remembered the Bennite left in the 1980s, needed to note the differences:

> If this really were a return to the eighties, as some suggest, then he would have a peace movement making his case for him against war and a vibrant trade union movement making the case against austerity. As it is he doesn't even have a party he can rely on. He did not emerge to the Labour leadership organically from a deeper organisational base but disorganically from a wider, amorphous, alienated sentiment.[9]

What Corbyn did have, however, was a new mass membership and a new message. This was what allowed the 'shock to the system':

> This election was the first time since the crisis that a mainstream party had offered principled opposition to austerity and shifted the conversation from immigration to investment in public services. We were told that voters would not buy it. We were told it was not possible. But when the clock struck 10, the tectonic plates shifted. And for just a minute, until we found our footing, we felt a little giddy.[10]

In the early hours of Friday 9 June 2017 in Lewes, 'a little giddy' was putting it mildly. I'd spent most of the previous day in Kemptown in Brighton, where the Tories were defending a 690 vote majority. We'd had a good campaign, with huge turnouts of supporters, youthful and enthusiastic: this was a seat Momentum had targeted for help, and it showed. Old hands had provided the tried and tested organisational infrastructure, newer ones trod the streets, knocking on doors, sometimes fired up by the helpful and inspiring training session with organisers over from the Bernie Sanders' campaign. On polling day I had had a recurrence of pessimism of the intellect, but I needn't have worried. Labour voters had queued up to tell us with unrestrained enthusiasm that they'd voted for the party, while on the Brighton University campus we were mobbed for anything to wear with Labour on it to show support, and at the campaign HQ throughout the day more and more activists had been turning up to help out, then coming back telling the same, positive story.

But there was still no real sense of the scale of the change to come, so, after a long day, as I checked the exit poll I was all ready for an early night. Wow! I hurriedly got dressed and jogged round to the Lewes Labour Party offices, where the optimists were already camped out for the night, with big screen, beer, wine and packets of Pringles. Tectonic plates shifting? When the Kemptown result came through it felt more like an earthquake. A Tory marginal had been transformed into a 10,000 Labour majority.

THERE ALWAYS WAS AN ALTERNATIVE

Throughout the long period of Thatcherism, Labour's capture by New Labour and its subsequent decline, there have always been alternative roads that could have been taken. There have been many debates about how to renew the left, and being critical of New Labour is not to deny that Labour in 1979 was in great need of new ideas. It is therefore worth revisiting some of these debates now, as an aid to thinking about what needs to be done to keep the Corbyn momentum going. Because that momentum, the pun is intended, should be about not accepting Labour as it is and was but what it could be and become.

The largely accurate and immensely uplifting film *Pride* is a good place to start looking for inspiration. It tells the stories of both the stalwarts of Lesbians and Gays Support the Miners (LGSM) and the communities who provided the backbone to the 1984-85 miners' strike in the Welsh valleys. Hywel Francis chaired the South Wales miners support group that features in the film, and with which LGSM twinned to such good effect in both film and actuality. In his book *History On Our Side*, he recalls the impact of 1984-5:

> The network of women and mixed support groups had given rise to an alternative, community-based system of food, clothing, financial and morale distribution which had sustained about half a million people for nearly a year. The social and political skills of organisation

and communication were akin to the experiences of people during a social revolution. Women, men and indeed children had learnt more about the strengths and weaknesses of the state apparatus, more about the problems of working-class solidarity and above all more about their own individual and collective human potential than at any time in their lives. The new links within and between coalfields, with non-mining areas in Britain and indeed internationally were all pregnant with possibilities.[11]

Francis is here writing about a very specific kind of geographical community in a very particular set of historical circumstances. Nevertheless, the creative solidarity which this strike sparked, and which is so memorably portrayed in *Pride*, offered at least the beginnings of the shape of things that might have become a new model Labour Party. In particular it showed how links could be made between older left constituencies and newer kinds of politics, with the effect of enriching the understanding of all involved.

Stuart Hall's essay 'The great moving right show', written in January 1979, was the first to take the measure of the crisis facing the left, as the age of neoliberalism was dawning with the onset of Thatcherism. Hall was a brilliant critic of both the wider left and the Labour Party at that time. He was very supportive of the kinds of creative political responses that developed during the miners' strike, as seen in *Pride*, but he was critical of the inadequacies of the kind of left response to Thatcherism he summed up as: 'Away with all those time-wasting theoretical speculations! The Marxist guarantees are all in place after all, standing attention. Let us take to the streets'. It was not only the Labour Party that needed new thinking, the old left, too, was stuck in a previous era. As Hall was at pains to argue, however, this was '*not* an argument against taking to the streets'. It was, rather, 'an argument against the satisfactions which sometimes flow from applying simplifying analytic schemes to complex events'.[12]

Hall pointed instead to an alternative left strategy, particularly as seen in the late 1970s popular campaigns against the National Front:

... the direct interventions against the rising fortunes of the National Front – local campaigns, anti-fascist work in the unions, trades councils, women's groups, the mobilisation behind the Anti Nazi

League, the counter-demonstrations, above all Rock Against Racism (one of the timeliest and best constructed of cultural, interventions, repaying serious and extended analysis) – constitute one of the few success stories of the conjuncture.

Rock Against Racism was probably the most memorable part of the campaign against the National Front.[13] Hall recognised that this was because of its nature as a cultural intervention: this was what enabled it to engage in action a broad new constituency. As with the support groups during the miners' strike, it was a movement that stretched far beyond the traditional horizons of the left.

Paul Gilroy provides an insightful understanding of RAR's significance:

> Unruly opposition was given creative expression not just in the musical cross fertilisation that came from the founding commitment in which black and white bands always shared audiences and performance space, but in the visual excesses of the RAR collective's graphics and the effervescence of what would now be drily called their 'branding' strategy. Badges, stickers and bright placards were all orchestrated around key colours, icons and slogans. There was an unprecedented connection between the spirit of political dissent and the novel ways in which it was being communicated and rendered. These tactics certainly drew courage and inspiration from the brazen confidence and reckless '1-2-3-4 let's get on with it' attitude of punk, but they also surpassed it in delivering viewers and participants beyond the limits of a world projected recursively in black and white.[14]

When I went up to London for the Rock against Racism Carnival in Victoria Park in 1978, a fresh-faced sixth-former straight out of Tadworth, Surrey, I didn't have the wherewithal to describe my experience as anything much more that discovering that politics could be fun. The appeal of the Carnival, of Rock against Racism, was that anybody could join: there was nothing to sign up to, no membership form, no committee, just a movement we could call – and make – our own. Analogue still ruled in those days, but RAR proved for a time at least to be the most (post) modern of social movements.

In 2017 something of this sort emerged once more. It is too early to be sure with any certainty what will happen next with

#Grime4Corbyn, but already it has made links between politics and popular culture in a way that has not been seen for years. And, like RAR, it is a do-it-yourself movement, framed first and foremost by the music and culture that generated it. Music and politics have come together in a shared breakthrough moment. It is a measure of both the music and the politics that they did, so that we once more had a glimpse of the potential for cultural change that Stuart Hall recognised in Rock against Racism all those years ago.

Following the Brexit referendum, John Harris wrote a brilliantly powerful piece in *The Guardian* against the rising wave of post-referendum bigotry:

> What is afoot is as much cultural as political, and it will take much more than conventional politics to turn it round. This is a moment: one that demands the attention of musicians, writers, dramatists, journalists – and the millions of people who surely feel a dismay about what is happening.

Harris, too, argues we should look for inspiration to the late 1970s:

> when a surge of largely English racism and bigotry was killed off by trailblazing creations such as Rock against Racism and the Anti-Nazi League, and a great counter movement of people that went right to society's roots. I do not know what a twenty-first century version of that fight will look like, but I do know we need one.[15]

Soon afterwards, when John came to a discussion meeting of Lewes Labour Party in early 2017, I asked him whether he could see the Labour Party getting involved in the kind of popular movement he had described in the article. His response was that, however popular Corbyn's populism might be on keynote issues such as housing, there was an almost universal disbelief that it would ever amount to anything, given that his leadership had put Labour so far from winning power. But this is precisely what the shift in tectonic plates has subsequently achieved. People now believe that Labour can win, and they also believe that it can bring about dramatic and meaningful change. So now is the time to start thinking imaginatively about how to build on this new sense of confidence.

A reconnection between parliamentary and extra-parliamentary campaigning will be a crucial way of making such change possible. As Tom Blackburn put it on the *New Socialist* website, we need a 'Corbynism from below'.[16] The new politics will need to involve more than leadership at the national level. Labour's mass membership needs to go local, forging a renewed bottom-up politics that proves, in practice, what Labour values can achieve on the ground. Such a shift could be the basis of a populist movement that is rooted in people-power, rather than in thrall to a demagogue, as is so often the case with right-wing populism. This is neither to decry or minimise Corbyn's role, but to understand that the role is that of representing our aspirations as a party: we all need to be involved on the ground, rather than waiting for him to do everything for us. As Blackburn puts it, Corbynism is a movement. It is not a personality cult, as some lazy critics describe it (and nor is it the kind of cult of personality seen in some left populist/hard-left traditions): 'To succeed, Corbynism must begin the vital process of rebuilding popular self-confidence, and the capacity of working-class people to take real collective control of their everyday lives'.[17]

Blackburn's article drew on the work of socialist-feminist writer Hilary Wainwright, one of the pioneers of the alternative modernisation tradition represented by RAR and the miners' solidarity groups. Wainwright was deeply engaged in these traditions, but this did not mean that change could not also be rooted in good old-fashioned political economy. In discussing the legacy of the Greater London Council (with co-author Maureen Macintosh), she argued:

> Any future political authority which thinks it can construct a progressive and successful economic policy without developing a model of constructing and implementing it in association with (and also sometimes in active contradiction with) those in whose interests it is intended to operate will be wrong.[18]

In other words, the way we do our politics shapes what our politics becomes. And this connects, too, with the necessity to show that popular power can operate effectively in the local arena, and so help dispel the myth that the left does not know how to govern. Lynsey Hanley argues for the huge potential that is released when a sense of incapacity is overcome:

Where politics fails, cynicism reigns, and the only way to negate that cynicism is to treat politics first as a local endeavour – in which voters have direct and regular contact with politicians whose experiences inform their parties' national policymaking from the bottom up.[19]

When Corbyn toured the country during the election campaign, he filled huge halls and parks with crowds desperate for precisely the kind of political engagement that Hanley describes. In this sense his is a practical vision that could appeal across some of the party's divides that so crippled Labour from 2015 to 2017. Many of the Labour MPs who lined up against him before the election also recognise this need, as can be seen in their constituency work and can be seen, when they are not undermining Corbyn, by their work in Parliament and more widely. They have practised and preached the beginnings of new and different ways of doing politics as much as, if not more than, some of Corbyn's own allies. Until the election the chances of any kind of dialogue with this group were next to zero, but there are now possibilities for co-operation.

This is to be welcomed, but we do no-one any favours if we fail to understand why the division erupted in the first place. We need to revisit the layers of support inside and outside Labour that Corbyn was able to give expression to and mobilise – not to re-open what we hope are old divisions, but to recognise what caused them. Jeremy Gilbert sums up the people energised by Corbyn as 'a body of opinion which has been widespread throughout the country for many years, but has been denied any kind of place in our public life since the early days of New Labour ... a body of opinion which believes, with good reason, that the embrace of neoliberal economics and neoconservative foreign policy under Blair was a disaster'. And he concludes, it would be better for all of us if Labour Party members had more say over policy and over who represents them in parliament.[20]

The successes of the 2017 election campaign have created the conditions for a new political settlement in Labour, able to bring together both sides of this long-standing argument – MPs, party members and voters – as the base from which Labour can go from a good second to a solid win next time.

THE BLAIR CUL DE SAC

There were varying models of modernisation available to Labour in 1994, when Tony Blair became leader after a series of failed attempts to remould the party. But the party under his leadership opted for an approach that combined a conservative version of modernity with a populist rhetoric that disavowed even the mildest version of social democracy. David Stubbs captures very well the problems of Blair's version of populism as it sought to draw on the pre-millennium mood of celebrating all things new, with the drive to reinvent and rebrand, connecting this mood to a technocratic managerialism divorced from the political. This embrace of the new was closely linked to a belief that the era was marked by the eclipse of left-versus-right politics: 'the End of History meant the end of the old struggle between top-hatted Capital and cloth-capped Labour'. This left us 'drifting backwards into a future in which a communal conservatism would see to it that the present, the Be Here Now, was maintained as long as possible'.[21]

At the core of this post-political Blairism was an uncritical reading of globalisation: 'I hear people say we have to stop and debate globalisation. You might as well debate whether autumn should follow summer'.[22] Blair portrayed the economic powers reshaping the world as a force of nature, unstoppable, irresistible; there was no point in expecting that they could be changed in any meaningful sense:

> The character of this changing world is indifferent to tradition. Unforgiving of frailty. No respecter of past reputations. It has no custom and practice.
>
> It is replete with opportunities, but they only go to those swift to adapt, slow to complain, open, willing and able to change. Unless we own the future, unless our values are matched by a completely honest understanding of the reality now upon us and the next about to hit us, we will fail. And then the values we believe in become idle sentiments ripe for disillusion and disappointment. In the era of rapid globalisation, there is no mystery about what works: an open, liberal economy, prepared constantly to change to remain competitive. The new world rewards those who are open to it.[23]

In other words, modernisation meant renouncing any hope of real change, and turning the government's attention, instead, to managing people's lives. Of course the Blair governments did many good things. But they were crippled by this embrace of neoliberalism, and it was this legacy that doomed Brown and Miliband when they unsuccessfully followed in Blair's wake. During the 2015 television election debate, Ed Miliband was forced to deny that he was the same as the Tories in face of united criticism from Nicola Sturgeon, Leanne Wood and the Greens' Natalie Bennett. As Sturgeon tellingly retorted, no Ed, you're not the same, but nor are you different enough.

As former *Marxism Today* editor Martin Jacques commented: 'For three decades the dominant themes were marketisation, privatisation, trickle-down economics, the wastefulness and inefficiencies of the state, the incontrovertible case for hyper-globalisation, and bankers and financiers as the New Gods'.[24] The election campaign of 2017 had finally turned Labour away from this legacy. As Jacques further commented: 'To be able to entertain a sense of optimism about our own country is a novel experience after 30 years of being out in the cold. No wonder so many are feeling energised again'.[25]

THE BENN HERESY

Blairism had been the logical conclusion of Neil Kinnock's leadership of the Labour Party; modernisation of the party – which was certainly needed – had already become identified with the repudiation of the left by the time Tony Blair became leader. But throughout the 1980s there was a strong rearguard action from the 'Bennite' left, who argued that only a democratic left renewal could defeat Thatcher. Not long before Corbyn first became an MP, in 1983, Alan Freeman described the mood in the Labour Party:

> Benn now had grounds for hope. The left seemed on the verge of complete triumph. It looked as if only the last bastion – the PLP – needed to be conquered, and with the right wing packing its bags and reselection entrenched in the constitution, this would surely fall in time.[26]

Benn's proposed electoral strategy was not so different from Corbyn's today:

Our road to victory does not lie in coaxing back half a dozen *Guardian* readers from their flirtation with the SDP, but in mobilising the 10 million people who don't vote but are our natural constituents because they are the ones, more than any other, who are repressed by our society ... We shall win by practical socialist arguments that begin with the experience of ordinary men and women. We must be there when they need us, and then assist them, as best we can, to learn from their experience and make something of it so that socialism and the vision that we have, and the revolution that we need, is constructed by the people, for the people and not one that drips down from above – to be imposed whether they like it or not.[27]

This is an extract from a debate with Stuart Hall in 1984. In his response, reflecting on the state of the Labour Party under Kinnock's leadership, Hall voiced a number of reservations:

If that looks like a party with enough political imagination and 'feel' for the current situation to put itself at the head of the different forms of struggle and to take that struggle, not just into its own organisations, but out into society and to generalise the case for socialism on the basis of it, then I yield to a more optimistic version of events. I honour Tony Benn's courageous efforts to 'gloss' the current situation in this way, but I regret to say that, on this issue, I believe he is whistling in the dark.[28]

Hall was reiterating his support for an alternative approach to that of both Kinnock and Benn, one that would be based on creating a more populist Labour Party, combining both radical politics and electoral appeal. But to suggest that Bennism was no longer the model to create the conditions for such a change was not very popular in 1984.

This debate took place at a packed out venue in Islington. Though I was there, I have no idea if the newly elected Labour MP for Islington North, Jeremy Corbyn was. But whether he was or not, I can be pretty certain that, as a convinced Bennite, he wouldn't have been in agreement with Hall when he argued:

The left must be able, on its own programme, with its own project, to engage the society as a whole, to generalise itself throughout society, to bring over strategic popular majorities on the key issues, to win converts, first of all among those sectors of its own class and those who can come into alliance with it, but who have in recent years not supported it. But secondly, to make converts to its case, to carry the case to a widening set of constituencies, to polarise the society in new ways towards the left, to connect with new experiences in society, to engage with its increasing complexity and in that way to make socialism grow in relevance to the emerging experiences as well as the traditional experiences of our time.[29]

As we now know, the Labour Party took the advice of neither Hall nor Benn, and in 1997 it was Blair's version of Labour modernisation that predominated. What do you do when the alternative to Thatcherism you've always believed in, a Labour government, turns out to be so much less than the stuff of your dreams? There were few answers as the years passed, and the left became ever weaker. The resources of hope were running on empty.

And then, in 2015, along comes Jeremy, a rank outsider. The other leadership candidates in 2015 were the same old faces or the same old politics, and in most cases, both. Corbyn represented a change, but he was never going to win – though he might be worth a flutter.

NOW THAT'S WHAT I CALL POLITICS

After Corbyn won, and when I had recovered from the rare experience of being on both the left and the winning side, I promptly became a full member of the Labour Party. To effect the change Corbyn now represented there was simply nowhere else to be.

My local Labour Party branch, as has been the case all over the country, was welcoming but a little unsure about who all these new members were. This is a party culture unused to the convulsions of change – or 'surge', to use the modern term. It sometimes seems as if, in the face of such a challenge, some of the old guard believe that bigger isn't necessarily better, and that the enthusiasm of the new members won't last. Why should an organisational culture more or less unchanged for the best part of a century adapt itself to what is probably no more than a bunch of fly-by-nights? Blair's modernisation had left most of this culture untouched: his objective had not been to modernise the party itself: in so many ways he ruled in spite of it, not with it. But if Labour really was now to become a social movement as well as an election-winning force, something would have to give.

Once again I rekindled my optimism by remembering some of my own experiences and influences, in this case Red Wedge, which was a hugely ambitious attempt to keep a culture of resistance on the road after all the benefit gigs of the 1984-85 miners' strike. The aim was to keep the flame burning of an avowedly political 'soulcialism', as us Red Wedgers liked to call it. I've got a strong memory of my first sighting of Billy Bragg – with his amplifier in his rucksack – at a gig in Birmingham on their first tour, and in 1986 I organised a gig on their comedy tour at what was then Wolverhampton Poly. The key thing about Red Wedge was that it was pro-Labour without being in and of the party, and it allowed a looser kind of association with them. Stuart Cosgrove described the Red Wedge audience in terms of geography, gender and class: suggested that the ideal image for Red Wedge was less a modified Russian slogan and design out of 1917 than a 'ginger haired typist from Carlisle who dances to soul music and has to save up for her holiday', adding, 'if Labour wins the typists' vote, who cares what art students do with their ballot papers?'[30]

This cultural initiative posed a challenge to the conservative organ-isational structures of Labourism. Cosgrove hoped that Red Wedge could become 'the animator not the afterthought', generating events, not simply providing them: 'Red Wedge has to chase the improb-able and fast. It has to unite the night away. Labour: it ain't nothing but a parrrty'.[31] But, of course, nothing of the sort happened. After Labour lost the 1987 election it reverted to type, most notoriously at the American-style rally in 1992 in Sheffield.

Red Wedge was a seriously ambitious attempt to effect change in the party's culture, but it wasn't factional in any traditional sense. It was very open: all who could see that Labour's ways of working and appealing weren't being effective could have a piece of the change it offered. Tony Mainwaring, at the time political assistant to the Labour Party's general secretary, describes what he now recognises to have been a lost opportunity:

> There was a moment of crystallisation of a new form of politics. It was brilliant and beautiful to see, and Red Wedge was reconfiguring the DNA. But I don't think the Labour Party had the reflective learning

capacity to draw and learn and honour what was being done. The Party was bound to let it down in some way because there wasn't a clear enough expectation and conversation about what 'good' would look like.

Yet thirty years on Tony remains convinced of the potential that did exist:

> The answer isn't what Red Wedge brought to the Labour Party, it's what kind of politics we could have created together. If it had developed for another few years it would have been extraordinary.[32]

Red Wedge eventually found the door slammed shut. But in 2017 a similar mood has appeared. In spite of the naysaying cynics, when Jeremy Corbyn took the Glastonbury stage he received the adulation usually reserved for rockstars. There are precious few politicians – now, or ever – able to attract such affection, and trust too, from young voters.

The success of the 2017 election campaign suggests a breakthrough, electorally and culturally, in generating the kind of connection between Labour as an institution and young voters that Red Wedgers could only dream of in the 1980s.

MOVEMENTISM VS LABOURISM

A core part of the Corbyn appeal is the idea that Labour can become both a party and a social movement. And to achieve this, a cultural politics is key. This is what will be able to project the party as more than the sum of its members, branches, annual conference and MPs, and put forward a vision for change which, in the here and now, defies all the limitations to practise its ideals.

David Graeber summed up the changes that would be needed for Labour to make the shift towards combining the electoral and the social:

> Over the past century it has gradually become like all the other political parties – personality (and of course, money) based, but the Corbyn project is first and foremost to make the party a voice for social movements once again, dedicated to popular democracy (as

trades unions themselves once were). This is the immediate aim. The ultimate aim is the democratisation not just of the party but of local government, workplaces, society itself.[33]

Corbynism, like Syriza, Podemos and the rest, has not emerged out of nowhere; it is in this sense part of a wider phenomenon. Each of the new movements and parties is different, but all have a base beyond, and sometimes in contradiction with, the left's traditional support, while still remaining part of the left. Paul Mason in part explains this shift in sociological terms, describing the base as 'the graduate with no future', equipped with access to social media and a flexible attitude to traditional leftist ideologies. This constituency is characterised by a rejection of rigid hierarchical structures, and a preference for 'horizontalism' and bottom-up politics: as a mix-and-match network, ad-hoc groups rather than organised factions are the norm; and within this group there is a thirst for knowledge of how to resist, no limits to the imagination, and no fear of the opposition.[34] This description certainly describes many of the new and younger Corbyn supporters, though part of Corbyn's success has been to engage with this group while also re-enthusing older Labour supporters and engaging other areas of support. Part of the task ahead is to hold these groups together in the broadest possible coalition.

Neal Lawson, a 'soft-lefter' back in the 1980s, surprised himself, and no doubt many of his friends, by voting for 'hard-left' candidate Corbyn. As he commented: 'Things change. There is no perfect wave, and Jeremy isn't perfect. But this is not about the person but the moment and the wave the Corbyn candidacy has unleashed. I voted for the wave':

> The Corbyn Wave is a window into what is possible. Its energy is breaking up the permafrosted soil that for thirty years has been too harsh for our dreams to grow in. Labour as a party and a movement cannot survive electorally or politically unless it holds out the hope of radically changing society. On this point, time has caught up with New Labour. If the best it gets is to slow the pace at which the poor get poorer and the planet burns, it's not enough to sustain us. A party needs high ideals and deep organic roots in society if it is to transform that society. This cannot be done from

the top down, but only when a party meets a groundswell from below.[35]

Since 2015 we have had that groundswell in the party, and after 2017, it has the potential to reach the country. For this to be sustained, Labour has to change so that it can ride the wave, and become part of it in every possible respect. But, as David Wearing warned in 2016, there is a danger that the Labour membership's potential to organise as an active social movement would be unrealised, 'given the exclusionary, aggressive and patronising attitude they have been greeted with by the party establishment'.[36]

There is a reason for the hostile attitudes to the new politics. It is caused by the existence of two fundamentally different conceptions of what constitutes the political, broadly speaking the parliamentary and the extra-parliamentary – though in my view they are by no means as incompatible as so many suggest. In a rebuttal of this mistaken counterposition, Rachel Shabi outlines one way in which Corbynism connects with a constituency seeking a Labour Party that is at one and the same time a social movement:

> This pursuit of collectivism, in the face of decades of rampant individualism, was always one of the more radical aspects of Corbyn's leadership. It was in evidence throughout his campaign speeches, where he often spoke of society's many cohorts as one community, binding together groups – young and old, black and white, nurses as well as builders and office workers – that are more often encouraged to compete against each other in the current economy.[37]

None of this would appear either new or all that threatening to those steeped in the Labour tradition of Keir Hardie and Ellen Wilkinson, the hunger marches, Cable Street, the International Brigades, Stafford Cripps, Labour winning the peace in '45, Nye Bevan and the foundation of the NHS, Barbara Castle on the picket line with the women striking for equal pay at Fords, Foot, Kinnock and Benn leading CND demonstrations, Bernie Grant standing with his community after the 1985 Broadwater Farm riots. But there has been a resistance to this kind of politics for a long time from the centre and right of the party, and many sitting Labour MPs share a distrust of social movement activism.

Progress, the grouping most identified with this position inside the Labour Party, some of whom identify as 'Clause One socialists', put it thus:

> In the 1930s, 1950s and 1980s Labour was pulled away from its true path by syndicalist social movements. At its founding, the party's intention was clearly spelled out for the world to see in the very first paragraph of the constitution: to 'maintain in parliament … a political Labour Party'.[38]

In contrast, there is a potential for Corbynism to create a party that has a lived experience of, and presence in, every community, at all levels of society. These days, in my small East Sussex town of Lewes, within ten minutes of setting out from my house I know I will come across a fellow member of the Labour Party – a neighbour, a market-stall holder, a fellow parent, a swimmer down at the pool, someone serving in a shop, the programme editor of the football club I support, all sorts. This is what the Labour Party is becoming – a mass membership party. We are everywhere. But if we are restricted to the kind of role that these Clause One socialists want to ascribe to us – passive supporters to be switched on and off when a canvassing session is required, extras rather than the actors – how many will choose to stick around?

What could have been more symbolic of the potential for Labour as a social movement than Saffiyah Khan's role as she introduced Jeremy Corbyn at the final outdoor rally of the 2017 election Campaign? A few months previously a photo of Saffiyah, a young Muslim woman, had gone viral: it showed her fearlessly facing down the English Defence League boot-boys in her Birmingham home town – and with a smile on her face. She had stood up for what she knew was right. Neither parliamentarianism nor protest politics can achieve changes in attitudes on their own. To make such resistance possible we need Saffiyah and hundreds of thousands like her, not as a stage army at the party's beck and call, but as individuals who, when they come together, become communities of change.

On 1 July 2017 I was at a rally in St Leonards-on-Sea at which Corbyn was a much anticipated speaker. He told the crowd that the world, Britain, our communities, didn't have to be divided in the ways they were: inequality was not the result of natural causes but of unnatural decision-making, and we now had the power to reverse all this. He made us feel we were all an important part of this movement that he had rather surprised himself by being at the head of. As he spoke, cars stopped so that drivers and passengers could listen, and residents stood on balconies and opened their windows, eager to hear the speech. But best of all, a fire engine pulled up and the crew disembarked to join in, welcomed by rapturous applause. Afterwards I caught sight of the firefighters in conversation with Jeremy. The crew were keen for the now almost obligatory selfies, but they also wanted to talk to Jeremy about their work, the attack on their conditions of employment, the cuts that had forced fire stations to close, the 1 per cent pay cap they, like all other public sector workers, had been forced to endure. Any politician in their right minds would have stopped and listened. But I could tell this was something different. This was a politician who has stood on those firefighters' picket lines, never condemning them or offering mealy-mouthed excuses when they've taken industrial action. He can count their union amongst his closest allies, and before he became an MP he was a trade union organiser himself. This is the kind of authenticity no marketing consultant or communications adviser can ever manufacture, because it's real. This, almost more than anything else, is Corbyn's appeal. His authenticity is rooted in his politics, and, as we've now learned, it has huge popular appeal. Jeremy Corbyn made Corbynism, but now it is ours, it belongs to all of us.

LET'S GET THIS PARTY STARTED

Our ownership of Corbynism, however, depends on Labour changing too. This risks driving politics towards the inward-looking. I doubt if many of the households whose doors I knocked in Kemptown and Hove during the election had heard of the 'McDonnell Amendment' (to change the percentage of PLP support needed to be nominated for leadership candidacy), let alone been stirred to action by it. But that doesn't mean the issues it raises don't matter, though perhaps not in the way either its supporters or opponents intended. Of course Labour is a parliamentary party: it is not, nor has it ever been, a revolutionary party, and that hasn't changed under Corbyn. Yet Labour has always existed outside parliament as well as within. For most of its history it has had the explicit ambition of a mass membership, not as an alternative to parliamentary representation but as a complement to it. So, now that it once more has such a large number of members, what role should be ascribed to us? A *New Statesman* leader in March 2017 made this helpfully clear:

> The absurdity of a leader opposed by as much as 95 per cent of his own MPs is incompatible with this mission [as a parliamentary party]. Those who do not enjoy the backing of their parliamentary colleagues will struggle to persuade the voters that they deserve their support.[39]

Under current Labour Party rules, for a leadership candidate to go on to the party ballot paper, 15 per cent of MPs and MEPs must nominate them. In other words it is possible for 85 per cent of MPs to be opposed to the winning candidate (not the 95 per cent of the *New Statesman*'s worst nightmares). But the problem is not that the party leader is out of kilter with the parliamentary party: it is, rather, that the right's domination of the PLP allows it to deny the possibility of standing to a leadership candidate of the left – a model more suited to a feudal party, with the MPs as barons and the members as serfs. It assumes a powerless party membership. This is not to deny that MPs have a special role, but rather to question the extent of their power over the rest of us.

Another area where many sitting MPs and their supporters seek too much privilege is the issue of *re*selection. I've lost count of the number of times I've read articles by otherwise well-informed political commentators who mistake the *re*selection of Labour MP's for their *de*selection. Quite why anybody finds the former in the least controversial is entirely beyond me. Local Labour members have the right to select parliamentary candidates, so it seems entirely legitimate that they should also have the right, once every five years, to review their role and confirm or not their candidacy for the next election. If this rule were applied automatically to all MPs, the process would be removed from factional motives. A job for life – which plenty of MPs in safe seats enjoy – should be the anathema of democratic politics. Labour MPs do need to represent all their constituents, of any party and none, in parliament. But the clue to the necessity of reselection is in the job title: they are elected as *Labour* MPs. There is no reason to believe that the vast majority of MPs wouldn't sail through reselection, but the importance of the process is that it asserts the principle of accountability, something that would help in the reshaping of Labour Party culture

A members-led party, bottom-up not top-down, is not, however, enough. Labour must also be a values-added party. And that means no more of the common-sense 'listen to the voters' mantra. In the aftermath of the 2017 election, Labour MP Graham Jones remained unimpressed by Corbyn's popularity. 'How thick does this party have to be?', he asked, before going on to answer his own question. His beef was that the party had not learnt 'the lessons' from the rise of the populist right: 'Our core voters cannot be taken for granted. These are people who have been let down by political elites for decades. They see themselves as being at the back of every queue.' Jones is convinced that he knows how to win these voters back: 'We have to talk about their concerns – counter-terrorism, nationalism, defence and community, the nuclear deterrent and patriotism'.[40] Jones is right to ask what kind of party Labour wants to be. It is just that his answer is wrong. He believes that, when faced with former voters who have switched to the BNP, Ukip or the Tories, Labour should simply go along with their reasons, regardless of their irrational – more likely racialised – underpinnings. If the concerns of all Jones's constituents are indeed as he lists them (which is doubtful), Labour does have a choice. It can nod sagely and agree that the rotten state of our nation is all down to those Muslims and their un-British habits, our unfettered borders, our lack of enthusiasm for nuclear war, and our failure to wave the flag at every opportunity. Alternatively, it can find a way to listen to people's grievances but choose to engage them in a discussion, seeking to convince them that we live in a potentially convivial multi-racial nation; that it is austerity and low wages that drive down our living conditions not immigration; that launching a first strike nuclear armageddon would destroy our own nation for no obvious reason; and patriotism means attachment to a place that we can all call home, wherever we come from, whatever our faith or lack thereof. This is not always an easy conversation, but, without it, the 'working-class appeal' that Jones and others in the Labour Party were calling for after the election will be based not just on a value-free politics, but on an attitude that has more than a whiff of something much nastier.

Labour isn't immune to other kinds of nastiness, within all sections of opinion. Social media has helped unleash a tidal wave of abuse at the click of a send button. None of this is excusable.[41] A party that is serious about social change, inside and outside parliament, must be one that forms ideas out of difference and argument. But it must also involve in the discussion people from as a wide a variety of backgrounds as possible, maximising the means of participation so that no-one feels excluded. This means both tolerance and limits to that tolerance. Name-calling doesn't get us very far down that difficult road of negotiation. Nor does heaping all the blame on one 'side' to score dubious points without examining our own behaviour. Ellie Mae O'Hagan put this very neatly in less than 140 characters: 'Time to draw a line under the disingenuous argument that there is a causal link between the left and bullying, and go back to debating ideas'.[42]

An ideas party is one that doesn't stand still. Labour needs to revise and adapt its ideas as society changes, but to do so based on a clear set of principles. Corbynism has sparked a wave of new thinking in and outside the academy, and across all the disciplines. Labour must find a way to constantly encourage this, never to be afraid of being challenged, both to surf change and to shape it too.[43]

Stuart Hall, a great populariser and adaptor of the thought of Antonio Gramsci, argued that a key purpose of intellectual discussion within a left party, 'the whole purpose of what Gramsci called an organic (i.e. historically effective) ideology' is to 'articulate … into a configuration different subjects, different identities, different projects, different aspirations'. The task is not to reflect back opinions, but to 'construct a unity out of difference'.[44]

To seek to create an organic ideology, built from the bottom up, is a risky, messy and unfamiliar proposition. But ideas, even the good ones in the 2017 manifesto, cannot be frozen in perpetuity. Ceasing to think is the death of any political party. If the party is to be effective this is the responsibility of us all, because not all intellectuals are academics (and not all academics are intellectuals).

Labour also needs to be a smart party. It needs to be modern not for the sake of cheap impact, but to do the best job it can in communicating, mobilising and leading. And right now there's no more important place to be doing this than in the sixty-six Labour target constituencies that will determine whether or not Jeremy Corbyn eventually enters number ten.[45] We also have to defend the nineteen seats with majorities of less than 1000. Under our rotten electoral system these seats are key. This is the place to turn rhetoric into reality; these are the communities in which we need to root the new mass membership party; in which we must take Labour out to those who have not yet been convinced, engaging with their fears and reservations. This represents an extra-parliamentary parliamentary politics of an entirely new type. And if people in those seats are convinced, more will surely follow.

THE GREAT MOVING LEFT SHOW

So, we need a bottom-up party, a values-added party, a conversational party, one that is brimming with ideas and thinking, and a party that is smart enough to know how to win, and able to inspire those who will make it happen. If this happens, it won't just be the Labour Party that is remade: our very understanding of the political will be transformed. It is Stuart Hall, once more, who confirms not only the implications but also the potential of such a change:

> One of the most important things that Gramsci has done for us is to give us a *profoundly expanded conception* of what politics itself is like, and thus also of power and authority. We cannot, after Gramsci, go back to the notion of mistaking electoral politics, or party politics in a narrow sense, or even the occupancy of state power, as constituting the ground of modern politics itself. Gramsci understands that politics is a much expanded field; that, especially in societies of our kind, the sites on which power is constituted will be enormously varied.[46]

None of this will be easy. As the movement grows, differences will surface, including some that are currently submerged in the excitement of living on the verge of success. Rachel Shabi is one of many thinkers urging the party to promote a more inclusive and participatory style, one which would 'represent a change in Labour's political culture'. This requires being open to challenge from groups that are often marginalised within the party:

> Because, as women, people of colour, or anyone else who sits outside the dominant group know all too well, inclusiveness within left movements does not happen organically. It does not just sort itself out. For member democracy to be a truly empowering venture, conscious

and continuous attempts to make inclusiveness and participation a built-in part of the programme are an essential part of the politics.[47]

In place of the militancy of the clenched fist, we need to embrace the majoritarian politics of open arms; we need a sense of human solidarity that increasing numbers can identify with, so that, as we join up to become part of a greater whole, we remain alert to the contradictions, anxieties and occasional fallings-out this will entail, and come together not simply as a party, but as a movement, a community.

Such an honest endeavour, and the best of motives, brings no guarantees of success. And it is made all the more difficult by the critics, who by their constant denigration risk expunging the sense of possibility that any radical politics has to cling on to.

The rise and rise of Jeremy Corbyn has been accompanied throughout by the conviction of his certain failure and misbegotten motives. But though this must resisted, we also need to be realists. Richard Seymour, writing in 2016, combined both the optimism of the moment and pessimism of the most likely outcome: 'In the final analysis, Corbynism will struggle to outrun the limits of Labourism. And it is those limits, above all, which have brought us to this impasse'.[48] Such circumspection was certainly justified in 2016, and even now, at the height of Corbynism's popularity, it remains necessary.

We need both hope and doubt: one without the other is not much good to anyone. But we need also always to remember that eras do come to an end. This is what Thatcher achieved when she overturned the postwar consensus to win consent for the forging of a free economy within a shrinking state. Blairism largely continued the trajectory of the neoliberal consensus it had inherited, and this continued with Brown, Cameron and Clegg. But the successes of 2017 are the beginnings of a reversal of all that.

The 2017 election showed, at least in part, the potential for a resurgent progressive majority. This did not come from a tactical voting stitch-up between the parties, or behind-closed-doors coalition deal-making: it was much more a question of a resurgent popular politics, embedded in values but not so rigidly that it set people apart. There is a long way to go, but there are signs that the momentum is continuing. Labour is putting itself at the cutting edge of oppositional politics, and it needs to continue to do this, winning support for its proposals in parliament and outside from the SNP, Lib-Dems, Plaid Cymru and the Greens' Caroline Lucas. They need to expose May's weakness, as well the Tories' deep-seated ambivalence about doing anything that serves the common good if they can possibly avoid it, while always being the first to defend the interest of the few.

Labour needs to win the next election, but an even bigger prize will be the creation of a radicalised majority that can embed a new, progressive, post-neoliberal, consensus right across civil society.

Stuart Hall summed up the way Thatcherism achieved its dominance:

> It works on the ground of already constituted social practices and lived ideologies. It wins space there by constantly drawing on these elements which have secured over time a traditional resonance and left their traces in popular inventories. At the same time, it changes the field of struggle by changing the place, the position, the relative weight of the condensations within one discourse and constructing them according to an alternative logic.[49]

A very similar strategy needs to be put into play to entirely different ends by Labour in 2017 and beyond.

Maybe revisiting the ideas that have framed my politics isn't such a bad idea – though not with the aim of freezing them in time. I've often considered the accusation of revisionism to be a compliment rather than an insult. But it is good to go back to Hall's militancy of uncertainty and his hard-headed recognition of the strength of the opposition. The ideas I have set out here, coupled with an unstoppable sense of optimism in the bleakest of times, have been my personal resources of hope. If Hall's words in any way sum up the prospects for Corbyn now, it is not, of course, that Corbynism has anything in common with Thatcherism. Nor is it the case that the idea of hegemony can ever be disconnected from the politics of the conjuncture that shapes it. Instead Hall's account should be read as the definitive account of what a hegemonic, transformative politics looks like.

In 1979 it was the right that understood and articulated such a hegemonic politics, to devastating effect. 'The great moving right show' went into excruciating detail in its forecast of the lengthy nightmare that Thatcher would unleash on us. In the intervening decades we've travelled from old times to new times, and with more than our fair share of hard times. Now, pregnant with possibilities, it is Corbynism that has the potential to become hegemonic and transformative – to 'work on the ground', 'win space', and in the process 'change the field of struggle' with an 'alternative logic'. We've waited long enough for such a moment. A great moving left show just might be about to take the stage, allowing the good times to finally roll. Cue: 'Oh, Jeremy Corbyn' (repeat).

NOTES

1. Jason Cowley, 'The Reckoning', *New Statesman*, 2-8 June 2017, p28.
2. See for example 'Leader: Corbyn's failure is no excuse for fatalism', *New Statesman*, 31 March to 6 April 2017, p 3; Nick Pearce, 'Corbynism is invisible now. It has no secrets to conceal', *New Statesman*, 31 March to 6 April 2017, p 36; Jonathan Freedland, 'Copeland shows that Corbyn must go' *The Guardian*, 25 February 2017; Owen Jones 'Polling and Labour's Prospects', www.medium.com, 21 October 2016 and 'Last words on the Labour Leadership', www.medium.com, 20 March 2017. And the most extreme example of the lot: Nick Cohen, 'Don't tell me you weren't warned about Corbyn', *Observer*, 19 March 2017.
3. John Harris, 'Back to the future', *The Guardian*, 29 September 2015.
4. See Marina Prentoulis's and James Doran's essays in this volume. Also James Doran, '5 Things you need to know about Pasokification', www. novaramedia.com, 28 January 2015.
5. Polly Toynbee, 'Never mind who leaked it, this Labour Manifesto is a cornucopia of delights', *The Guardian*, 11 May 2017.
6. Editorial, *The Guardian*, 17 May 2017.
7. Michael Rustin, 'The prospect of change', *Soundings* blog, www.lwbooks. co.uk, 16 June 2017.
8. Peter Kyle MP, quoted in Cowley, *ibid.*, p28.
9. Gary Younge, Stuart Hall Foundation Keynote Speech, www.stuarthall-foundation.org, 28 November 2015.
10. Gary Younge, 'A shock to the system', *The Guardian*, 17 June 2017.
11. Hywel Francis, *History on our Side: Wales & The 1984-85 Miners Strike*, Lawrence & Wishart: London, 2015, p80.
12. Stuart Hall, 'The great moving right show', *Marxism Today*, January 1979, p15.
13. For an account of my experience in RAR see Mark Perryman 'Straight out of Tadworth' in Roger Huddle and Red Saunders (eds), *Reminiscences of RAR: Rocking Against Racism 1976-1982*, Redwords: London, 2016, pp179-181.
14. Paul Gilroy, 'Rebel Souls: Dance-floor justice and the temporary undoing of Britain's Babylon', in Syd Shelton, *Rock against Racism*, Autograph ABP: London, 2015, pp24-25.

15. John Harris, 'Don't allow England to be recast as a nation of bigots', *The Guardian*, 10 October 2016.
16. Tom Blackburn, 'Corbynism from below?', www.newsocialist.org.uk, 12 June 2017; see also Deborah Hermanns, 'Labour's reinvention needs to come from the bottom up', *The Guardian*, 7 March 2017.
17. Blackburn, *ibid.*
18. Maureen Mackintosh and Hilary Wainwright (eds), *A Taste of Power: The Politics of Local Economics*, Verso: London, 1987, p19.
19. Lynsey Hanley, 'Labour's heartlands aren't racist. They need listening to', *The Guardian*, 17 February 2017.
20. Jeremy Gilbert, 'Is Momentum a mob? No – this is what democracy looks like', www.opendemocracy.net, 18 July 2016.
21. David Stubbs, *1996 & The End of History*, Repeater Books, 2016, p140.
22. Tony Blair, Labour Party Conference speech, 27 September 2005.
23. *Ibid.*
24. Martin Jacques, 'A leader for the new times', *New Statesman*, 16-22 June 2017, p31.
25. *Ibid.*, p31.
26. Alan Freeman, *The Benn Heresy*, Pluto: London, 1982, p125.
27. Tony Benn, 'Who Dares Wins', *Marxism Today*, January 1985, p15.
28. Stuart Hall, 'Faith, Hope and Clarity', *Marxism Today*, January 1985, p19.
29. *Ibid.*, p17.
30. Stuart Cosgrove, 'Winning the Wedge Heads', *New Socialist*, March 1986, p9.
31. Stuart Cosgrove, 'Bands on the Wagon', *New Socialist*, March 1986, p10.
32. Quoted in Daniel Rachel, *Walls Come Tumbling Down: The Music and Politics of Rock Against Racism, 2 Tone and Red Wedge*, Picador: London, 2016, p513.
33. David Graeber, 'The elites hate Momentum and the Corbynites', *The Guardian*, 5 July 2016.
34. See Paul Mason, *Why It's Still Kicking Off Everywhere*, Verso: London, 2013, pp261-296.
35. Neal Lawson, 'I voted for Jeremy Corbyn today – and here's why', www.newstatesman.com, 19 August 2015.
36. David Wearing, 'Ignore the patronising naysayers, Labour members can drive a revolution', *The Guardian*, 23 September 2016.
37. Rachel Shabi, 'Momentum's grassroots democracy can make Labour an unstoppable force', *The Guardian*, 14 June 2017.
38. Editorial, 'Clause One socialists will win the day', www.progressonline.org.uk, 22 September 2016.
39. New Statesman, 'Leader: The Divisions within Labour', *New Statesman* 24-30 March 2017, p3.
40. Graham Jones MP quoted in Rajeev Syal, 'Senior Labour Figures clash over concerns of working class voters', *The Guardian*, 4 July 2017.

41. For an excellent account of the emergence and impact of online abuse see Owen Jones, 'How online abuse is politically hijacked', www.medium.com, 13 July 2017.

42. @misselliemae, Twitter, 12 July 2017.

43. See for example Nick Srnicek and Alex Williams, *Inventing the Future: Postcapitalism and a World Without Work*, Verso: London, 2016.

44. Stuart Hall, 'Gramsci and us', *Marxism Today*, June 1987, p19.

45. See 'Labour Target seats 2022', www.electionpolling.co.uk.

46. Hall, 'Gramsci and us', p20.

47. Rachel Shabi, 'Opening Labour', www.jacobinmag.com, 16 July 2016.

48. Richard Seymour, *Corbyn: The Strange Rebirth of Radical Politics*, Verso: London, 2016, p219.

49. Hall, 'The great moving right show', p20.

The Absolute Corbyn

Jeremy Gilbert

Even at the start of the June 2017 election campaign, nobody expected Labour to achieve the vote share of over 40 per cent that it eventually won. This was a 10 per cent increase on the last election, just two years previously. Labour hasn't seen such a large increase in vote share since 1945, when then there had not been an election for ten years. How did it happen? How did this historic turnaround occur, and what did it mean? To answer this question, we have to understand the genesis of Corbynism, some of its internal dynamics, and where they might be heading in the future.

It's easy to forget now how unexpected Jeremy Corbyn's election as Labour leader was in 2015. At the start of the leadership campaign, bookies were offering odds of 100/1 against Corbyn winning. Neither he nor his closest advisors thought his chances any better than that. Two years on, after Trump's election, the Brexit vote and the surprise of the general election, we are becoming accustomed to unprecedented and unexpected outcomes. In fact, it is becoming clear that we are now in a new historical moment, wherein many of the typical assumptions of the previous era no longer apply, even if it is not yet wholly clear what our new assumptions should be.

This new era is one in which digital platform technologies are increasingly becoming central to the organisation of many forms of social life. The election campaign was no exception. Mobile and online apps and platforms have vastly reduced the costs traditionally associated with organising large numbers of campaigners, making it possible for Labour and Momentum to mobilise thousands of activists at minimal cost. Online platforms similarly reduce the cost of producing and circulating media content, allowing fantastically successful viral campaigns to challenge the mainstream media's antipathy to Corbyn and his politics. All of this has coincided with the end of the long period of neoliberal hegemony in Britain. Just two years previously, Ed Miliband was derided as a marxist for proposing some regulation of the domestic energy market. In 2017, the Tories offered to do something remarkably similar themselves.

LABOUR AND PARLIAMENT

The UK is governed according to a classical parliamentary model, such that executive authority rests with the prime minister, who is almost invariably the leader of the largest party in the House of Commons (the elected legislature). Each Member of Parliament (MP) represents a single, geographically-defined constituency with a population of around 100,000. Unlike almost every other parliamentary system in the world, and unlike even the systems for election to all of the more recently created legislative bodies in the UK (such as the Scottish parliament), there are no proportional mechanisms in place to overcome the inevitable discrepancies which arise between the share of the popular vote won by each party nationally and their actual representation in the House of Commons. So a party, in theory, can achieve close to 20 per cent of the national vote without achieving any parliamentary representation, if that vote is not concentrated in any particular constituencies. This produces a situation not entirely unlike the American party system, and less like that in most European countries, such that the two main political parties are, by necessity, large and at times quite incoherent aggregations of different political traditions and interests. In any normal parliamentary system these disparate views would be represented by distinct political organisations.

Within the Labour Party itself, the group of Labour Members of Parliament – the Parliamentary Labour Party (PLP) – has a specific role, in that the party leader must be drawn from this group. All leadership candidates must secure nomination from at least 15 per cent of the PLP membership to be allowed to stand in a national leadership election. During the Blair years, the party leadership took great pains to ensure that only individuals fitting a very narrow set of criteria, both ideologically and presentationally, were selected as MP candidates in winnable parliamentary constituencies – which of course influenced the membership of the PLP. There was less that the Blairite leadership could do to ensure that the actual overall membership of the party conformed to their idea of what good citizens should look like. Instead, various mechanisms were introduced to ensure that that membership, and particularly the local party organisations in which an activist culture tended to be strong, lost almost all influence over either policy-making or candidate-selection.

THE INTERNAL POLITICS OF THE LABOUR PARTY

Broadly speaking, there are four main political currents which can be identified as having been active in the Labour Party over recent decades: the hard left, the soft left, the old right and the Blairites. The old right has historically tended to support social democratic redistributive programmes and Keynesian industrial strategies, while being ideologically committed to NATO, Atlanticism and nuclear deterrence, and having no interest in any radical anti-capitalist programme or in indulging the democratic demands of grassroots members or other political and social constituencies. In class terms, this tradition is arguably the product of the historic post-war alliance between organised labour and industrial capital.

The hard and soft lefts emerged from the bifurcation of the traditional left after the moment of its greatest success in the party to date, the early 1980s. The hard left are still sometimes referred to as Bennites, a reference to their iconic leader Tony Benn, who came close to taking the deputy leadership (and arguably even the leadership) of the party at that time. Bennism is an odd mixture of marxist analysis and aspiration, a hypothetical commitment to working with social movements, and a Labourist political strategy little different from that favoured by the old right: in other words, this is a strategy which assumes that the Labour Party alone, seeking to win parliamentary majorities within the existing parliamentary system, is a largely sufficient vehicle for the implementation of the hard left's programme. That programme has traditionally been conceived as a classical left-Keynesian one of nationalisation, exit from the EU, imposition of capital controls and increased taxes on the rich. Less predictably, the Bennites were always also interested in more radical-democratic measures such as the extension of co-operatives and workers' control in industry.

Soft left is the name still sometimes given to a tendency which crystallised in the wake of the battles between the hard left and the old right in the early 1980s.[1] Historically, this tendency shares much of the analysis and aspiration of the hard left, but traditionally tries to combine this with both electoral pragmatism and a more open attitude to political strategy. If any tendency represents the political centre-of-gravity of the actual Labour Party membership over the past few decades it is this one, and at least two of the party leaders during that period (Neil Kinnock and Ed Miliband) have been identified with it. Whether the soft left is still a coherent force is an open question. 'Soft left' remains a popular way in which members and MPs identify themselves if they do not wish to publicly side with the right of the party, but seem to have no significant policy differences from it. On the other hand, the radical wing of the soft left (exemplified in parliament by popular MP Clive Lewis) has been largely absorbed into Corbynism, while continuing to agitate for a more Europhile and more democratic agenda than that embraced by traditional Bennism.

The Blairites only emerged in the 1990s, never had much of a base in the party, and remain committed, like their 'Third Way' counterparts in countries like the US and Germany, to a neoliberal socio-economic programme boosted by some meritocratic social reforms. In class terms, they represent a historically novel alignment between a professionalised political elite and sections of finance capital. Their current weakness in the party was shown by their candidate (Liz Kendall) coming a humiliating last in the 2015 leadership election with a mere 4 per cent of the vote. Their public behaviour even since the election suggests that, like their counterparts in the US Democratic Party, they remain in abject denial about the reality of their historic marginalisation.

Policy documents from the party in 2016 and 2017, including the widely-celebrated general election manifesto, give some indication of the current balance of influence between these tendencies. The Blairites are nowhere, having relatively little power in the party bureaucracy (always dominated by the old right) and no influence among the membership, outside of the inevitable local personality-cults which form around certain sitting MPs. The organisation that co-ordinates and supports their activities, Progress, has been abandoned by its millionaire sponsor, Lord Sainsbury, and while there have been rumours of plans to form a break-away party, there is no prospect of them regaining influence within the Labour Party in the foreseeable future. On the other hand the old right, led by the deputy leader of the party, Tom Watson, is the force with whom the Bennites most routinely have to negotiate. It continues to exert considerable influence, while showing an ongoing capacity to obstruct progress where it wants to.

A fantastic, innovative document, *Alternative Models of Ownership*, published by Labour in 2016 put forward the speculative case for implementing a new economic programme based on a vast extension of co-operative models in corporations and public bodies.[2] This delighted the more radical legatees of the soft left and those Bennites who remember fondly Benn's advocacy of workers' control in industry and the spread of co-operatives. But the absence of almost any of those proposals from the actual manifesto demonstrated how little influence such ideas really have. That document essentially put forward a Keynesian programme of national re-industrialisation, along with the re-nationalisation of railways, education and other services that have been fully or partially privatised in recent years. To all intents and purposes this represented a compromise between the centralising current within Bennism and the traditions of the old right. However, as a clear rejection of forty years of neoliberal doctrine, it was nonetheless warmly embraced by all but the most fanatically Blairite tendency in the party.

HOW JEREMY CORBYN BECAME LEADER

It is crucial to remember that up until the summer of 2015, for several decades, any such mapping of Labour's internal politics would have presented Bennism as an almost entirely marginal and residual force. In this context, how did it ever come about that a figure from this smallest and weakest of these internal party tendencies find himself leader of the Labour Party? It seems clear now that two key changes in the culture and constitution of the Labour Party since 2010 made Jeremy Corbyn's eventual shock victory possible.

Throughout its history, the Labour Party has been an organisation composed of multiple elements and informed by competing ideas as to what kind of organisation it should be. Founded at the beginning of the twentieth century, explicitly in order to achieve the goal of getting working-class trade unionists into parliament, Labour was from the beginning a federation of other organisations, principally unions and socialist societies. Indeed, in its earliest iteration there was no such thing as an individual member of the Labour Party – only by joining one of its federated components could an individual become a member.

From the very beginning, therefore, there was a marked tension between the idea of the party as a vehicle for a democratic mass movement, and the understanding that its sole function was to create, maintain, service and serve the interest of the Parliamentary Labour Party. The latter view largely prevailed at a national level until the beginning of the 1980s. The exception was those many municipalities in which Labour had been able to transform local communities without access to or support from national government. Throughout this period, electing the leader remained the sole prerogative of the PLP.

The early 1980s saw both an influx of left-wing activists to the party and a radicalisation of key sections of its membership and of the trade unions: this was the high water mark of Bennism. The 1974-9 Labour government had capitulated to an IMF-imposed structural adjustment plan in an attempt to stabilise the currency, becoming the first major government in the 'developed' world to do so. Widespread disillusion within the party and particularly with its old right wing, from which the prime minister and chancellor during this period had been drawn, was therefore understandable, and fierce battles were subsequently fought between right and left over issues ranging from policy and programme to the presence of entryist Trotskyites within the party.

Perhaps the bitterest of these fights emerged from the struggle to empower both members and affiliated organisations (in particular the unions) in the election of the party leadership. The compromise outcome of this battle was the creation of an electoral college, which granted one third of votes for the leadership to the PLP, one third to the unions, and one third to the 'constituency parties' (local party organisations controlled by and representing individual members). Although the Labour left was not satisfied with the amount of power which the parliamentary party retained under this dispensation, it was enough of a blow to the right of the PLP that a significant section of it split off to create the ill-fated Social Democratic Party (SDP).

Importantly, the other key demand of the left at this time was for mechanisms which would reduce the outright independence of MPs from their constituency parties. Labour MPs have traditionally not been bound by mandates from their members and have not been easy to remove once in office; this independence has been jealously guarded by Labour MPs since the formation of the party, and has always been resented by its more radical rank and file. Some concessions were made to the demand for more accountability for MPs, but these were largely rescinded and even reversed over the course of the 1990s, as the parliamentary party became more and more compliant to an increasingly-centralised leadership, while local parties lost almost all of the power that they had once had.[3] In practice, the electoral college also allowed the PLP to remain by far the most important section of the party when it came to electing that leadership.

Here is where things become ambiguous and rather complex. The Blairites had always understood the weakening of local constituency parties as central to their goals, believing them to be a breeding ground for activists who were by their very nature unrepresentative of, and isolated from, the wider public. The Blairites were always more complacent, however, about the idea of empowering individual members, believing (with some reason) that the typical individual Labour Party member was not an activist, did not participate in the culture of their local constituency party, relied for political information mainly on national media outlets and on the party's centralised communications structures, and so could be expected to be largely compliant with the leadership's programme at any given time, and to support programmes and leaderships which were more likely to be popular with a wider public.

This coincidental history explains why there was very little opposition when the then Labour leader Ed Miliband – who had been elected by the electoral college in 2010, despite his rather weak support within the PLP – introduced a radical change to the leadership rules, granting equal authority to all party members, while creating a new category of registered party 'supporter' who would only have to pay a nominal registration fee, £3 at the time, in order to acquire full voting rights. This was widely seen as an attack more on the continued influence of the trade unions (the other third of the electoral college) than on the PLP, and neither the PLP nor the right of the party generally seem to have perceived the changes as any threat to them. Tony Blair welcomed them enthusiastically.

This was the first change which made both Jeremy Corbyn's 2015 victory, and his re-election in 2016, possible. The other change was subtler, but almost as important. It must be understood here that Corbyn's actual support in the PLP – the proportion of PLP members who openly campaigned for him and cast their votes for him as individual party members – does not come close to 15 per cent. Under normal circumstances he would not be expected ever to have achieved enough nominations to get on the ballot. However, there was an important precedent set during the previous leadership election. The then favourite to win the leadership, Ed Miliband's more right-wing brother David, the darling of the Blairites and of the PLP, had made a gesture of asking a proportion of the MPs who had been planning to nominate him, instead to nominate Diane Abbott, at that time the only black woman in parliament, and a well-known public face of the hard left.

There were a number of motivations for the gesture. On the one hand it was impelled by an honest commitment to liberal feminism and liberal anti-racism which the Blairites share with other 'left' neoliberals around the world, Hilary Clinton being the best example. That there were no women or black people on the ballot therefore was an embarrassment that they genuinely wished to avoid. On the other hand this move signified the total confidence of the Blairites – and indeed the rest of the party – that the hard left had absolutely no hope of even impacting on the contest in any significant way, never mind actually winning it. In this sense, it was symptomatic of the widespread belief that the left was effectively dead as a political force in the UK, and the belief among Blairites that the New Labour project to isolate and neutralise the left within the party had been successfully completed. This is not to say that the Blairites entirely controlled the party. It was fully recognised at the time that David Miliband's younger brother Ed, associated with the soft left, might, as he eventually did, win the 2010 leadership election. But it was assumed that the Bennite tradition represented by a handful of MPs – most of them, like Corbyn and Abbott, representing London constituencies – was an irrelevance, and thus its vanquishers could now afford to indulge it with some opportunities to campaign and make speeches.

In 2015 the situation was slightly different. No candidate had quite the level of support from the PLP that David Miliband had enjoyed in 2010, and the leading candidate – Andy Burnham – had less reason to be complacent about a rival candidate coming from his left (given that he hoped to draw much of his support from the left). Jeremy

Corbyn was a more personally popular figure with the party and the PLP than Diane Abbott (who of course has to contend with racism and sexism in ways which Corbyn never has), in that he was widely perceived as an extremely decent human being and a highly conscientious campaigner and constituency representative. But it was widely assumed that Jeremy Corbyn would be destined to come a distant last in any leadership contest. So with the help of some votes lent by supporters of other candidates, following the 2010 precedent, Corbyn got on the leadership ballot at the last possible moment (having been pushed to stand by colleagues who felt it important that a left voice was heard in the contest). We can be fairly certain that given what followed, this is a precedent which will never be acted on again.

What followed was an unprecedented influx of members and supporters into the party, almost all of whom joined or registered in order to vote for Corbyn. Although huge rallies in support of Corbyn were held around the country, there is little dispute that social media played a decisive role in enabling his otherwise disaggregated potential support base to coalesce and recognise their collective potential. Most evidence suggests that the new members seem to be roughly equally divided between older former members returning to a party which had become too right-wing for them under Blair's leadership, and younger members, most of whom have never previously belonged to a political party, although some of them may have been members of the Greens or small far left groups. At the same time, evidence also shows that a significant section of the existing membership, most of whom would have voted for Ed Miliband in 2010, voted for Corbyn rather than the perceived front-runner and soft-left candidate, Andy Burnham.[4]

This switch of allegiance from a small but strategically significant section of the membership is notable here. The success of the New Labour project was always predicated on the willingness of both the old right (who will traditionally support any programme or leadership they think likely to deliver electoral success) and the soft left to defer to the leadership of the Blairites, many of whose key figures were former members of the soft left themselves. Indeed, Blairisim arguably emerged from the attempt of the soft left in the late 1980s to develop a programme and an electoral strategy which responded effectively to the UK's transition to a largely post-industrial economy.[5] As such it took a long time for many members of the soft left tradition to accept that rather than being a radical project for egalitarian and democratic modernisation, New Labour in government amounted to little more than a total capitulation to the hegemony of finance capital.[6] By 2010, however, this fact had become apparent to a large enough number of them to enable Ed Miliband to confound predictions by beating his Blairite brother to the leadership.

In 2015, the over-caution, incoherence and ultimate electoral failure of Ed Miliband's leadership had led a significant section of the established membership to the conclusion that perhaps the Bennites had been right all along. For many, including those like myself who had previously been associated with the more radical end of the soft left, our position was, as it remains, that the soft left strategy had now been tested to destruction, and that the only logical response was to support Corbyn's bid for the leadership, while arguing for a more imaginative strategy than the Bennites had ever previously shown themselves capable of implementing.[7]

NEOLIBERALISM AND ITS CRISIS

In a larger historical context, both the Brexit vote in 2016 and the success of Corbynism in 2017 must be seen as symptoms of the complete breakdown of neoliberal hegemony in the UK.

The emergence of neoliberalism as an actual political project was in large part a reaction by capitalist elites to the terrifying upsurge of democratic demands which emerged in the 1960s.[8] There was nothing inevitable about the adoption by those elites, from around the mid-1970s, of the general neoliberal programme: a set of ideas and proposals which had been issuing from the Mont Perelin Society and its legatees for several decades by that point. Rather those ideas and policies provided a convenient set of discursive tools with which to respond to a new historic situation. This situation was characterised both by an incipient technological revolution which offered capital the opportunity of rescinding many of the concessions made to governments and organised labour in the post-war period, and by a rising tide of democratic demands to which capitalism had to find an answer if it was to survive the 1970s at all.

From the late 1960s onwards, the automation of manufacturing, as well as outsourcing opportunities created by new communications technologies and the containerisation of shipping, created historic opportunities to shift the balance of power between capital and labour in the core manufacturing countries. At the same time, the possibility that socialists might use the new computer technologies to facilitate their own objectives was something of which certain sections of the capitalist elite were themselves acutely aware.[9] Liberal democratic capitalism appeared to face a genuine existential threat due to the scale of material expectations from populations who were becoming used to ever-rising living standards, and the intensity of the democratic challenges to existing distributions of power and authority issuing from new social movements. 'Actually existing neoliberalism' – to which ever-expanding private consumption and debt was always fundamental – was a response to this situation which both neutralised many of those demands (by enabling private consumption and facilitating a pluralisation of consumption-oriented lifestyles),[10] and re-asserted the supremacy of finance capital over both industrial capital and the rest of the population for the first time since the great crash of 1929.[11]

A crucial element of this process has been the gradual evisceration, since the 1970s, of democratic institutions and almost all forms of public and collective agency. Again, this is a situation in which neoliberalism and the interests it expresses have taken advantage of an underlying social and cultural shift. The pluralisation of lifestyles and the democratisation of values which came to characterise 'postmodern' societies was clearly anticipated by the cultural revolution of the 1960s. But the most far-sighted ideologues of that revolution always saw its impetus to cultural pluralisation as inseparable from a certain collectivism. This collectivism was expressed most clearly by demands for a genuine democratisation of both culture and politics, which would have seen that pluralisation become the condition of possibility for the extension of radically participatory and deliberative mechanisms of self-government across much of society. The achievement of the neoliberal response was to make this process of pluralisation instead the context for an individualisation and marketisation of politics and culture which would ultimately undermine many of the democratic gains of the previous century.[12] In the place of the 1960s promise of radical democracy, from Students for a Democratic Society and Black Power to Paris May 1968 and the Prague Spring, we ended up with a process of ongoing and ubiquitous privatisation, administered by a technocratic elite accountable only to their masters in the bond markets and the banks.

Throughout the era of neoliberal hegemony neoliberal policies have rarely enjoyed a significant popular mandate. In the UK, for example, no opinion poll since the mid-1980s has shown majority support for the extensive programme of public-sector privatisation which has been arguably the defining government policy of the period. The social groups who have benefitted from this programme and in whose interests it has been conducted – finance capital and those class fractions in the media, the tech industries, retail, etc who are most directly in its orbit – are routinely deferred to by politicians and policy makers. But the wider public does not regard them as possessing any special legitimacy or moral authority.[13] Instead, a vast and continuous expansion of credit-financed private consumption is what has secured consent to the continuation of this basically unpopular programme amongst large sections of the public. Across most of Europe, only relatively small, though strategically-significant populations (senior executives, for example) ever really bought into the neoliberal worldview. As such, from the mid-1970s until the crisis of 2008, it was neoliberal capitalism's promise of private luxury which was the basic condition for consent to it, rather than any real ideological enthusiasm for it, or even any widespread acceptance of its norms.

Under such circumstances, even those groups who were most opposed to neoliberalism were until recently forced to accept it as something that effectively could not be challenged at a public political level, except in purely symbolic or rhetorical terms. In the UK one of the institutional forms which this acceptance took was the fact that the most traditionally radical sections of Labour's natural support base and the vast majority of its membership, effectively acquiesced to the leadership of the Blairites, or at least declined to challenge their legacy in any serious way.

The 2008 crisis manifested the inability of financial elites and governments to reproduce a growth model based on continual expansion of private debt, and this ability has really not returned since. Unsurprisingly, it is precisely in those places and amongst those social constituencies where their capacity to keep offering compensations for the gradual erosion of democracy and social solidarity has been weakest, that political opposition to neoliberalism has emerged most dramatically. The obvious examples here are Greece and Spain, but even in the UK, among those sections of the population who either cannot be bought off (because there are no resources left to buy them off with) or won't be, a left resurgence has been under way and seems unlikely to abate any time soon. This is a particularly widespread phenomenon among the young, who across Europe have seen social and economic entitlements gradually eroded since the 1970s, to the point where many now have very little left to lose.

In the specific case of the UK, it is notable that most opinion polls and social attitude surveys have demonstrated the existence of a pretty consistent bloc of public opinion since the beginning of the 1980s that in effect endorses a marxist perspective on all important issues. It probably consists of around 20-25 per cent of the electorate. A recent extensive survey of contemporary political opinion showing the same finding was widely reported to demonstrate how out of touch Corbyn and the new Labour membership are with 'ordinary voters',[14] because only about 20-25 per cent of such voters agree with them on all (rather than just some) major issues.[15] But in any normal parliamentary democracy, a body of opinion shared by a quarter of the population would be expected to have significant public representation. It is symptomatic of neoliberal hegemony at its height that this 20-25 per cent was pretty much denied any representation altogether, and that it largely acquiesced to this denial. Furthermore, it is now symptomatic of its total breakdown that this portion of the electorate was able to mobilise itself so effectively to achieve over 40 per cent support for Labour's break with anti-neoliberal politics in the 2017 election.

The electoral coalition that Labour was able to motivate to achieve this result was arguably unique in British electoral history. Both demographic data and specific constituency results showed a clear pattern.[16] It has been obvious since 2015 that Corbyn's base was in that 20-25 per cent, who are largely drawn from what we might call 'the metropolitan left'. In part, this consists of the London-based liberal intelligentsia so despised by conservative commentators in all parties, but it also includes large numbers of low-paid workers in cities such as London, Leeds and Manchester, especially in the public sector. It also includes smaller university cities, Canterbury and Brighton for example, as well as certain 'traditional' working class populations in former industrial and mining areas where socialism was traditionally popular (parts of the North East and South Wales, for example). These are Corbyn's people. It came as an extraordinary shock to the

professional political classes to find, in 2015, that they had not disap-
peared, but had merely been acquiescent in recent decades. What has
been even more unexpected has been their capacity to win support
from almost the entire electorate under the age of thirty-five, and
from large numbers of affluent professionals (traditional supporters of
liberal Toryism).[17]

What is quite unclear about the latter constituency is what is
really motivating their support for Labour. In part, Theresa May's
courting of working-class Ukip voters and her apparent preference for
a 'hard' Brexit had drastically alienated that constituency, culturally
committed as they are to liberal cosmopolitanism. If this is their main
motivation for backing Labour, then Labour has a problem; May will
almost certainly be replaced at some point, quite possibly by a more
palatable, Cameron-like alternative. On the other hand, all but the
very wealthiest of affluent professionals can now see that the forty-
year neoliberal assault on social privileges and wages has reached a
point where even their own privileged offspring are severely threatened. If this is their main motivation for backing Corbyn, then they
are unlikely to withdraw that support soon, and we really have passed
a historical rubicon.

CHALLENGES AHEAD

In the immediate aftermath of the general election, Labour stood at
an incredible 46 per cent in the opinion polls, with an 8 per cent
lead over the Conservatives: a situation which few of even Corbyn's
most ardent supporters ever thought likely to materialise. But if this
is not to prove a temporary high-water mark, and a missed historic
opportunity, then several key challenges must be overcome. The fact
is, May won the election because she did succeed in winning over a
core section of Labour's traditional constituency: older working-class
voters in smaller towns in the post-industrial areas and on the coast.
These are the people still most likely to read and be influenced by the
Conservative print press, and most likely to feel thoroughly alienated
by almost all of the cultural, social and economic changes of recent
decades. For them, the fact that Corbyn represents – among other
things – metropolitan cosmopolitanism, is a source of incomprehen-
sion and hostility. The greatest challenge for Labour's new organising
model will be to become part of these communities and win them

over with a different analysis of their condition to that offered to them by the *Daily Mail*, persuading them that neoliberal capitalism – rather than social liberalism, immigration and Europe – is the source of their woes. This can be done, but it will require an effort in public political education and socialist proselytisation such as Labour has not undertaken since the 1940s.

Figures on the right of the party are already claiming loudly that only the adoption of an explicitly conservative position on defence and security (and, of course, Brexit) can hope to recover Labour's position in these 'traditional' working class communities.[18] This is wrongheaded for more than one reason. Firstly, it simply ignores the reality that Labour actually gained votes in most of those communities,[19] although the Tories gained more. Secondly, it ignores the fact that the Tories winning support there is not a new phenomenon. There is a long tradition of working class-conservatism and Toryism in this country. Labour has only ever prospered by beating it politically and winning over its adherents to more progressive positions.

At the same time, if it is to undertake such a task without alienating or fragmenting its existing electoral coalition, then Labour will have to keep appealing to youth, to the metropolitan left, and to highly-educated, self-consciously modern, affluent professionals. It is doubtful that it will be able to do this if it ties itself to a programme which could have been implemented in 1951. From this point of view, there was nothing in the June 2017 manifesto that a twenty-first century socialist should object to, but there wasn't much to get excited about either. Co-operative housing, workers' self-management, decentralised media and democratised public services: these should surely be key features of a socialism appropriate to the platform era. These ideas are well known to the Labour leadership, but they weren't in the manifesto. They need to be next time.

It may well be that Labour's greatest challenge will be to hold together a coalition – of the metropolitan left, the 'traditional' working class, disaffected but optimistic youth and cosmopolitan professionals – while the most divisive issue in British politics since the 1930s plays out: Brexit. Whatever the outcome of the Brexit negotiations, Labour will have to convince all of its constituencies that there is something in it for them. Even Corbyn loyalist Rebecca Long-Bailey MP has publicly acknowledged that Labour's policy on Brexit is to 'have our cake and eat it': effectively retaining all the economic benefits of single-market membership without any of the political costs. Whether or not this is a viable political strategy will depend not on the balance of payments or the future rate of immigration, but on a fundamentally political question: what is our strategy for defeating neoliberalism in Europe? If 'lexit' (left-wing Brexit, which some of Corbyn's closest advisors were hoping for long before the referendum) is to become a plausible reality, then it will have to be explained how a pro-lexit Labour government would propose to deal with the inevitable hostility of the entire European Union (and US, and WTO, and IMF, and, in all probability, China) to its project. Those hoping to forestall Brexit altogether (and their numbers will grow as the weakness of Britain's negotiating position becomes apparent) will have to answer much the same question, and explain how remaining within the EU would help.

Internally, the issue which will no doubt prove most divisive for Labour, but which is not going away any time soon, is the question of party reform. Members are frustrated by an archaic internal bureaucracy whose main function and intention always seems to be to frustrate them; or at least to obstruct whatever desires they may have to claim accountability on the part of officials or elected representatives. Momentum ran the most successful political campaign in living memory despite that bureaucracy, not because of it. In the process, it has demonstrated what can be achieved when members are given tools with which to self-organise rather than being presented at every turn with institutional obstacles to them doing so.

MPs and party officials, the entrenched networks of the Blairites and the old right, are terrified of letting the members have any more power. They are right to be: given half a chance, the members would treat them with the contempt that so many of them have so evidently earned, with their constant and simply wrong-headed efforts to undermine Corbyn's leadership. It is hard to see how Corbyn and his followers can achieve everything that they want to, without some reckoning coming sooner or later. There is very little appetite for internal conflict among Corbyn supporters or Momentum members, however, most of whom just want to be able to organise as they see fit to further the party and its cause. How many of the right-wing refuseniks will accept the new historical reality, and how many of them will have to be forced into doing so, remains to be seen, and will be largely up to them.

Beyond the party, Corbyn himself seems well aware that only a full-scale social movement is likely to be able to bring about and sustain political, economic and cultural change on the scale that he and his supporters seek. Radical reform of the party will be one necessary prerequisite for such a movement developing critical mass, but it will not be a sufficient one. Parties and movements are simply not the same kind of thing. Parties fight elections. Movements organise in communities, challenge widespread cultural assumptions, develop dynamic internal intellectual cultures, and disseminate their ideas and their practices at multiple levels of society. These are not mutually-exclusive types of activity, but they are also not simply interchangeable.

The highly decentralised modes of organisation and campaigning pioneered by Momentum,[20] and the vision of a future society implied by the *Alternative Models of Ownership* document, all seem to point towards the possibility of a radically democratic political movement supporting the most radical government in British history: a prospect which looks more likely now than at any time since 1981. For that to happen, a movement committed to radical democracy in many areas of social life – education, local government, the media, parliament – will have to develop, and to acquire a dynamism which no centralised party leadership can contain. For example, demands for local selection of MPs will carry far more authority if we are seen to campaign for democracy in other local institutions as well.

A large-scale campaign of political education would certainly be required to enable activists to achieve real effectiveness in challenging neoliberal assumptions in their everyday communities. At the present time, the level of political debate even on the Labour left rarely rises above the level of moral condemnation of austerity. It is not an abstract proposition to say that this has to improve: all successful social movements – from women's liberation to animal rights – have changed attitudes by promoting more sophisticated ways of understanding certain issues than the ones which went before them. The endemic, historic anti-intellectualism of English political culture remains an obstacle which Corbynism will have to overcome if it is to catalyse the movement that it needs, in order to realise its goals.

It is quite clear that not all of Corbyn's supporters or close advisors share this vision, preferring a centralised party and a statist form of social democracy. These two tendencies can co-exist, and even sustain a productive tension, for a while, as long as the work of displacing neoliberal hegemony requires them to co-operate. The June 2017 general election would not have been such a success for Labour if they had not done so. But sooner, or later, Corbynism as a movement and as a project for the party is going to have to decide whether it wants to simply relive Labour's glory days of the mid-twentieth century, or truly re-imagine socialism for the twenty-first.

NOTES

1. See Neal Lawson, 'Without the soft left, Labour is doomed to splinter', *The Guardian*, 24 July 2015.
2. 'Report to the Shadow Chancellor of the Exchequer and Shadow Secretary for Business, Energy and Industrial Strategy', *Alternative Models of Ownership*, Labour Party, 2016.
3. For example, the process of making party policy was changed so that constituency parties played a far less significant role; rather than policy being decided by the annual national conference, to which constituency parties could send motions and voting delegates, it was passed onto a body known as the National Policy Forum (NPF), which included some representatives who were elected by members voting individually through postal ballots, but lacked any organic connection to the everyday life of local parties. The NPF in effect came to be completely under the control of the central leadership, especially as very few members voted in the elections to it, not knowing anything about most of the candidates, who tended to be party hacks (i.e. activists who were always loyal to the leadership and usually in search of political career advancement), and none of the ordinary membership had ever heard of them.
4. See Peter Kellner, 'An anatomy of Corbyn's victory', www.yougov.co.uk, 15 September 2015.
5. See Jeremy Gilbert, 'The unfinished business of New Times: Reflections on the political legacy of *Marxism Today*', www.jeremygilbertwriting. wordpress.com, 17 November 2013.
6. See Jeremy Gilbert, 'The second wave: The specificity of New Labour neoliberalism', www.jeremygilbertwriting.wordpress.com, 3 November 2004.
7. For a full explanation of my own position, then and as it remains now, see Jeremy Gilbert 'What hope for Labour and the left? The election, the 80s and aspiration', www.opendemocracy.net, 28 July 2015.
8. See Jeremy Gilbert, *Common Ground: Democracy and Collectivity in an Age of Individualism*, Pluto: London, 2014 and Jeremy Gilbert. 'Moving on from the market society: Culture (and cultural studies) in a post-democratic Age', www.opendemocracy.net, 13 July 2012.
9. For an explanation of this potential, Eden Medina, 'The Cybersyn Revolution', www.jacobinmag.com, 27 April 2015.

10. See Jeremy Gilbert, 'What kind of thing is neoliberalism', *New Formations*, Vol. 80/81, 2013, pp7-22.
11. See David Harvey, *A Brief History of Neoliberalism*, Verso: London, 2005.
12. See Wendy Brown, *Undoing the Demos: Neoliberalism's Stealth Revolution*, MIT Press: Cambridge, 2015, and Colin Crouch, *Post-Democracy*, Polity: Cambridge, 2004.
13. See Datablog, 'Social Attitudes Survey: What does Britain think about inequality, bankers and the NHS?', *The Guardian*, 13 December 2010.
14. For background see 2017 British Social Attitudes Survey, www.bsa. natcen.ac.uk.
15. Peter Kellner, 'The gap between Corbyn's support and Labour's target voters', www.yougov.uk, 25 September 2015.
16. See BBC News, 'General Election 2017: Why people voted the way they did' www.bbc.co.uk, 20 June 2017.
17. BBC News, *ibid*.
18. For example John Mann MP, 'Jeremy Corbyn proved me wrong, but now he must answer the Bolsover question', www.politicshome.com, 12 June 2017.
19. See Andrew Murray, 'How do we build on Labour's election results: Not by misunderstanding our position with working class voters', www.labourlist.org, 14 July 2017.
20. See Michael Savage and Alex Hacillo, 'How Jeremy Corbyn turned a youth surge into general election votes', *The Guardian*, 10 June 2017.

The Resistible Rise of Theresa May

Andrew Gamble

Some election results are genuine surprises, but most are not. 1979 and 1997 were hugely significant elections but the results were widely anticipated. The real surprises include 1970, 1974 (February), 1992 and 2015. But these have all been outdone by the general election of 2017. When Theresa May announced at the beginning of April that she planned to hold an early election, she had been in office for a little over eight months. But she was riding high. She had just received the backing of both Houses of Parliament to invoke Article 50 and start the negotiations over Britain's withdrawal from the European Union. The Conservatives enjoyed leads in the opinion polls of more than 20 per cent. May herself had positive popularity ratings, and according to those same polls, was overwhelmingly regarded by voters as the party leader who would make the best prime minister. The Conservatives were also far ahead of the Labour Party on economic competence. They had just won the Copeland by-election, a working-class seat which had been Labour since the 1930s, the first gain for a governing party in a by-election since 1982. May had the enthusiastic support of most British newspapers, and a much better funded and more organised electoral machine than her opponents. Many colleagues had been urging her to go the polls to give herself a strong personal mandate, and to increase her authority in the forthcoming Brexit negotiations. In the local government elections held on 5 May, the Conservatives had an 11 per cent lead over Labour. The result of the election was therefore not in doubt, the only questions were what the size of the Conservative majority would be and how great would be the scale of Labour's defeat. Labour, internally divided and with an unpopular leader, appeared to be facing an even worse defeat than 1983, when it polled 28 per cent of the vote and was reduced to 209 seats. Many in

Labour thought the party might fall below 200 seats for the first time since the 1930s, and receive less than a 25 per cent share of the vote.

But instead of their expected landslide, the Conservatives lost seats and lost their parliamentary majority, even though they recorded their highest vote share since 1983 and their highest number of votes since 1992 – almost 14 million. They also made twelve gains in Scotland against the SNP, their best result since 1983. In England, their strategy targeted Labour marginals in the North of England and the Midlands, particularly in those seats where the Ukip vote had been strong in 2015. They calculated that the Ukip vote was soft and could be won by Conservative candidates, given that the party was promising to deliver Brexit. Part of this strategy worked. The Ukip vote share did indeed collapse by eleven percentage points, and their votes fell from 4 million to 600,000. The Conservatives took more than half these votes, but they only won five of their target seats. A significant minority of Ukip votes went to Labour, which was also buoyed by the support of most of its 2015 voters and by a huge surge of support amongst a new turn out of young voters. Labour increased its share of the vote by almost ten percentage points, narrowing the gap with the Conservatives to two and a half points. They won more than 40 per cent of the vote for the first time since 2001, and for only the third time since 1970. Labour lost the election but its thirty net gains put the party back in contention. It lost traditional Labour seats like Mansfield but won in improbable places like Canterbury and Kensington. The Conservatives won fifty-five more seats than Labour but this was not enough to secure an overall majority. Like Edward Heath in 1974, they had called an early general election expecting to be endorsed by the electorate, and instead had been rebuffed.

Theresa May's authority as leader was shattered. She had seemed on the brink of establishing an unassailable personal dominance. Her campaign, unwisely in retrospect, reflected that expectation. It was all about her. Other members of the shadow cabinet had limited roles in the campaign or, like Philip Hammond, were denied a platform altogether. There was much talk about the reshuffle planned for the weekend after the election; Hammond was expected to be one of the main casualties because of his hostility to central tenets of Mayism, notably on Brexit and on industrial strategy. Despite May's departure from Thatcherite economic principles, her firm commitment to Brexit persuaded the Conservative tabloids to anoint her as the new Thatcher.

The *Daily Mail, Daily Express, The Daily Telegraph* and *The Sun* gave her the kind of unconditional backing they had withheld from all of Thatcher's other successors. When Trump was elected, they speculated, somewhat improbably, that he would be the new Reagan to her Maggie, and together they would renew the 'special relationship' and strengthen the Anglosphere. She revelled in the epithet of being 'a bloody difficult woman', just as Thatcher had delighted in being called the 'iron lady'. But all this was changed dramatically by the election result. Speculation focused on how long May could remain in her position, and few believed she could lead the Conservatives into another election. All political careers are notoriously uncertain, but rarely has a fall been so precipitous or vertiginous as Theresa May's.

THE MAY RISING

Theresa May became leader of the Conservatives and prime minister by accident. David Cameron had planned to step down in 2019, handing on to a preferred successor from his circle, most probably George Osborne, in time for the next general election in 2020. After winning what was a widely unexpected overall majority in 2015, he was obliged to hold a referendum on the EU because it had been one of his pre-election pledges, and he decided to hold it early, after fairly perfunctory negotiations. It seems evident that he did not think he would lose the vote, but, since he had campaigned so strongly to remain in the EU, he resigned as soon as the result was announced, triggering a frenzied fight for the succession. At the same time, the Labour Party also went into meltdown, embroiled in a second leadership contest in a year, after most of the shadow cabinet resigned in a bid to force Jeremy Corbyn to stand down, citing amongst other things his lukewarm support for the Vote Remain campaign.

May had been a 'remainer', but a very low-key one; she rarely surfaced during the campaign. Having been home secretary for six years, she was known for a tough rhetorical stance on immigration, although any success she could claim for bringing figures down to the government's target of 'tens of thousands' was slight. Her anti-immigration rhetoric at the 2015 Conservative Party Conference was markedly out of step with the pro-European messages other ministers were trying to convey ahead of the referendum. Before she became leader, she was hard to place in the Tory political spectrum. She had not shown much interest either in the economy or in foreign affairs. She had not been part of David Cameron's inner circle, but was also not part of the more traditional Tory right. One of the few occasions on which she was prominent, that had stuck in political memory, was when, as party Chairwoman in 2002, she told a rather surprised Conservative Party Conference: 'you know what some people call us: the nasty party'.

The leadership campaign in July 2016 seemed to bear out her description of the Conservatives. By the time it was over, the party resembled the final scene in *Hamlet*, with bodies strewn everywhere. Only Theresa May was left standing, and the party united around her, arguing that she could give the party and the country stability and reassurance. Initially, there was some dismay among Conservatives, who had voted and campaigned to leave the EU, that Theresa May had backed the Vote Remain campaign. Many 'leavers' argued that only someone who had voted to leave could be trusted to deliver Brexit. Some prominent leave campaigners like Christopher Grayling did back Theresa May, but few others from that circle were behind her. They preferred anyone but May; Boris Johnson, Michael Gove and Andrea Leadsom, all briefly aspired, with support, before ultimately disappearing. May thus succeeded to the leadership without having to win the endorsement of the party members. The speed of her election meant that she was not obliged to reveal very much at all about what she believed, or make promises that she might have regretted.

Pro-remain Conservatives were at first happier than those who were pro-leave, when Theresa May was confirmed as prime minister. There was much talk about the government being in the hands of a 'grown-up', and May was expected to be cautious and favour continuity. Appointing Philip Hammond as her chancellor appeared to guarantee that the interests of the City and the wider economy would shape the government's Brexit negotiating strategy, and that some of the wilder fantasies of pro-Brexit campaigners would be dispelled. The appointment of such 'Brexiters' to head departments closely involved with Brexit was seen as necessary to ensure party unity, but also as skilful, binding them in to the negotiating strategy agreed by the whole government. May made it very clear that she was going to be in overall control of policy, aided by her two chiefs of staff, Fiona Hill and Nicholas Timothy, and was not intending to delegate key decisions to any other ministers.

As the months passed however, it was those who were pro-leave who found much more to cheer than 'remainers'. They were impressed with her performance as prime minister. She had apparently seen the light and been reborn as pro-leave. She tilted the balance of government policy firmly towards the demands of the Vote Leave campaign and explicitly ruled out the soft landings favoured by 'remainers'. Her position was set out in her two speeches to the Conservative Party Conference in October 2016. She stated that she had believed before the referendum that the case to remain in the EU was superior, but after the vote to leave, she accepted the new political reality. Her declaration that 'Brexit means Brexit' attracted derision, but, for her, this slogan had a very precise meaning which she set out in her Lancaster House speech in January 2017. She dismissed the idea that there was a choice between a soft and a hard Brexit. For her there was only Brexit. The vote on 23 June 2016, she repeatedly declared, was 'clear and decisive', and gave the government a mandate to implement Brexit. It was quite evident, she said, what the people had voted for, namely that Britain should be a 'sovereign' nation again, with all the attributes that sovereign nations have, particularly control of their borders.

Theresa May's position was dictated by the nature of the party she had come to lead. John Major and David Cameron both struggled to stop their party 'banging on' about Europe. May concluded that in the light of the referendum result, it was futile to try to limit these conversations. YouGov estimates that 61 per cent of Conservative voters in 2015 voted to leave the EU.[1] The ministerial payroll voted strongly to remain, but a small majority of Conservative backbenchers did back the Vote Leave campaign,[2] as did most Conservative newspapers, and a large majority of Conservative associations and members. Theresa May knew that as leader her vote to remain made her suspect, and knew that if she appeared lukewarm about Brexit, her party would quickly become unmanageable. She chose instead to allay the fears of the Conservative 'leavers' and the Conservative tabloids. Ending free movement became a red line for her, because, as suggested, it involved sovereignty. Negotiating a good trade deal for the City and protecting universities were defined as secondary issues. They might be important national interests, to be secured if possible in the negotiations, but they could not be allowed to compromise the sovereignty of the British state.

May took the decision that her political future and the future of the Conservative Party depended on delivering a Brexit which the pro-leave elements of her party would accept. We can assume that she was well aware of the economic costs and risks of Brexit, but she was even more aware of the political costs of not delivering a Brexit which satisfied pro-leave Conservatives; the people had spoken and their wishes had to be respected. Britain was to be a sovereign nation again. It might be significantly poorer than it would otherwise have been, and the deficit in the public finances significantly larger, but if there was a price for Brexit it had to be paid. In public she still claimed, along with the more optimistic 'Brexiters', that she could deliver Britain's exit from the customs union and the single market (and therefore an end to free movement), as well as a free trade deal with the EU. But she never presented it as a trade-off. Sovereignty came first. If she had to choose, borders would come before trade. In this way she hoped to end the great Conservative civil war over Europe.

This hope was dashed by the 2017 election result, along with much else. With a larger parliamentary majority May might have hoped to see off any dissent within her own party during the course of the negotiations. Lacking a majority, and reliant on the Democratic Unionists, left her at the mercy of a divided and fractious party and an unruly Cabinet. Brexit has dominated British politics since the referendum, and the election result offered no escape. This was presumably frustrating for May, as she did not want to be remembered just for Brexit. Her team had crafted an ambitious agenda for changing Britain, laid out in the ill-fated manifesto. It involved much greater reliance on the state to create a 'shared society', dealing with the grievances of those who felt they had been ignored, tackling 'burning injustices', removing obstacles to social mobility and increasing the availability of well-paid jobs through an industrial strategy. It aimed for a more socially conservative and retro Britain, with plans to open new grammar schools, bring back fox hunting, reduce the numbers of immigrants and set limits to cultural diversity. All of that has now had to be abandoned.

MAY AFTER THATCHER

The Conservative Party still lives in the shadow of Thatcher and the Thatcher years, and seems incapable of escaping them. It has not won a convincing parliamentary majority since 1987, Thatcher's third and final election victory. There have been seven elections since then. In three (1997, 2001 and 2005) the party suffered major defeats, in two it won small majorities (1992 and 2015) and two have resulted in hung parliaments (2010 and 2017). Since Thatcher ceased to be leader, the party has had six leaders, and has been riven by disputes over Europe and over how far it should continue to be guided by Thatcherite principles. Every leader has been compared to Thatcher and every leader has been found wanting.

Thatcher was claimed by both sides in the EU referendum. Charles Powell, her former foreign policy adviser, argued she would have voted to remain in the EU because of her pragmatic estimate of where the balance of advantage lay. But this was bitterly disputed by Norman Tebbit and other keepers of the Thatcherite flame. The problem for Conservatives is that they have turned Thatcher into a myth, and much of the nuance and contingency of the Thatcher years has been lost.[3] The Thatcher years seem so special in retrospect because during them, the party sensed it was not just in office but in power. Between 1979 and 1997, it won four elections, and its programme and ideology gradually became hegemonic, although not without some mighty struggles. The Thatcherites had the satisfaction of not only dismantling many of the key institutions and policies of the post-war era, but also of fashioning a new set of institutions and policies, which have subsequently constrained their successors.

Prior to 1979, the Conservatives had had long spells in government, notably the thirteen years between 1951 and 1964, but Thatcherites condemned that period as one of accommodating Labour's priorities, and lamented that their governments had done so little to challenge those expectations. Thatcher was different. Although she was much more pragmatic and cautious than her image suggested, she always had a vision of the direction she wished to go, and she was never satisfied with what had been achieved. She always wanted to go further. This characterised her leadership and her time as prime minister, and if anything it grew more marked as time went on. As a result, her government transformed Britain in many ways, and not always the ones she intended. She restored an idea of the market as the dominant institution for assessing public policy, and although she did not reduce the size of the state very much, she did change attitudes to what it was appropriate for the state to do, and identified areas from which the state should be withdrawn. The passionate intensity of the Thatcher years, which saw Thatcher both demonised and sanctified, helped to ensure her passage into myth.

Dealing with a myth was a heavy burden for her successors to carry, as John Major and every succeeding leader has discovered. Each leader has tried to manage the legacy in different ways, and the more time has elapsed, the bolder some of them have become. David Cameron and Theresa May stand out as the two leaders who tried hardest to break the hold of the Thatcherite orthodoxy, but neither has ultimately succeeded. They needed a big personal mandate to do so; May thought this was in her grasp but at the last moment, it slipped away.

CHANGING TIMES

As discussed, before the election, Labour was facing an existential crisis. The Conservatives had united under their new leader after the Brexit vote, and presented themselves as the only possible party that could offer 'strong and stable' government. May planned to win back all those who had defected to Ukip, as well as making a pitch for Labour voters. She wanted the Conservatives to become the new party of the working class. Labour seemed hopelessly divided. 65 per cent of Labour voters had voted to remain in the EU, but 70 per cent of all Labour constituencies had voted to leave.[4] Labour had already lost its Scottish heartland to the SNP in 2015, and now its English and Welsh heartlands looked vulnerable to the Conservatives.

Conservative unforced errors and a highly successful Labour campaign turned Labour's existential crisis into an existential crisis for the Conservatives. Brexit has proved double-edged. It unleashed a tide of anti-establishment sentiment that first took down Cameron and the liberal elite and has now been turned against the Conservatives and the Brexit elite. Anti-austerity and class politics, which had not provided Labour with much traction in 2015 suddenly roared into life. Labour's manifesto promised extra spending and support for every public service from the armed forces and police to the NHS and education, and made targeted promises to particular groups, including abolishing university tuition fees and the public sector pay cap, all to be funded by rather modest tax increases for companies and the rich. The content was broadly social democratic, consistent with Labour manifestos over the last fifty years, but the appeal was populist; it rejected the political establishment and its ruling ideas. The manifesto did not spell out the intellectual case for that rejection, but instead it focused on practical policies to help different groups struggling with austerity and debt.

The contrast between this and the Conservative manifesto was stark. The latter contained an intellectual defence of Mayism, and argued for the central place of the state in managing the economy. Nigel Lawson denounced it as 'social democratic' and Norman Tebbit called it 'anti-Thatcherite'.[5] What was even worse, was the lack of specific offers to target voters; this had been a prominent feature of the 2015 Conservative manifesto. Apart from the promise to deliver Brexit the manifesto was largely negative, taking things away from voters, such as free school lunches and threatening to tax the assets of the elderly to fund their social care.

The tide turning against austerity puts the Conservatives on the defensive. Support for public spending, higher taxation and even redistribution has begun to increase again.[6] Yet the government is still running a high deficit and the UK's national debt has reached 80 per cent of GDP, alongside growing household debt. There are increasing calls to ditch austerity, increase spending and even increase some taxes. Most economists argue that there is scope to do this. But politically this will make the government look weak, because they will be moving on to Labour's ground, and here, Labour will always outbid them. Feeding the growing popular desire to be rid of austerity will only allow that desire to grow stronger. The Grenfell Tower disaster, and May's fumbling response, has created more problems for the Conservatives, because of the widespread perception that spending cuts and deregulation played a part in making the impact of the fire so devastating.

This is all very bad news for the Conservatives and specifically for those who were pro-Brexit, many of whom expected that leaving the EU would allow a return to the Thatcherite agenda of low taxes, small state and less regulation. Radical reform of the NHS and education would at last become possible. Brexit Britain would be global Britain, a land of enterprise and individualism. But this vision was not shared by many who voted for Brexit; many of the people whom Ukip mobilised as well as many older Labour working-class voters wanted more security and protection, particularly from free movement of people but also from the free movement of goods and capital, which had caused so many of them to be left behind and excluded. Many voting to leave wanted a closed rather than an open Britain. They want their country back. Taking back control, from their perspective, did not mean handing it over to foreign multinationals and hedge fund traders.

The dilemma for the Conservatives in their weakened state is that it seems impossible to deliver a deal which can keep the Conservative Party united, and still less one which can unite the country, and keep England, Scotland, Wales and Northern Ireland together. Many citizens who voted to leave the EU wanted Brexit to happen without delay, and cannot understand why it is taking so long. Business lobbies on the other hand are pressing for lengthy transition arrangements to make the change as smooth as possible. The political risk for the government is that the more they listen to business lobbies in order to protect jobs and prosperity, the more 'Brexiters' will start wondering whether the decision to leave the EU has made any difference at all. Britain's already semi-detached status in the EU does not help in this respect. If Britain was a member of the eurozone or had signed the Schengen agreement, then the decisions to leave the euro and reintroduce the pound, or to reimpose hard borders, would provide quick and easy symbolic reassurance that Britain had, in fact, left the EU. But with Brexit very few citizens will be able to tell what difference it has made. The continuing flow of goods, capital and migrants is likely to be greater than many of the people voting to leave were expecting. To negotiate new trade agreements, the UK will have to be prepared to abandon many regulatory and environmental protections, and to reduce taxation, potentially weakening still further the fiscal basis of its welfare state. Promoting a global Britain and at the same time a more sharing society work in opposite directions, and appeal to different parts of the coalition of leave voters.

FUTURE PROSPECTS

After the unexpected Conservative election victory in 2015 and still more after the unexpected referendum result, the Tory right was jubilant. Now, the unexpected 2017 election result has cast them into despair. The threat of a Labour government led for the first time by the party's left, is terrifying enough, but they also fear that Brexit may be diluted or even abandoned altogether. Charting a way back to Conservative recovery looks hard. Some Conservative writers like

Allister Heath in *The Daily Telegraph* console themselves with the argument that the six months after the general election will turn out to be 'peak Corbyn', after which the surge of support for Corbyn's Labour will subside.[7] Others think that the Conservatives will need to elect a new leader once the first part of the Brexit negotiations is complete in 2018 or 2019, and then set out a new programme for the electorate. But there is little agreement on either who or what that should be. One of the biggest electoral problems for the Conservatives is that they have become heavily dependent on older voters, and they have lost support in the higher income groups and among those with university degrees. Their appeal to the young has plummeted, so they need to find new ways to connect with these younger voters, particularly over student debt, housing and pay.

Whatever now emerges it is unlikely to be Mayism. Theresa May's shortlived experiment with industrial strategy and an active state to protect all its citizens, intervening in markets, controlling borders and investing in public services, was an audacious attempt to move on to Labour's ground. But it was always unclear how much support such a strategy commanded in either the Cabinet or the parliamentary party. After its chief architect, Nicholas Timothy, who helped run the most dysfunctional Downing Street in British political history, was forced out after the election defeat, Mayism seemed doomed. The Treasury had never liked it, and May no longer had the authority to push it through. The Red Tory dream of the Conservatives as the party of the working class, the successor to both Labour and Ukip may be hard to resuscitate now.

Difficult too will be any return to the project of the Cameron/Osborne years, which sought to combine economic and social liberalism, modernising the Conservative Party to keep it in tune with those new sectors, entrepreneurs and lifestyles that emerged so strongly in the 1990s and early 2000s. Cameron and his supporters continued New Labour's social liberal reforms, but broke with New Labour economic policy, repositioning themselves as fiscal conservatives, pinning the blame for the crash and recession on Labour profligacy. This worked politically but it provided no stable basis for government, because they had no strategy for overcoming the structural weaknesses of the economy, which the crash highlighted. Their misjudgement of Brexit destroyed their grip on the party and on government. And this will be hard to restore.

The most likely instinct of Conservatives in the short term will be to move right, rekindling the Thatcherite flame. This might even be led by Theresa May, if she can achieve a relatively quick and successful negotiation of Brexit, but that seems unlikely. Whether it is May or her successor, a Conservative leader is likely to ditch Mayism and re-embrace Thatcherism, recommitting to a small state, low taxes, free trade, national sovereignty and strong defence. Is the nation ready to hear that again? It has become a hard one to sell after ten years of austerity and squeezed household incomes, and thirty years of rising inequality. The 2010s are not the 1970s.

Conservative prospects now depend in part on what Labour does. That in itself is a huge change from the recent past. The initiative has passed to Corbyn's Labour, but the party still has a big task ahead. It need to hold all of the 9.6 per cent swing achieved in 2017 and then add a further 3.5 per cent swing to capture the additional sixty-four seats (twice as many as it won in 2017) to have even a majority of one in the next Parliament.[8] The seats Labour would need to win mostly have fewer young voters, fewer students, fewer ethnic voters and fewer public sector workers than the seats they currently hold. They will have to win back C2 voters where the Conservatives still have a majority, and make inroads into the older vote, as well as winning back more seats in Scotland.[9] Even just to become the largest party in a hung parliament Labour would need to win as many new seats again as it won in 2017. Either of these is a huge, but not impossible, task. The party has a pathway to achieve this, but it will need a still broader coalition than the one it achieved in 2017. Labour's manifesto was very successful, but it is unlikely the Conservatives will fight another election with so little focus on the economy. As a prospective government, the credibility of Labour's proposals on tax and spend will be subject to much greater scrutiny. Because it is a social democratic manifesto and not a socialist one (the few nationalisation measures barely scratch the surface of structural economic power), the party will need to form alliances with businesses and the City to implement it.

In mid-2017, the world economic situation does not look particularly benign for an experiment in left social democracy or any other form of social democracy. There were repeated warnings, including from the Bank of International Settlements in June 2017,[10] of the increasing risks of a new financial crisis. The underlying problems in the international economy have been contained but not overcome.

Corbyn's Labour will also face much greater attention on its policy on Brexit. As Matt Bolton has argued, the manifesto cleverly triangulated the issue,[11] and the party managed to please both those who were pro-leave and pro-remain by promising to leave the single market, leave the customs union, end free movement but still secure the same access to EU markets as the UK currently has. This cost-free Brexit will not stand up in the negotiations, and at some point Labour will have to make challenging choices which will divide its voters as well as its MPs. The election has reunited the Labour Party, but it is a precarious unity.

This is a highly volatile political situation. The public mood keeps changing in unexpected ways, and will change again. We have seen the triumph of Trump and Brexit, but also of Macron and Trudeau, as well as populist insurgencies of right and left in many parts of Europe, including Corbyn's Labour. Populist insurgencies can very quickly lose their momentum, and the challenge for Corbyn's Labour is to prevent that from happening and to win the power to form a government. If it falters, the initiative could pass back to the Conservatives again. They are a chameleon party with a very strong instinct for power, and the old political order which was resilient for so long after the crash, has begun to crack, but it has not yet collapsed. The political impasse throughout the western world is profound, because while neoliberalism appears exhausted and increasingly threadbare, the shape of a new framework is still very unclear. There remains doubt as to whether any agency can resolve this crisis, in the face of the intractable nature of the problems in our political economy, problems that circulate around international governance, growth and legitimacy.[12]

NOTES

1. 'How Britain Voted', www.yougov.co.uk, 27 June 2016.
2. 'Europe. How Conservative MPs break down final remain estimate. 185 Tory MPs, 91 on the patrol, 94 not', www.conservativehome.com, 23 June 2016.
3. See Richard Vinen, *Thatcher's Britain*, Simon & Schuster: London, 2009.
4. Chris Hanretty, 'Most Labour MPs represent a constituency that voted leave', www.medium.com, 30 June 2016.
5. Nigel Lawson, 'Margaret Thatcher understood the secret of winning elections: free market economic policy', *The Telegraph*, 10 June 2017; Norman Tebbit, 'Theresa May arrogantly abandoned Thatcherism – this is her reward', *The Telegraph*, 9 June 2017.

6. Patrick Butler, 'UK Survey finds huge support for ending austerity', *The Guardian*, 29 June 2017.
7. Allister Heath, 'This political chaos doesn't scare me – It's a sign of Britain Growing Up', *The Daily Telegraph*, 28 June 2017.
8. See George Eaton, 'Why a Labour Majority at the next General Election has become far easier', *New Statesman*, 10 June 2017.
9. See Patrick Diamond and Charlie Cadywould, *Don't Forget the Middle: How Labour Can Win a New Centre-Left Majority*, Policy Network, 2017.
10. See Bank for International Settlements, Eighty-Seventh Annual Report.
11. Matt Bolton, 'Reassessing Corbynism: Success, Contradictions and a Difficult Path Ahead', SPERI, 13 June 2017.
12. Wolfgang Streeck, *How will capitalism end? Essays on a failing system*, Verso: London, 2016; Andrew Gamble, *Crisis without end? The unravelling of western prosperity*, Palgrave Macmillan: London, 2014.

Labour's New Model Party

Jessica Garland

The Labour Party entered the snap general election of 2017 with over half a million members and supporters, the highest official support base the party had enjoyed for over four decades. Previous party leaders had sought to expand membership with some success but this doubling of membership represented the most numerically successful recruitment exercise in the party for decades. Yet changing the incentives for partisan support in order to attract new participants can have consequences for parties. It can shift the locus of representational authority in the party and affect the type of organisational resources the party can draw on. The relationship between supporter numbers and party strength is not straightforward. Moving to an organisational model of expanded and more open affiliation is a delicate balancing act, in which parties are moving with the tide of individualisation and fragmentation of party support yet are bound by party traditions and culture. The expansion of partisan support appears to have delivered in the 2017 election, particularly the mass canvassing campaigns, but how successful will the party be in engaging its new half-a-million-strong support base in the future?

Party membership numbers have long been associated with party strength. Members are a crucial operational resource for parties, making up the available pool of candidates for elections, providing an 'on the ground' campaigning resource and providing funding through membership fees and individual donations. Membership numbers are also seen as enhancing legitimacy by demonstrating an important link between the party and the electorate, particularly if party members reflect the sections of electorate the party seeks to represent. In this way, a party's membership is valuable even if it is largely inactive. Party members provide both a functional and a legitimising resource to party organisation and, on this basis, a decline in numbers clearly weakens party strength. Indeed, the downward trajectory of party membership numbers in the major European parties over the last fifty years has led many commentators to herald the end of the mass membership political party.

Yet the death of the mass membership party may have been announced prematurely. Labour, the SNP, the Liberal Democrats, Ukip and the Green Party have all seen membership increases in the last five years. Following the Scottish independence referendum, SNP membership rose to over 100,000 from less than 10,000 a decade previously. Both the Green Party and Ukip have had significant membership growth in the last few years, particularly following the 2015 general election. The Liberal Democrats, having lost members after the 2010 general election, gained enough members in the aftermath of the EU referendum to reach their highest membership since the early 1990s.

Recent membership changes in UK parties would suggest that significant political events have had more effect on party recruitment than specific membership drives, yet parties do invest in attracting members, often changing the membership incentives to do so. Sustaining mass membership has required parties to rethink the nature of partisan support. By adapting to models of support more familiar to newer parties, traditional parties like Labour are moving towards open affiliation structures and expanding intra-party democracy. In many ways, this is a natural response to changes in society that have made formal party membership less attractive; declines in class and social ties, and changes in leisure opportunities and communities mean that party membership had become an increasingly unusual choice, even for politically motivated citizens. Parties have responded by expanding affiliation options and making it easier to get involved in party activity outside of formal membership. Across Europe, parties have been changing the way they engage with supporters, opening up affiliation options to include 'light' or temporary support status and in some (albeit rare) cases, opening up political rights to these wider constituencies of supporters, such as offering voting rights in leader selections and policy development.[1] Yet whilst attracting new support, these organisational changes have consequences: in changing the incentives to join, parties also change the shape of the party and partisans within it.

LABOUR AS A MASS PARTY

For Labour, mass membership has not always been the primary concern. The steady decline in numbers between 1953 and 1983 was largely ignored. Membership was not seen as a critical source of organisational strength during this period, as developments in polling and media-led campaigning together with the dominance of trade union funding, appeared to leave members with little role in campaigning or in financing the party. It was under the leadership of Neil Kinnock that the link between membership and party strength took on new significance. Kinnock stated an intention to return membership to over a million and introduced schemes to convert trade union affiliates to full membership. Whilst this recruitment drive only saw modest increases, the focus on membership growth continued and recruitment of new members was given sustained attention under Tony Blair's leadership. By 1996, Labour's membership exceeded 400,000 from a low of just over 260,000 in 1991.

Elected leader in 2010, Ed Miliband made rebuilding the party as a mass movement a strong theme in his project to renew Labour post Blair and Brown. The 'Refounding Labour' review, initiated in 2011, aimed to 'rebuild a mass movement ... to reach out to a wider range of individual supporters, community groups and national organisations' and led to a change in the party's rules.[2] This change, for the first time, formalised the role of non-member support in achieving the party's primary aims. It paved the way for the introduction of a one-member-one-vote (OMOV) model for leadership elections but with a crucial addition: non-member registered supporters would also be included. In this way, whilst finalising the long-awaited move to OMOV, the party also took a significant step beyond formal membership.

This procedural change, and the leadership contest that followed in 2015, set in process the largest increase in membership the party has witnessed in recent decades. The first leadership election under the new rules saw 553,954 members and registered supporters combined (both £3 registered supporters and trade union members who had opted-in) take part. Jeremy Corbyn attracted the votes of 251,417 of these members and supporters. Less than a year later, by the midpoint of 2016, Labour had over half a million members alone. Not quite a return to a million members but enough to make Labour the largest party in the UK with more members than all the other UK political parties put together.

However, this period in the party's history demonstrates the challenges of expanding party democracy. The Labour Party more than doubled membership numbers during 2015-16 yet few would argue that this period saw the best of party organisation; there were widening internal divisions between MPs and members, local parties were suspended and the NEC was challenged in the High Court when it backdated a cut-off point for members and supporters to qualify to vote in the leadership election.

CHANGING THE 'NARRATIVE OF REPRESENTATION'

The changes in party organisation that are needed to attract a wider group of supporters have consequences for party organisation. Susan Scarrow has coined the term 'multi-speed membership' to describe the way many parties are opening up support structures and moving beyond formal membership. However, Scarrow also notes that for most parties, the move to 'multi-speed' organising is not a complete transformation but a 'layering' of new affiliation options on top of traditional party structures. It is this layering that has the potential to create tensions within the party. When member rights and privileges are extended to a wider group of supporters, questions about the distribution of influence arise: the change brings into question the party's 'narrative of representation'.[3] Parties that have grown out of a cleavage representation model (defending group interests and using membership to reinforce links to the groups they represent) have difficulties with the shift to a 'multi-speed' membership model. In such parties, the widening of membership presents a significant shift in the party's notion of political legitimacy, that is, who the party represents and who should define its values.

The Labour Party is still very much in the cleavage representation model, despite having moved away from it through various periods of modernisation. This tradition is imprinted in Labour's organisational culture and it helps explain the difficulties the party has experienced in dealing with the consequences of moving to 'multi-speed' membership. These matters are not confined to issues of left and right, they encompass the very 'narrative of representation' within the party.

In 2015, during the leadership contest, the party initiated a vetting procedure that involved the rigorous checking of supporter sign ups, their social media activity, past political behaviour and support. Whilst this may have been aimed at avoiding a legal challenge (and was no doubt fuelled by those who publicly sought to undermine the process, such as high-profile members of other parties), it also suggests the party had a problem with the full implications of a 'multi-speed' way of organising. A year later, the party re-instituted and backdated a six- month cut-off for membership rights to vote in leadership elections, restricted the period for registering as a supporter to a two-day window, and raised the price of doing so from £3 to £25. The six-month cut-off rule was successfully challenged in the High Court in a case brought by new members but reversed in the Court of Appeal in favour of the NEC. Despite this hike in registration fee, over 180,000 supporters registered in the two-day window, earning a significant amount for the party coffers but moving some way from the aims and ideals of an open contest.

Whilst some of these reversals can be put down to a struggle between factions within the party, the act of establishing rules for who can and cannot have a vote (especially rules based on previous affiliations and social media activity) is indicative of an underlying organisational conflict. These are the actions of a party that seeks to demand pure allegiance and commitment, a party in the cleavage representation model, a party not entirely comfortable with 'multi-speed' organising or indeed 'multi-speed' partisans. By contrast, such issues have not presented a problem for newer parties that have embraced open affiliation, participation and engagement structures from their inception. Environmental parties and parties of the left that have grown out of social movements often have participatory mechanisms built into their structures from the outset. Yet even with these parties, such mechanisms are often put under strain when parties rapidly expand or pursue an electoral strategy.

CHANGING INCENTIVES, CHANGING PARTISANS

Changing party structures not only challenges a party's representational traditions, it changes partisans. Remodelling how a party engages support is likely to have implications for what a party can expect from its members and supporters. In countries where primaries for candidate and leader selection are more established, such contests can increase membership but they may also lead to a less attached support base. Membership increases around these contests, but partisan support can be weak and volatile. Moving to 'multi-speed' membership requires a shift in how the party views individual support. It is not possible to embrace a more open model of organisation, opening-up engagement and participation, whilst also demanding unwavering, lifelong loyalty from members and supporters. Indeed, the notion of lifelong support misunderstands the nature of partisan attachment; the relationship between partisan identity and political interest is far more fluid. Parties unwilling to allow that their current supporters may have previously placed their political support elsewhere will close themselves off to a vast number of politically interested citizens.

So 'multi-speed' parties not only need to balance open structures with party traditions but also accept that this opening of structures comes with a more fluid support base. The fluidity of partisan support is not necessarily a new phenomenon for the Labour Party. In 2010, a year containing both an election and a leadership contest, of those signing up as members that year, only 50 per cent were still members five years later; 25 per cent of these members didn't last the year.[4] The growth in membership of other UK parties around national referendums and elections supports a sense of membership in flux that can have consequences for all parties' future organisation.

Following the huge growth in membership and support in the two years following the 2015 general election, the key question for Jeremy Corbyn's Labour Party going into the snap election was what the party could expect from its expanded and potentially less attached support base. The decision to move to a more open model of affiliation not only challenges the nature of representation in the party, changing who the party is responsible to, but can have consequences for organisational resource: what the support base does for the party.

The expanding of leader selection rights to individual members in the 1990s, whilst increasing membership numbers, did not lead to equivalent increases in active support. Patrick Seyd and Paul Whiteley's seminal work on Labour Party membership during this period finds that whilst membership increased, average rates of participation declined. Their research concludes that expanding opportunities for plebiscitary activity is 'ultimately self-defeating' if the aim is to encourage wider grassroots activity.[5] Research on the activity of new supporters and members suggests that non-member supporters are less likely to engage in 'high-intensity' activities such as canvassing: activities that remain crucial for parties during elections.[6]

During the first leadership contest in 2015 and after the election of Jeremy Corbyn as leader of the party, I had the opportunity to interview members of the party who were or had been participating in 'high intensity' activity for the party. These members were aged between eighteen and eighty and had been members from three months to over fifty years. All interviewees had at some stage been active in campaigning (offline), attending meetings or had stood as representatives of the party and all had joined before the general election in 2015. In my interviews with these active party members we explored when, how and why they joined, their first impressions, their expectations, what they do and what they did, what it means to them to be a party member and what they expect from the party in return. The interviews also directly addressed the issue of political rights, the leadership contest, and the new registered supporter scheme which gave these same political rights to a group of Labour supporters outside the membership.

Interviews with these active members revealed some unexpected dynamics between partisans and their party. Firstly, many were encouraged to join the party because of selective incentives (motivations stemming from personal benefit and opportunity, such as career opportunities or benefits accruing from the process of participation itself). These incentives featured more prominently in members' narratives of how they came to join than the existing, predominantly quantitative, literature on membership has revealed. These personal incentives are particularly important for younger and newer members. Secondly, these active members were not especially motivated by political rights; if anything, they saw them as peripheral. That is not to say they would be happy to lose them, but that they were of little value compared to other forms of engagement; they played little to no role in drawing these members to the party. It is perhaps unsurprising to say that active members value opportunities for activity in the party, but it does matter when it comes to the incentives parties offer to partisans. It was also surprising to discover that, on the whole, most members cared little about political rights being extended to supporters.

SIGNING UP TO WHAT?

I decided I actually wanted to join the party as well but that came secondary to wanting to work on the election campaign

In describing their routes to party membership, members draw on a number of incentivising factors: their paths to the party are complex and yet there are patterns. All of the incentives categorised in the oft-replicated General Incentives Model devised by Whiteley and Seyd were mentioned by participants: selective process and outcome incentives, collective incentives (positive and negative) and ideological, expressive or altruistic ones.[7] However, some motivations played a more significant role and there are similarities across members' narratives. Collective, ideological, values-based incentives have consistently come out on top in party member surveys.[8] Yet while collective incentives were mentioned in my interviews, selective incentives, personal benefits derived from activity and participation, appeared to have a more influential role in prompting joining. Whilst there was often a tendency to downplay these personal benefits (perhaps because of a party culture that suggests them unacceptable), they were important in providing members with a reason to join the party. That opportunities to be politically active are valued by active members is to be expected, but it is nevertheless important to bear in mind particularly for parties who need volunteers to undertake crucial organisational functions.

By contrast, political rights such as leader selection or policy rights did not feature in interviewees' accounts of their routes to party membership. Though these rights clearly play a huge role in attracting partisan support (and not just in the last few years), for those who are active in the party and have been for some time, these rights don't appear to have drawn them to the party in the first place. Political rights are being used by parties to attract wider constituencies of support, but an in-depth reading of what motivates the most active members suggests that organisationally, parties may not be offering the right incentives to attract 'high-intensity' participants.

IN THE PARTY INTEREST

> I personally feel discomforted by it, but actually I think it's probably, as a strategy, the right thing to be doing at this time.

A shift in political rights within a party is no minor administrative tweak: it raises important questions about influence and ownership. Scarrow highlights the potential conflict in trying to retain existing

members as well as attracting a looser affiliate support; parties wishing
to keep longstanding members would be advised to limit these looser
affiliates' rights to intra-party democracy, whilst those seeking to
mobilise a wider support base would benefit from opening them up.[9]
We have already witnessed the tensions created in the Labour Party
from a shift towards 'multi-speed' membership. Whilst it is true to say
that the expansion of political rights to supporters was not universally
welcomed, the true extent of the tension amongst individual members
is at risk of being overstated. In my interviews, beyond the results of
the leadership contest itself, party members were surprisingly relaxed
about their rights being offered to non-members. Party members'
commitment extends well beyond what they get out of it themselves.
Whilst many expressed some concern or discomfort with the supporter
scheme, they on balance discounted these views in favour of an assessment of what was best for the wider interests of the party.

This willingness to discount personal concerns in favour of what
is best for the party as an organisation suggests that we need to move
beyond a cost-benefit assessment of party membership and party
incentives. A dual preference structure is present in party members'
assessment of organisational change; it is part selfish, part altruistic. This dual preference structure is fairly uniform across ages and
amongst both new and longstanding members. Even for those disap-
pointed by the outcome of the leadership election and those whose
long service far outweighed the contribution of the £3 supporter,
the value to the party was paramount and they could rationalise the
change from the party's perspective.

INCENTIVES AND REPRESENTATION

So why shouldn't they elect the leader or help elect the leader as
it would really be no more disproportionate than union members
having two votes.

It seems odd that members of the party who have contributed many
years of service (or indeed a very intense level of engagement over
shorter periods) would care little about their rights being extended
to partisans who may have contributed nothing beyond a £3 fee
(raised to £25 after these interviews took place), particularly given
that one-member-one-vote has been such a long time coming. An

explanation for this may possibly be found in the examination of member incentives. The presence of selective outcome and process incentives is key: active members join for active opportunities and new supporters are not able to derive these benefits without getting involved face to face. After all, new skills and job opportunities can only be gained by on the ground experience and benefits derived from joining in campaigns with like-minded people, cannot be realised without participation. These benefits are not diminished by extending political rights to supporters.

We might also look to the history of the party itself for an explanation. I have argued that the traditions of representation in a party matter when organisational structures are changed. Representation within the Labour Party has always involved affiliation as well as membership. In fact, being founded on collective affiliation, the party itself predates individual membership. The supporter and member distinction has therefore always been more complicated in the British Labour Party than in other mass *individual* membership parties. Until the introduction of OMOV in 2015, the number of Trade Union affiliates with a vote far outnumbered the membership. Perhaps for Labour Party members, sharing political rights is simply part of the party's 'narrative of representation'. Looking to the future, this is a party whose representational traditions might just be broad enough to move to 'multi-speed' membership successfully.

'MULTI-SPEED' MEMBERSHIP AND THE 2017 GENERAL ELECTION

The move to 'multi-speed' membership clearly has consequences for both party cohesion and organisational resource and it was the latter of these that was unexpectedly put to the test in the 2017 general election. Would new members and supporters attracted by the plebiscitary opportunities presented by the two leadership elections be out engaging in 'high-intensity' activities such as canvassing?

One lesson from the election is that such a question is potentially out of date. The extensive use of online campaigning through social media, to encourage supporters to vote, appears to have been a success. Whether Labour's new army of members and supporters went out door-knocking becomes an interesting but irrelevant question in campaigning terms if activists can have a significant effect online. But it is also clear that many new members and supporters also went out 'on the doorstep'.

By employing a 'multi-speed' model of membership and support, Labour successfully attracted a range of new participants who, come the election, were inspired to campaign in a range of ways. And it did so whilst maintaining the support of its longstanding members who continued to provide essential voluntary campaign expertise and effort. The 2017 election appears to provide us with an example of 'multi-speed' organising at its most effective.

NEW WAVE LABOUR

Embracing a 'multi-speed' model of participation can reap rewards for party organisation. Utilising the interest created by a leadership election and the opportunity for democratic participation it affords, parties can attract new members and raise funds. The 2017 general election campaign demonstrated the potential strength of this model of organising, providing the party with a mass of activists both on the ground and online, and a source of multiple campaign donations.

However, the move towards a more open 'multi-speed' way of organising has wider consequences. Adopting this model marks a shift from group aims to individual interests, from loyalty to a party to loyalty to a leader. For a new wave member, encouraged by political influence and opportunity, the routines of party business may not provide the engagement they envisaged. When not tethered by the bonds of time and of loyalty, it may not be long before the winds of a different political cause blow supporters elsewhere. As the party moves forward, can the new wave Labour members stay the course or withstand a change in leadership or in this new more fluid model of partisanship, does it not matter?

The changes Labour made to the supporter scheme after its first outing, introducing time limits and raising the fee, suggest that having embraced the ideals of 'multi-speed' membership, the party was drawn back to the comforts of a traditional mass membership model. This may be a recognition of the value of linkage and loyalty or perhaps an unconscious reversion to the model of political participation that feels most comfortable. The significant step the party took towards a more 'multi-speed' way of organising with the introduction of more open selection perhaps demanded too great a change to party culture. After the 2017 general election, will this more open model of organising be recognised as a strength and can the party cope with a more fluid support base?

The greatest challenge for the party now is the need to strike a balance between maintaining the traditions of the party, one founded on collective representation, and embracing a more fluid support model: a support model appropriate for today's politically motivated citizen.

The year 2018 will be the centenary of the introduction of individual membership of the Labour Party. If current membership numbers are maintained, the party will reach its hundredth year with the largest individual membership since the mid part of the last century. By changing what it means to support a party and embracing the needs of twenty-first-century partisans, the Labour Party has moved party membership into the 'multi-speed' era, but still has to find a way of striking a balance between the party's history and its future.[10]

NOTES

1. Susan Scarrow, *Beyond Party Membership: Changing Approaches to Partisan Mobilisation*, Oxford University Press: Oxford, 2015.
2. *Refounding Labour to Win: A Party for the New Generation*, Labour Party, 2011, p5.
3. Scarrow, *ibid.*, pp207-209.
4. National Executive Committee, 21 July 2015.
5. Paul Whiteley, Patrick Seyd, *High-Intensity Participation: The Dynamics of Party Activism in Britain*, University of Michigan Press: Ann Arbor, 2002, p147.
6. Paul Webb, Monica Poletti, Tim Bale, 'So who really does the donkey work in "multi-speed membership" parties', *Electoral Studies*, Vol. 46, 2017, pp64-74.
7. Patrick Seyd, Paul Whiteley, *Labour's Grass Roots: The Politics of Party Membership*, Clarendon Press: Oxford, 1992; Paul Whiteley, Patrick Seyd, Jeremy Richardson, Paul Bissell, 'Explaining party activism: The case of the British Conservative Party', *British Journal of Political Science*, Vol. 24, 1994, pp79-94; Paul Whiteley, Patrick Seyd, *ibid.*
8. See Anika Gauja, Emilie van Haute, 'Members and activists of political parties: A comparative perspective', 2014, presented at the IPSA World Congress of Political Science panel 'What is party membership', Montreal, 19-24 July 2014; Knut Heidar, '"Little boxes on the hillside". Do all party members look the same?', 2014, presented at the ECPR Joint Sessions of

Workshops, 'Contemporary meanings of party membership', Salamanca, 10-15 April 2014; Karina Pedersen, Lars Bille, Roger Buch, Jørgen Elklit, Bernhard Hansen, and Hans Jørgen Nielsen, 'Sleeping or active partners? Danish party members at the turn of the millennium', *Party Politics,* Vol. 10, 2004, pp367-383.

9. Scarrow, *ibid.*

10. This is a much revised and updated version of Jessica Garland, 'A New Politics? The Challenges of Multi-Speed Party Membership', *Renewal,* Vol. 24 No.3, 2016, pp43-47.

The Coming of Caledonian Corbynism

Gerry Hassan

Scottish politics through the years has been seen through many different prisms. Once Scotland was meant to be a Labour, even socialist nation, then a nationalist country on the brink of independence. Neither were completely accurate and instead were partial truths and caricatures. But what they did capture was a profound sense of difference and the notion that Scotland was a land of restless natives just waiting to boil over and rebel at the slightest wrong decision from Westminster and the British ruling classes.

The Scottish Labour Party at its peak, was portrayed both within and without Scotland as omnipotent: Labour carrying all before it in its reach, appeal and power. It was represented as a party that understood the need to be an electoral 'machine', while being deeply embedded in the social values and constituencies of the nation, in a way which British Labour clearly wasn't in the 1980s.

There was a sureness and certainty about Scottish Labour, but also a smugness and self-importance. It didn't have to engage in the zigzags and compromises that Labour down south did. Not for it the Bennite wave of the 1980s, nor the subsequent New Labour experience. Indeed, elements of the party believed that its ballast and centredness saved the party in the 1980s from implosion, and provided the perspective and many of the talents for the coming out of the wilderness after eighteen years of Tory rule under Thatcher and Major.

However, this viewpoint jars with the last two decades when the party hasn't exactly had an easy time. It has struggled to adapt to a more competitive Scottish politics; seen power and dominance snatched from it by the SNP; experienced decline, confusion and marginalisation, and skirted irrelevance and ridicule. How did this happen if it once was so seemingly impregnable and powerful? And after it fell so steeply, how was its mini-recovery in the 2017 UK election able to happen?

A BRIEF HISTORY OF SCOTTISH LABOUR

The Scottish Labour Party once dominated Scotland – a history that has provided a folklore, mythology and set of stories for the party, and just as importantly, for its opponents. This context has contributed to the rise, fall and present condition of the Scottish party, but so, critically, has the state of British Labour and its leadership, from Clement Attlee to Harold Wilson, Tony Blair, and now Jeremy Corbyn.

Scotland, in many accounts, has been characterised as a socialist country. It was progressive, even radical, more left-wing and collectivist. This was the land of Red Clydeside, Highland radicalism, non-conformism and deep seated anti-Toryism.[1] Of course that was only one version of Scotland. Another would pose the role of imperialism, empire building and unionist Scotland. It would recognise that the left-wing clarion calls of 'Red Clydeside' were used, not just by the left, but by the right, to mobilise middle class voters with the universal fear of the revolutionary mob.

As a party, Scottish Labour was never as popular or as strong as it thought itself to be, or as many of its opponents believed. It never won a majority of the popular vote, only coming near once in its history (49.9 per cent in 1966), was never a party of mass membership and outward campaigning, and was never even at its peak a truly national party – instead being limited and concentrated in its appeal to the West of Scotland central belt. This matters as Labour Scotland was always a minority, and due to the vagaries of the first past the post system (FPTP) at Westminster and local government, thought and acted as a majority. It meant the party didn't have any need to understand the nature and strength of non-Labour Scotland – who were always, even at the party's peak, a majority of voters.

The culture of Labour Scotland at its zenith became inward-looking and self-referencing for good reason. The party stacked up enough piles of votes to not have to look outward and win over floating voters or opponents. This was particularly true in the West of Scotland Labour citadels such as Glasgow, Lanarkshire and Ayrshire, and less true in places such as Edinburgh and Dundee that were much more electorally competitive.

The weakening of Labour's political antenna and failure to understand non-Labour Scotland carries a salutary warning for the SNP and their future direction. The SNP, for a decade in office, looked like they carried all before them in party political terms. Their opponents were divided, weak and in disarray. But beyond this, the party's appeal was as limited as Scottish Labour's was at its peak, perhaps in many respects weaker given the volatility and turbulence in present day politics, and which became evident in the 2017 election.

The SNP, as with Labour, at their height have never won a majority of the popular vote; they came closest when they won 49.97 per cent in the 2015 Westminster election. Just like Labour, this produced huge distortions because of FPTP, with the SNP winning fifty-six out of fifty-nine seats (95 per cent). Nationalist Scotland at its peak, like the previous Labour version, has always been a popular minority – one where non-Nationalist Scotland has always remained a majority.

This isn't a side issue for the SNP, but about political antenna and instinct, pluralism and building alliances, and planning how it can put together a coalition to win a second independence referendum. Labour realised in the 1997 devolution referendum that it couldn't win the vote by relying on its supporters alone, and needed to make overtures to Lib Dem and SNP voters. The same is true of the SNP, which knows it cannot win an independence referendum on its own base: it needs Green, Lib Dem and Labour voters. But over-bearing dominance, as with Labour, weakens political sensitivities, and leads to arrogance and insensitivity, and resultant voter rebellion. The story of Scottish Labour's long-term decline carries with it a warning for the SNP – one they have not so far adapted to, as the politics of the fifty-six SNP MPs, with all its hubris, turned out to be what looks like a brief spasm.

THE HOUSE THAT SCOTTISH LABOUR BUILT AND WHY IT FELL

Labour's dominance was built upon three pillars – local government, trade unions and council housing. This is the analysis myself and Eric Shaw advanced in our book *The Strange Death of Labour Scotland.*[2] We posed the idea of 'Labour Scotland' as different in character from 'Scottish Labour'. The former was a version of political dominance via a party that at its core was not large in members or resources but could extend its influence across the country through patronage and clientism. This allowed a minority party to appeal to, represent and speak for majority Scotland.

Post-1980 the three pillars began to slowly erode, hollow out and finally crumble, leaving Scottish Labour with no support systems to aid its long-term survival. The last pillar to crumble came in 2007 when the first local government elections were held under proportional representation (PR), at a stroke removing an entire layer of Labour councillors who had for years provided the backbone of the party. Without this and with the simultaneous loss of power in the Scottish Parliament, the party was in a mess: 2007 was a watershed for the party, one it did not initially recognise and respond to.

Even the above must be seen as one in a series of events which contributed to Scottish Labour's predicament and decline. These include the following ten moments:

1979: Scottish Labour general secretary Helen Liddell formally declares that in the first devolution referendum the party will not support any cross-party campaign which contributes to the inconclusive nature of the result.

1980: Thatcher government introduces the right to buy council houses for sitting tenants. After initial Scottish Labour opposition this is legally forced through by the Scottish Office.

1988: Labour agree to enter cross-party Constitutional Convention, which the SNP decide to boycott.

1991: Scottish Labour conference agrees that a future Scottish Parliament should be elected by PR.

1995: Labour and Lib Dems agree a Scottish Parliament elected by PR.

1996: Tony Blair announces a referendum on a Scottish Parliament without consulting the Scottish party.

1999: First Scottish Parliament elections see Labour as the biggest party and herald eight years of Labour-Lib Dem coalition government.

2002: Labour propose PR for local government.

2007: SNP narrowly wins Scottish Parliament elections and forms government; first local government elections held under PR.

2011-14 After SNP form majority government Scotland faces a three-year independence referendum campaign.

The above illustrates Scottish Labour's painful struggle to adapt to a country with an increasing culture of multi-party politics and pluralism. The first trend was an environment where, despite the SNP breakthrough at Westminster in 1974, Labour was still the leading party until 2007 but had to compete in an increasingly competitive electoral landscape. To take a couple of examples – in the first devolution referendum of 1979, Labour refused to support any cross-party pro-devolution campaign with then general secretary Helen Liddell declaring that 'the achievement of an Assembly will be ours, and it would be wrong to allow our consistent opponents ... to claim credit for this constitutional advance'.[3]

By 1988, the party was committed to cross-party co-operation in the Constitutional Convention; a stance that made many in the party uneasy. It led to a commitment to PR for a Scottish Parliament, and ultimately, first, Labour entering coalition with the Lib Dems, and second, providing a platform for the SNP to become a credible opposition and then government.

The second trend has been the party's inability to become autonomous: a combination of British Labour not letting go and Scottish Labour, even when popular, not having the resources to run itself. Critical here are the events of 1996-99 and the establishment of the Scottish Parliament. Public trouble began in June 1996 when Blair announced there would be a two-question referendum: on a Scottish Parliament and tax raising powers. No proper consultation took place with the Scottish party or Gordon Brown, George Robertson and Robin Cook.

This marked a third trend – the Blairite Labour contradiction, between favouring both devolution and centralisation at the same time. Labour prevented Rhodri Morgan becoming Welsh Labour leader and blocked Ken Livingstone from being the party's candidate for the London Mayoral election of 2000. Further examples include the party's manipulation of the selection process of Labour candidates for the Scottish Parliament, but just as importantly, the Scottish party did not fully control the campaign or manifesto for the first Scottish Parliament elections in 1999.

These three trends linked with other predicaments. Labour has showed over the twenty years from the 1997 devolution referendum, a glaring chasm when it comes to answering the question: what should the Scottish Parliament do? This impeded the party's prospects as the SNP had an answer – the Parliament was meant to be the main body of an independent, self-governing, progressive nation. Labour's only real motivations for a Parliament were deeply negative – to continue and protect Labour hegemony, block Thatcherism, and forestall Scottish nationalism. It was the Parliament as a defensive barrier, whereas the SNP saw it as potentially a catalyst for further change. The SNP talked a good story about Scotland and the Parliament, one which was often different from their record in office post-2007, but for a long period it was more than enough, given the paucity and lack of convincing story from Scottish Labour.

WHO SAVED SCOTTISH LABOUR?

Fast forward to the present day. Scottish Labour has had a terrible couple of years following the 2014 independence referendum. It was reduced to one MP and 24.3 per cent in the 2015 UK election, losing forty seats. In the 2016 Scottish Parliament elections it won a share of just 22.6 per cent of the constituency and 19.1 per cent of the regional vote – in the latter and in some seats finishing third behind the Tories. To put this in context, the party had not finished third in votes in Scotland for a Westminster poll since 1918, or behind the Tories in the popular vote since 1959. Things looked grim for the future of the party.

Everything seemed to be going against Labour. The SNP were entrenched as the dominant centre-left party for the foreseeable future. The Tories had a new-found popularity under Scottish Conservatives' leader Ruth Davidson and for the immediate period after Brexit Theresa May came over as having a British-wide appeal including Scotland. If that wasn't enough, Labour had leaders in Scotland and the UK, Kezia Dugdale and Jeremy Corbyn, who not only had problems with their own parties, but didn't see eye to eye on much either, including Scotland.

While 2017 looked to be another difficult year in the life of Scottish Labour, it didn't work according to the script. First came the May 2017 local elections where the SNP did not carry all before them. Instead, they won 32.3 per cent of the vote, the same share they had in the previous local elections five years before, while the Tories won 25.3 per cent and Labour 20.2 per cent. This wasn't by any measurement a good performance by Labour, as its vote fell by 11.2 per cent, and it lost the last of the councils over which it had previously held overall control (including Glasgow).

Yet, this wasn't the annihilation many had thought and Labour feared. Only three months before the contest, Labour's own internal polling put the party on 15 per cent and the SNP on 45 per cent. While the party lost control of its last major stronghold, Glasgow, the SNP failed to win it outright. The Nationalists won thirty-nine seats to Labour's thirty-one, Conservatives eight, Scottish Greens seven – the SNP winning 41 per cent of the vote to Labour's 30.2 per cent across the city. The SNP's supposedly all-conquering electoral machine did not carry all before it, and this was reinforced by SNP denial and blinkeredness, with even first minister Nicola Sturgeon declaring 'We won Glasgow', when the party had patently failed to do so.

All of this occurred against the backdrop of the UK election which Theresa May unexpectedly called to strength her Brexit negotiating hand. What began as an unchallenged coronation soon turned out to be very different as Theresa May's Conservative campaign self-destructed and Jeremy Corbyn's Labour produced a populist and effective challenge.

Scotland followed a different course to the rest of the country. The Scottish Tories, already believing their years of being a pariah force were coming to an end, felt that challenging the SNP on their plans for a second independence referendum post-Brexit, gave them a popular cause which spoke to many Scots. Ruth Davidson ran her campaign as 'the Ruth Davidson Party' – with shades of how Theresa May began her campaign, but unlike May she kept to this and combined it with the message 'We said no to Independence. We meant it'.

Scottish Labour entered the campaign in a poor state. Kezia Dugdale and Jeremy Corbyn had publicly contradicted each other several times on a second independence referendum prior to the election. At the time of the Brexit vote, Dugdale had floated that it might be conceivable she would support independence: a position she now denies she ever had. Corbyn has made various comments on independence, and in the middle of the campaign stated that he would be 'opening discussions' with the SNP on a referendum.[4] This was announced when Dugdale had reverted to her hard, pro-unionist position saying she would 'never support independence'.[5]

A defining and surprising feature of the Scottish election was the lacklustre SNP campaign, with no clear strategy, spine or message, beyond that it wasn't meant to be about independence. This allowed the Nationalists' opponents to define what the election was about. For the Tories, it was about 'a divisive second independence referendum', while Labour concentrated on the failings of the SNP on education and health after ten years in office. This created a classic two-way pincer attack which disorientated the SNP.

The Scottish campaign, like the British one, made a difference. The SNP, starting from a high base and expecting losses, played a defensive game, but went further back. The Tories advanced, continued to do so, and weren't affected by the May meltdown. And the Corbyn surge nationwide, registered in the last few days, crossed the border, surprising nearly everyone, Scottish Labour included.

The final Scottish result saw the SNP fall from fifty-six to thirty-five seats, the Tories rise from one to thirteen, Labour rise from one to seven, and the Lib Dems one to four. In the popular vote, the SNP fell to 36.9 per cent (-13.1 per cent), Tories rise to 28.6 per cent (+13.7 per cent), Labour 27.1 per cent (+2.8 per cent) and the Lib Dems fell to 6.8 per cent (-0.8 per cent).

The SNP bandwagon had been halted and reversed, the Tories continued to advance from the previous year and bucked the UK trend, but Scottish Labour's mini-recovery caught everyone off-guard. Immediately, an open debate began within the party about who should take most of the credit – Kezia Dugdale or Jeremy Corbyn. We have at least some evidence which points to this mostly being a Corbyn-led phenomenon. For one, Corbyn's ratings began to shift upwards in Scotland, as they did across the UK in the campaign, whereas Dugdale's remained on the floor; and in the latter stages, as polls put Labour in second place to the Tories, they detected a significant surge of younger voters away from the SNP and towards Labour.

These results beg many questions about the future of Scottish Labour which have many similarities to the British-wide picture. What would a 'Corbynified' Scottish party look like, what would it say and do differently, and critically, what would its attitude to independence be? Presently we have little idea of the potential nature of a Corbynite Scottish agenda because until the 2017 election, politics north of the border had been largely immune to such an approach.

There are broader issues to consider. The party has had, over eighteen years of the Scottish Parliament, eight leaders and has to elect its ninth. British Labour over the same period has had four. Of the eight, three – Donald Dewar, Henry McLeish, Jack McConnell – were first ministers, with five in opposition – Wendy Alexander, Ian Gray, Johann Lamont, Jim Murphy and Kezia Dugdale. Labour is behaving like a failing, declining football club constantly changing managers as it goes from regularly tasting success to relegation and lean times. It seemingly knows no other strategy than plotting, moving against and firing the existing leader.

Scottish Labour has been regularly derided as 'London Labour' – a party which defers to British Labour. Johann Lamont, when she resigned as Scottish Labour leader after the independence referendum, brought this out into the open when she said the party was treated as nothing more than a 'branch office' of British Labour.[6] Many Scottish colleagues were furious, believing she had just given enormous propaganda to the SNP by conceding one of their main arguments. They were also furious because she had made something public that everyone knew had the air of truth.

Then there is the immediate picture which still holds after the 2017 election. Scottish Labour hasn't experienced the influx of new members, proportionately, that has been a feature of Corbyn's party across the rest of Britain. The Scottish party is coy about membership but claims it went up from 13,500 after the 2014 referendum to 18,824 towards the end of 2015 – hardly a dramatic uplift.[7]

Furthermore, the contours of left politics have been dominated by independence since 2014, and this boosted the SNP's membership – which saw the party increase from 25,000 members in September 2014 to 120,000 by the end of 2015. Many of these new members were exactly the sort of people who in England would have been swept along by Corbynism: left-wing, influenced by social media and network politics, and anti-austerity.

Finally, the Scottish Labour left remains a rather timid, conservative force. The politics associated with Momentum have not translated north of the border, with the group not even organising in Scotland. Corbynista politics have coalesced around the much smaller Campaign for Socialism set up in 1994, which has been characterised by a defensive, oppositional and tribal Labour left politics.

THE BIG SQUEEZE OF SCOTTISH VS BRITISH NATIONALISM

The politics of 2014-17 aided not only the SNP, but also the Scottish Tories. The dominance of the Scottish Nationalists electorally over the last decade, disorientated many in Scottish Labour, who regard the SNP as interlopers, 'tartan Tories' and worse. They have been unable to come to terms with an SNP occupying the centre-left, emphasising their progressive, social democratic credentials. This was true of Alex Salmond, first minister from 2007-14, but he also pivoted towards a pro-business, low tax and regulation climate. Under Nicola Sturgeon's leadership since November 2014, the SNP has sat more unambiguously on the centre-left while still retaining a 'Big Tent' national appeal.

Labour critics point out the gap between SNP rhetoric and action: the absence of redistribution, not taking on vested interests. This is all true, but the exact same points could be made about previous Labour-Lib Dem devolved administrations.

Labour has never managed to accommodate itself to the SNP, to normalise it so it can effectively oppose it, because, in many respects, independence apart, the two have been so alike. Labour members have looked at the SNP in its popular years and been reminded of earlier, better, more idealistic versions of themselves: mobilised by a cause – independence, principled on issues like Trident, and because of these causes, prepared to make the day to day compromises of politics for the longer term.

If these were not enough problems, the long referendum campaign and its aftermath, combined with the election in 2011 of Ruth Davidson has given renewed spirit to the Conservative Party in Scotland. A politics increasingly centred on the constitution – independence versus the union – has allowed the Scottish Conservative and Unionist Party (to give the party its full name), to make an apologetic pitch for its core *raison d'etre*.

This resulted in Labour being squeezed by two forces of nationalism: the Scottish led by the SNP and the British advanced by the Scottish Tories. In the 2016 Scottish Parliament election 'No' supporters split 36 per cent Conservative and 31 per cent Labour; the following year in the UK election they divided 53 per cent Conservative, 22 per cent Labour; when asked which party 'No' voters trusted on independence they said 57 per cent Conservative, 16 per cent Labour. At the same time, the edge began to wear off the SNP: in 2015, 89 per cent of 'Yes' supporters backed the Nationalists, but by 2017 that fell to 75 per cent.[8]

This culture of competing nationalisms has become a problem for Scottish Labour.[9] There has been a glaring Labour failure to find a space between the SNP and Tories for a politics that isn't about nationalism or the Union, but is instead about Labour values.

This political environment has been a regular feature in Scotland since 1997. The Labour Party didn't adapt to devolution; it didn't become autonomous. And it didn't have a distinctive story to tell about devolution beyond a kind of 'be grateful Labour legislated for a Scottish Parliament for you'. Moreover, in the 2014 independence referendum campaign, as harmful as sharing platforms with Tories was, there was the complete absence of a distinctive Labour message on the Union.[10] The Tories are unionists to their core and could unapologetically pitch their tent, but Labour was meant only to be pragmatically pro-unionist as a means to an end: that end being greater equality. That message hit barren ground in the Scotland of the early twenty-first century.

Prominent Scottish, Labour figures such as Gordon Brown can wax lyrically about the union as 'a force for social justice' and the progressive qualities of 'pooling' and 'sharing resources'. But this rhetoric didn't connect to the realities of a grotesquely unequal UK. It left Labour on the disastrous terrain of arguing for the union as an end in-itself rather than as a means-to-an-end: a unionist message and one which went against everything in the party's DNA. It was a cul-de-sac for the party and one which left it nowhere to go and with little distinctive to say. All this needs to be seen as part of a bigger story: of how Scottish Labour ended up being unable to articulate a social democratic case for the union, and that failure has to be situated in British Labour's long retreat from the progressive values it once championed. Part of this equation was to change sooner than people thought.

THE FORWARD MARCH OF SCOTTISH NATIONALISM HALTED?

Labour once thought it would rule Scotland forever. Then the SNP came to think likewise, that they were the future and independence inevitable. The election of 2015 was seen by many as a permanent realignment and Nationalist hegemony, whereas it now appears as a one-off 'tartan tsunami', while 2017 is a salutary corrective to determinist views of politics. Just as it was myopic for Labour supporters to believe in a mechanistic, machine 'the forward march of labour' so the same has been proven true for the Nationalists.[11]

These are times of flux and uncertainty in Scotland and the UK – of anger and fury at the state of Britain, seven years of austerity, what we are told we can and cannot afford in the sixth richest economy in the world, and the deceptions of the political, business and managerial classes. It isn't an accident that even senior Tories are openly acknowledging people are tired of austerity, or that *The Economist* reluctantly conceded that 2017 was the first post-neoliberal election in Britain – a harbinger of the still undefined politics of the future.[12]

Corbyn's Labour caught that wave in the 2017 campaign; a historic opportunity to remake a populist left politics. But given the limits of Corbyn and the main protagonists in the leadership, divisions in Labour, and the kind of opposition any radical agenda would face in office, the prospects may be slender that they will successfully ride this wave of change for long. But even if my pessimistic account turns out to be true, their success tells us something we should have long known: even at its peak, neoliberalism didn't win hearts and minds, and now its failures have been laid bare it has little to fall back on.

There remains a set of fault-lines and geo-political challenges in relation to where the UK sees itself in the world: Brexit is only the most obvious. Within the UK there are other points of division, about the global class version of London, the unequal growth and prosperity across the union, and the different agendas of the numerous regions. Fundamentally, all of this points to the continued crisis of the British state – in politics, governance and statecraft – and the collapse of the neo-Conservative and New Labour ways of advocating 'modernisation' in the narrow interests of the elites.

This leaves the UK at an impasse where we cannot go back to the future: not to traditional 'One Nation' benign Toryism, nor to conventional centralist and statist Labourism. This is therefore a watershed era in which all sorts of tensions, developments and surprises may emerge, for which the British political classes and establishment seem supremely unaware and unprepared.

Post-2017, the Scottish question remains unresolved and unanswered – namely the expression of the desire for Scottish self-government and autonomy, whether as an independent nation state or in a fully reformed, democratised union. The SNP have experienced a significant reverse but they are still, for the moment, Scotland's leading party, and the cause of independence, while linked to them and their popularity, isn't completely the same thing.

All of this offers a window for Scottish Labour, one which until very recently no one expected to emerge.

In the 2017 Westminster elections, although Labour once more came third in Scotland (it has fewer MPs in the Scottish Parliament than the SNP or the Tories), it succeeded in closing the gap on the second-placed Tories to a mere 1.5 per cent of votes (down from 3.8 per cent in the 2016 Scottish election). The election in 2017 provided Scottish Tories with the opportunity to consolidate their position as the unchallenged opposition to the SNP, but, despite everything, they somehow didn't manage it.

Scottish politics has long been defined by an anti-Tory ethos which hasn't gone away despite the right's recent revival. The combination of this with the more recent anti-SNP popular mood, leaves the Labour Party well placed to speak for the large constituency which is anti-Tory and increasingly disillusioned with the Nationalists. It is also true that the long tail of wanting to kick and punish Labour as the political establishment, while still evident in some quarters has weakened, pro-independence opinion has mostly waned.

The emergence of a Corbyn Labour effect in Scotland and the UK alters some of the dynamics of politics north of the border. The double SNP charge that Tory governments will be elected in perpetuity and that the Labour Party is a Blairite sell-out is no longer very plausible. The argument that the SNP sit to the left of Labour has been shown to be a fallacy by the new model Corbyn party, depriving it of one of its most effective political messages.

All the above has come at a time when the 2017 election showed how very human and mortal the SNP were, and that talk of their powerful electoral machine and discipline, had been overstated. The SNP have been in office ten years, and are showing the wear, tear and limitations that comes with incumbency.

And none of this can be divorced from the SNP's problematic relationship with centre-left values and social democratic policies. In government there has been a growing discrepancy between rhetoric and practice.[13] The SNP's social democracy has been thin, self-congratulatory and contradictory, buying into giving vested interests and the middle classes selective universal goods, while not advancing any kind of redistribution. This has become more obvious and salient with the passing of time and length of tenure of the SNP in office.

Who then speaks for Scotland – if any political party can? The SNP claim of exclusivity is much diminished on a mere 36.9 per cent of the vote, and after successive reverses in the 2016 Scottish and 2017 Westminster elections. Who speaks for Scottish Labour – and how? And who do they speak for? These have now become the more interesting questions. One critical dimension of a future Scottish leadership is the loyalty they will be expected to pay to Corbyn and his agenda.

So far, the Scottish Labour leadership has shown little hunger to map out a new political terrain, and the Corbynites were inclined, until June 2017, to write Scotland off as unfertile territory. The contours of any Labour perspective in Scotland are already self-evident: breaking with the past of traditional Labour, embracing insurgency, and railing against the limits of closed, networked, insider Scotland – whether of the old kind or the newer nationalist variety. Nearly two decades of devolution haven't altered the main characteristics, dynamics and inequalities of Scottish society, and the Scotland that remains disadvantaged, excluded and on the outside, yearns to have someone speak up for it, give it voice, and challenge the cosy consensual arrangements which for too long have been called 'progressive'.

Does Scottish Labour or the UK Labour leadership have the capacity to shake things up and challenge the politics of the few which has operated in the notional name of the many, for so long in Scotland? Any answer will require that Scottish Labour change nearly everything about how it has done politics, both when it was on top, and then on the way down. It needs to learn how to campaign, advocate, win new supporters and members, make coherent policy and disseminate new ideas. Most importantly, it needs to find a new story about the Scotland it wants to see, distinct from Tory unionism and SNP independence, and which dares to challenge the divided kingdom of the UK which has so aided power, privilege and the plutocrat class.

British politics are set for some turbulent times ahead, and in this period the Scottish question will be pivotal. The Scottish Labour Party hasn't quite come back from the dead, because it was never completely dead, but it has earned the right to have a second chance. Scottish Labour learnt the hard way that no party has the divine right to rule. But neither do the Nationalists. It has been a helter-skelter ride in Scotland and the UK these last few years, and there is no sign that this will stop anytime soon.

NOTES

1. See for example Anon., *The Scottish Socialists: A Gallery of Contemporary Portraits*, Faber and Faber: London, 1931.
2. Gerry Hassan and Eric Shaw, *The Strange Death of Labour Scotland*, Edinburgh University Press: Edinburgh, 2012.
3. Alan Macartney, 'The Protagonists', in John Bochel, David Denver and Alan Macartney (eds), *The Referendum Experience: Scotland 1979*, Aberdeen University Press: Aberdeen, 1981, p17.
4. *BBC News*, 29 May 2017.
5. *BBC News Scotland*, 25 February 2017.
6. *Daily Record*, 25 October 2014.
7. Membership figures as quoted in the *Sunday Herald*, 9 November 2014; *The Scotsman*, 27 September 2015. The Scottish party has been vague about its membership since the end of 2015, issuing no official figures to correspond with the period of the Corbyn membership surge.
8. *Sky News,* 30 May 2017.
9. See Gerry Hassan, *Caledonian Dreaming: The Quest for a Different Scotland*, Luath Press: Edinburgh, 2014 and Gerry Hassan, *Scotland the Bold: How Our Nation Has Changed and Why There is No Going Back*, Freight Books: Glasgow, 2016.
10. See Joe Pike, *Project Fear: How an Unlikely Alliance Left a Kingdom United but a Country Divided*, Biteback Publishing: London, 2015.
11. See Eric Hobsbawm, 'The forward march of Labour halted?' *Marxism Today*, September 1978.
12. 'The summer of discontent: Britain's election offers little respite for its woes', *The Economist*, 3 June 2017.
13. Gerry Hassan and Simon Barrow (eds), *A Nation Changed? The SNP and Scotland Ten Years On*, Luath Press: Edinburgh, 2017.

Corbyn Framed and Unframed

Des Freedman

Jeremy Corbyn has been comprehensively framed by the media. I mean this both in the sociological sense where frames are a key part of the process whereby journalists and editors attempt to 'order' the world through the inclusion (and exclusion) of particular narratives *and* in the more basic sense: that Corbyn has been stitched-up by a hostile press corps. This started the moment he announced his intention to stand in the 2015 Labour leadership election, continued through both his victories and reached into the general election campaign. Given that in 2017 Labour earned both its biggest share of the vote since 2001 and its biggest increase in vote share since 1945, this attempt at character assassination hasn't worked that well.

Indeed, the election result blew a hole, not only in the arguments of Corbyn's many critics who had argued that his leadership would lead to 'annihilation' and 'meltdown' for the party, but also in the view, long held by sections of the left, that a biased media makes it impossible for the left to perform well electorally.[1] In this case, some 13 million people simply refused to believe the narratives offered up by mainstream outlets and voted instead for a distinctively progressive, anti-austerity programme. Much as they huffed and they puffed, the 'great' and the 'good' of the media elite were unable to blow down the house that Corbyn was building. The bias was intense but, ultimately, ineffectual. The result, therefore, punctured two major myths that had long held back the left: first, that press oligarchs are all-powerful and second, that 'parties only prosper if they stick to the middle ground (usually defined as the neoliberal political consensus)'.[2] Instead, here was vindication that a radical leader could take on a media system that had done so much to diminish him – through a continuous barrage of misrepresentation and mockery – and still come out on top.

One example of the distorted news frames that have surrounded Corbyn from the start was when he was condemned for showing disrespect at the 2016 Remembrance Day ceremony by dancing a jig at the Cenotaph. 'Is this really the day to audition for *Strictly*, Jeremy?' asked the *Mail Online* while the *The Sun* (online) ran a headline insisting that 'Jeremy Corbyn dances his way down Downing Street as he attends Remembrance Sunday' (13 November 2016). Both titles had cropped their photos to hide the fact that Corbyn was actually walking next to a ninety-two-year-old constituent and Second World War veteran. It was an episode that epitomised a recurrent theme of the coverage of Corbyn: that it has never been in 'full frame' and that it has never sought to understand the reasons for his election as Labour leader. As Gary Younge argues, the press's lack of interest both in Corbyn himself and in the reasons for his success is an example of the 'most egregious professional malpractice'.[3]

A QUESTION OF IMBALANCE: FOR THE FEW NOT THE MANY

The attacks on Corbyn and his supporters from the British media establishment came in thick and fast – hardly unexpected given that his overwhelming success in both leadership contests was predicated on a desire to challenge establishment rule. His resounding victory in 2015 was greeted by headlines arguing that he was a 'danger to Britain' (*Daily Express*), that his union friends were plotting 'strike chaos' (*Daily Mail* and *The Daily Telegraph*), that he was planning to scrap the army (*The Sun*) and that his victory was responsible for dividing the Labour Party (*The Times*). In the first week following his election, *The Daily Telegraph* called Corbyn's shadow chancellor a 'nut-job' while the *The Sun* attempted to smear Corbyn for illegitimately seeking public funds for Labour (a claim that has been comprehensively refuted). Famously, many front pages condemned his refusal to sing the national anthem which, given Corbyn's reputation as a republican, put him in an invidious position: either he would be denounced as a hypocrite for singing or condemned as disrespectful for not.

The Media Reform Coalition (MRC) conducted research into press coverage of Corbyn's first week as Labour leader and found that out of 494 news, comment and editorial pieces, 60 per cent were overtly negative, 27 per cent were neutral while only 13 per cent were positive leading the MRC to conclude that the 'press set out to systematically undermine Jeremy Corbyn … with a barrage of overwhelmingly negative coverage'.[4] The most damning part of this press coverage was 'hard' news where a mere 6 per cent of stories were positive in contrast to 61 per cent that were negative. Any notion of simply 'reporting the facts' – about the unlikely prospect of a backbench socialist campaigner, supported by thousands of young supporters, actually winning the leadership – appeared to have had a restraining effect only on positive stories suggesting that the default, 'common sense' position was based on overwhelmingly negative assumptions about the new Labour leader.

Subsequent studies of press coverage tended to confirm this initial judgement. In July 2016, researchers at the London School of Economics assessed over 800 articles in eight leading newspapers. They found that most of the coverage was either 'critical' or overtly 'antagonistic' and argued that the press had moved from a 'watchdog' to an 'attack dog' role that was aimed at delegitimising the Labour leader because of his willingness to challenge the political establishment.[5]

Central to this delegitimation project was *The Guardian* – because it has long provided a space in which debates about Labour strategy can be thrashed out. While the paper was initially supportive of Corbyn's right to stand in the first leadership election, it soon changed its tone when it realised that a Corbyn victory was a realistic prospect. At this stage, the paper went into overdrive, handing over its comment pages to a series of anti-Corbyn voices and flying in the face of a readership that overwhelmingly took the opposite position. When asked by *The Guardian* in July 2015 which candidate readers were intending to vote for, 78 per cent replied that they were backing Corbyn with the next most popular candidate, Yvette Cooper (*The Guardian*'s preferred choice) receiving a mere 9 per cent of the vote.[6] Yet this discrepancy failed to dent the enthusiasm of leading commentators including Jonathan Freedland, Martin Kettle, Polly Toynbee and Rafael Behr, for knockabout routines aimed at Corbyn and his supporters.

Broadcast coverage was not quite as vitriolic but equally incredulous that Corbyn was a figure to be taken seriously or understood. The BBC's chief political correspondent, Laura Kuenssberg, seems from the off to have had a problem with reporting Corbyn in impartial terms. She 'sealed the deal' for the shadow foreign affairs minister to resign live on TV in order to maximise embarrassment for Corbyn and then reported the subsequent reshuffle by describing it as a pantomime in which 'Corbyn is *meant* to be the boss' but lacks the clout to deliver the desired changes (BBC, *News at Ten*, 6 January 2016). Kuenssberg was then heavily criticised for her reporting of the local elections in May 2016 – as if they were solely a referendum on Corbyn's leadership as opposed to one on a government weakened by the impending EU referendum – and was even censured by the BBC's former regulator, the BBC Trust, when she misleadingly edited a package to make it seem as if Corbyn was against 'shoot to kill' in absolutely all circumstances. This has led to exasperation from some surprising places. 'There have been some quite extraordinary attacks on the elected leader of the Labour party, quite extraordinary', wrote Sir Michael Lyons, former chair of the BBC Trust. 'I can understand why people are worried some of the most senior editorial voices in the BBC have lost their impartiality on this'.[7]

Further research by the MRC focusing on broadcast and online reporting of the 2016 leadership campaign found that twice as much television airtime was given to critics of Corbyn than to his supporters. The research identified a tendency within BBC bulletins to use pejorative language when referring to the Labour leader with his supporters regularly described as 'far left' and 'hard core'.[8] It noted the reliance of the media on a form of militarised discourse and highlighted 'the degree to which the Labour leadership and its supporters were persistently talked about in terms that emphasised hostility, intransigence and extreme positions'.[9]

Impartiality rules enforced during the general election campaign changed the balance of coverage from an exclusive focus on Corbyn as 'danger' to a consideration of party policies, particularly in the light of the popularity of the Labour manifesto and the poverty of the Tory one. Corbyn took advantage of this shift, easily winning Channel 4/ Sky's *Battle for Number Ten* in which a live audience questioned both main party leaders before one-on-one interviews with a flailing Jeremy Paxman, and out-foxing Theresa May by appearing on the live leaders' debate at the last minute after May had refused to appear. So, while Corbyn exploited the opportunities previously denied to him, May's absence – and her wider failure to interact effectively with either voters or journalists – simply reinforced a sense of isolation and growing panic inside the Conservative campaign. That said, while broadcasters were less explicitly partisan than the press, they nevertheless happily reproduced memes about Corbyn's 'unelectability', his alleged links to terrorists and his reluctance to commit mass murder by pressing the nuclear button. Through endless 'two-ways' and 'vox pops' where ordinary people were encouraged to reflect on Corbyn's leadership qualities (or lack of), broadcasters continued to engage in 'the editorial construction of public opinion' – a public opinion that, despite the broadcast narrative, was rapidly shifting towards Labour.[10]

Corbyn supporters have often been accused of 'conspiratorial thinking' when they highlight the levels of negative coverage of the traditional media. Bias, however, should be understood, not so much as the product of conspiracy or conscious manipulation, but of something far more simple and innocuous: the routine marginalisation of ideas that challenge received wisdom about the existing political order. It is, as Paul Myerscough argues:

> more a matter of the everyday, the gradual accretion of decisions taken and declined, the issues thought worthy of discussion, in what order, in what way and by whom, a line of questioning, an inflection in the voice: unquantifiable things which form the ideological weave of broadcasting as much as headlines and the arrangement of text and images on a page do of print.[11]

In that sense, the negative coverage of Corbyn is hardly an accident or the product of 'bad' journalism but is in-built into a media system that is heavily intertwined with class interests and market ideologies. Peter Oborne described the process when he was the political editor of *The Daily Telegraph*: a highly unequal society means that 'British journalists will almost always favour the rich, powerful and glamorous over the poor, weak and unfashionable'.[12]

Some journalists liked to argue that the bad press Corbyn received wasn't ideological but pragmatic: it simply reflected his low standing in the polls and what they saw as his poor leadership skills. The amplification of his critics in the 2016 leadership election was inevitable, they claimed, given the fact that it followed the mass resignations of his critics inside the shadow cabinet. For *The Guardian* commentator Gaby Hinsliff, the prevalence of negative coverage reflects not structural bias but simply the professional instincts of political reporters to gravitate towards familiar stories of power and success: 'It's more that most journalists – rightly or wrongly – simply don't expect Corbyn to win an election'.[13] To the extent that the news environment tends to favour those politicians who occupy the 'centre ground' (and to marginalise those who challenge it), Hinsliff accepts that audiences may be increasingly ill-served at a time when the centre is shrinking:

> Unwittingly, the news agenda can end up rather like a sagging mattress where everything naturally rolls towards the middle, leaving voters on left and right with less orthodox views feeling excluded and ignored.[14]

Given the media's hostility to Corbyn, some sympathetic commentators called for the development of a more purposeful and professional media strategy that, while recognising the bias against the left, would engage more positively with popular news outlets. Owen Jones, for example, urged Corbyn to go on a 'media offensive' and highlighted what he saw as the lack of a coherent approach to the media by the Corbyn leadership leading to entirely avoidable mistakes. Warning that 'if you do not define yourself, you will be defined by your enemies', he advised Corbyn's team to draw up some simple, positive messages, to repeat them endlessly and to take advantage of every media opportunity, especially broadcast appearances given the continuing size of their audiences.[15] Social media, he added, may have been vital to Corbyn's leadership campaign but it is by no means an adequate substitute for a 'coherent media strategy' that aims at winning power. Indeed, according to the *New Statesman*'s Helen Lewis, an over-reliance on social media can be counter-productive if existing supporters are locked into impenetrable 'echo chambers' that provide reassuring but unrealistic assessments of Labour's electoral fortunes and of Corbyn's leadership qualities.[16]

The general election result, of course, blew away many of these misconceptions, not least the arguments that Labour would be unable to make gains in the face of such determined media opposition and that only centrist policies would attract support. Just six weeks before the election, *The Daily Telegraph* was triumphantly boasting that 'Theresa May [is the] most popular leader since the late 1970s as Jeremy Corbyn hits all time low' (26 April 2017). The Tory press hammered away at Corbyn (even if they were increasingly demoralised by Theresa May's disastrous performance) but saw his campaign, boosted by the manifesto, go from strength to strength. In the end, some 13 million people rejected the preferences of press moguls and the negativity of the commentariat and voted for a programme of hope and change.

Labour's electoral success was predicated on precisely the opposite of what Corbyn's critics had urged him to do. Far from turning towards a disappearing centre, Labour produced a radical, anti-austerity manifesto that created a pole of attraction for millions of voters. Instead of brushing up his image and avoiding controversial statements, Corbyn was praised for his authenticity and for his determination to stick to foundational principles even when it came to issues of terrorism and defence policy. And rather than pursuing a conventional media-first strategy, Labour returned to its roots with enormous rallies that galvanised local audiences and attracted mainstream media coverage, comprehensive canvassing facilitated by a growing party membership, and an information strategy that was focused, above all, on circulating its own messages via social media. Judging by the amount of humble pie consumed in the days following the election – where even some of Corbyn's most acerbic critics reluctantly acknowledged their error in underestimating him – the election campaign confounded virtually everyone.[17] Even *The Guardian* was affected by the Corbyn surge, endorsing Labour ('the party might be the start of something big rather than the last gasp of something small', 2 June 2017) and opening its pages following the election to pro-Corbyn voices in order better to relate to a changed political atmosphere.

A BIT MORE THAN MAKING IT UP AS JEREMY GOES ALONG

Of course, Corbyn's team has neither focused exclusively on social media channels nor have they totally ignored established media sources. Corbyn has taken his anti-austerity message up and down the country, hoping that his presence in front of thousands of people at public events would generate the kind of buzz – online and offline – that is worth more than a single interview with a journalist in which he is, all too often, painted as the 'extremist' while they ask 'probing' questions about the 'divisiveness' of his 'radical' programme.

Frustratingly for most of the commentariat, Corbyn refused from the outset to play by the normal rules of media engagement. The appointment of *The Guardian's* associate editor Seumas Milne as his Director of Strategy and Communications was designed less to build bridges with the media than to secure a firm ideological ally who was familiar with, but hardly sympathetic to, the existing media landscape. Corbyn highlighted the abuse of media power in his very first speech as Labour leader, warning journalists not to 'attack people who didn't ask to be put in the limelight'.[18] Three months later he gave an interview to the *Morning Star* in which he promised to develop a media policy which would stimulate cooperative ownership, community access and break up 'single ownership of too many sources of information, so that we have a multiplicity of sources'.[19]

On the day of his first labour leadership election victory in September 2015, he showed up in Parliament Square to speak at a rally in support of refugees and, the following day, Corbyn turned down the opportunity to appear on the BBC's *Andrew Marr Show*, the main Sunday politics programme, in favour of attending a mental health fundraiser. He then announced key shadow cabinet appointments late on Sunday night – keeping journalists up past their bedtime and not playing ball with their deadlines. Indeed, his first broadcast interview as leader was not with one of the usual news heavyweights at all but with the BBC Radio One's *Newsbeat* programme – aimed at young people – in order to pay them back for the huge support they had given him in the leadership campaign.

This refusal to adopt a business-as-usual attitude towards the media was deliberate. It was not just New Labour market-oriented domestic and interventionist foreign policies but also New Labour's relationship with the media that was buried by Corbyn's victory. Unlike Tony Blair, who cultivated a very close relationship with Fleet Street (sic) newspaper proprietors, Corbyn decided that he had little to gain from cooperating with a media culture that he believes is too insular and that, by and large, will patronise, misrepresent or simply denigrate what he says. Criticising what he describes as the 'golden circle of the media establishment', Corbyn has adopted a critique that echoes the widespread distrust of 'official' sources and elite agendas that is at the heart of the growth of populist movements. The traditional media, argues Corbyn:

> frame all political debate around rumours that abound in the Palace of Westminster and the discussion that takes place between journalists who have very much the same ideas, same backgrounds and same attitudes towards society. We are doing things very differently.[20]

Instead, Corbynites have placed enormous faith in social media networks that allow them to shape their own message, to bypass traditional media and to communicate directly with supporters. These channels involve some significant numbers. By the time the general election was over, Corbyn had managed to accumulate 1.2 million Facebook 'likes' (nearly three times as many as his opponent, Theresa May), 800,000 followers on his personal Twitter account, and a popular Snapchat account to engage with a younger audience that has dramatically turned away from traditional news sources. Labour used these channels to great effect, with Corbyn's Facebook page attracting a weekly reach of 29 million people in the final week of the campaign and pro-Labour content dominating traffic on Twitter (and that's not even mentioning the supportive memes that flooded social media).[21]

Corbyn himself is clear that his campaign's use of social media is a direct response to the limitations of relying on the establishment media: it is 'a way of reaching past the censorship of the right-wing media in this country that has constrained political debate for so long. And so we begin to reframe political debate'.[22]

This full-blooded engagement with social media reflects advice offered to Corbyn by former Greek finance minister Yanis Varoufakis on a visit to London where he argued on *Channel 4 News* (14 September 2015) that the left, if organised openly as a movement, should not fear the media: 'the media can be bypassed if the message is right and if sincerity defeats hypocrisy'.

HAVE WE GOT NEWS FOR 'THEM'!

This approach to the media resonates less with traditional political communications strategies than with social movement practices designed to promote autonomous channels of communication and to neutralise the impact of a hostile media landscape. The strategy adopted by Corbynites thus appears to resemble the typology of responses proposed by the German sociologist Dieter Rucht that is aimed primarily at activist movements:[23]

> Abstention which arises out of the indifference or outright hostility of traditional media towards social movement activities;
>
> Attacks on traditional media agendas and frames;

Adaptation, where movements comply with dominant agendas and routines in order to secure minimal amounts of sympathetic coverage;

Alternative media where movements produce their own media.

It could be argued that Corbyn's media strategy has veered, at different times, between all of these responses with a special emphasis on the latter. Embracing a social movement communications strategy, however, accentuates the tensions that, despite the election result, remain between those who want to see Labour prioritise its immediate electoral fortunes by creating a 'broad church' and those who believe that Labour needs to mobilise around social justice issues in order to popularise left-wing ideas. While 'pragmatists' criticise the latter strategy for neglecting the importance of the need to win political power and for cultivating a conspiratorial view of the media as structurally anti-Labour, social movement campaigners dismiss the 'pragmatists' for wanting to curb Labour's radical policies to appease the media and 'middle England' and to win power at all costs (a theory that was decisively defeated in the general election).

Corbyn, like Bernie Sanders in the USA and Jean-Luc Mélenchon in France, is a cipher for wider discontent about rising levels of inequality, deep frustration with neoliberalism and growing mistrust of establishment voices. There is a similarity in their core constituencies: the young and the disaffected. In this situation, the task for Corbyn is not *first* to develop a 'clever' media strategy and *then* to mobilise his networks to extend his support but precisely the other way around. Indeed, Corbyn has shown that by confidently and ably using all channels of communication to propose a clear and relevant set of messages – for example, opposition to welfare cuts, opposition to scapegoating of immigrants, increased investment in local services and large infrastructure projects – the media, despite a continuing reluctance to understand both his politics and his success at generating so much enthusiasm, are more likely at least to acknowledge the presence of such narratives. This was, of course, helped by the legal requirement during an election time to give equal broadcast time to both main parties.

The emphasis, therefore, ought to be on political imagination and boldness more than professionalisation and triangulation. Corbyn ought to continue to articulate the concerns of the movements and constituencies that propelled him to his position, to devise and reiterate policies that address their interests and then to communicate with the public using all the channels available to him: from the biggest talk shows to the most local bloggers, from mass rallies to his own videos.

Furthermore, in a situation in which news – at least as provided by its most established outlets – is far from a neutral or transparent space but one framed by the agendas and priorities of those who control it, Corbyn can never afford to pander to the routines of Westminster journalists nor to organise policy development simply around what will 'play well' with leader writers and broadcast journalists. Indeed, it is this latter group, not Corbyn, that is woefully behind the times and out of touch with the anger of their audiences. What would be the point of softening his approach to the media in the hope that they would be more generous to him in the future, given that would then be interpreted by both existing members and potential supporters as bowing down to media power and therefore feeding the hand that is set on biting him? Given its attitude towards him, he is entitled not to respect a media establishment that has shown little signs of respecting him.

The biggest danger in these circumstances is not that Corbyn will buckle under the weight of press attacks, but that future internal squabbles may distract him from doggedly pursuing the popular policies around health, education and welfare that were contained in Labour's election manifesto. Corbyn can't always expect to win sympathetic media coverage nor, outside of election periods, necessarily high levels of broadcast visibility, but it is possible to construct a bold and radical programme that at least provides journalists with a clear narrative of where Labour stands. Corbyn needs to continue to invoke the 'spirit of 1945' for the twenty-first century and to declare unambiguously his principled opposition to neoliberalism and militarism and for a more just and equal society in order to maintain the momentum that is attracting more and more hits, column inches and views.

There are four lessons to be learned from this analysis.

First, the power of the media in restricting political opportunities for the left shouldn't be overstated – the general election showed that political life hasn't (yet) been subsumed into a carnival of entertainment and sensation. Indeed, media power is far more contingent than many (on both the left and the right) believe it to be. Media influence is connected to the ideas that people hold at any one moment in time – a consciousness that is not fixed or immutable but subject to constant change in the light of everyday experience. And in any case, radical politics has *always* had to contend with an intrusive and hostile media and it has, at times, made huge gains despite entrenched opposition by powerful opinion formers. The Chartists didn't have an easy ride from newspapers when pressing for labour rights in the 1840s just as the suffragettes failed to win much support from Fleet Street when campaigning for votes for women a century ago. Progressive movements have always had to organise in the face of sustained attacks from the dominant media of the times. It is less the sophistication of a media strategy or a movement's appeal to commentators than the strength of grassroots support and the ability to neutralise opposition that best determines the prospects for meaningful change.

Second, although a left politics can be built in the face of the most hostile media, movements will – especially at times of intense political debate – be required to confront hostile media landscapes with their own images and narratives. All major campaigns for social change have, after all, had their own media: the Chartists had the *Northern Star*, the Suffragettes had their own self-titled newspaper and the Bolsheviks had *Pravda*; Gandhi founded *Harijan* to help build his anti-colonial struggle, while Solidarity in Poland had *Robotnik* and the Algerians had the unofficial radio station *Voice of Fighting Algeria* during their struggle for independence from the French in the 1950s, brilliantly described by Frantz Fanon. When the anti-colonial movement took off in Algeria in the mid-1950s, the status of the radio changed overnight:

> Almost magically the radio receiver lost its identity as an enemy object. The radio set was no longer a part of the occupier's arsenal of cultural oppression.[24]

Instead, a new media, the unofficial *Voice of Fighting Algeria*, brought the war in to every village and market. Jammed by the French and constantly closed down, it nevertheless allowed Algerians to imagine the spreading of resistance: 'behind each modulation, each active crackling, the Algerian would imagine not only words but concrete battles'. For Fanon, 'having a radio meant *going to war*'.

None of these initiatives were commercial enterprises but instruments with which activists communicated with each other, publicised their activities and spread their vision. They were the organising frameworks of emergent mass movements designed not to supplant the news outlets of their enemies but to strengthen their own campaigns and, in so doing, to reach out to new audiences. That is the kind of model which left movements ought to adapt today: a rigorous and imaginative use of social media – involving everything from targeted Facebook campaigns to a more expansive approach to Instagram – combined with a commitment to exploit any opportunities for more mainstream coverage. Of course, hashtags and memes alone do not topple governments and win elections but they can help solidify and give confidence to movements whose trust in, and capacity to use, traditional communications channels is limited.

Third, for all the rhetoric about a 'paradigm shift' from traditional to social media,[25] and for all the talk, following the 2017 general election of the collapse of press power and the irrelevance of media bias, it is not the case that the mainstream media have lost their ability to influence the conduct and the coverage of public affairs. Academic research on the agenda-setting influence of right-wing newspapers on the broadcast coverage of the 2015 general election,[26] together with the domination of those same voices of coverage of the EU referendum,[27] points to the continuing ability of established voices to distort conversations about contemporary politics and to systematically undermine progressive arguments. And despite the crucial role played by an emerging network of pro-Corbyn online media outlets in the 2017 general election, television news – and the BBC in particular – remains the most popular source of information for most people. 'In other words, broadcasters still matter in election campaigns'.[28]

For this reason, the Labour leadership should not lose sight of the need to stand up to entrenched media power: to challenge the anti-Labour agendas inside the BBC's newsroom and to deal with the 'anti-democratic virulence of Britain's tax-dodging media monopolists' (as Seumas Milne so elegantly calls them).[29] Millions of people voted for Corbyn's Labour in the hope that the party would lead an uncompromising opposition to inequality, poverty and war, and they would also welcome a challenge to a media establishment that has been intimately associated with support for neoliberal policies.

Finally, given the complex interaction between media and left politics, the key task for a popular and radical left is to grow the movements on which it gathers its strength in order to extend and deepen its appeal. As such, the danger for the Corbynite left is a rather old one: the temptation to put 'pragmatic' politics, seamless communication campaigns and exclusively parliamentary manoeuvres ahead of a commitment to challenge the status quo and to represent more effectively those who have been marginalised and victimised in recent years. This is a form of politics that is unlikely to emerge from, or to be contained within, 'insider' spaces but will grow out of the movements themselves. Of course, traditional media – with their intimate links to 'official' politics – will never be the bedfellows of social movements and radical politics but, as we have seen most vividly by the Grenfell Tower fire which exposed 'the extraordinary gulf between the media class and those they report on', dominant frames can be challenged by movements that are sufficiently strong and vibrant.[30]

Repeated attacks from the media – mocking, marginalising and misrepresenting him – together with the relentless criticism from MPs from inside his own party obviously made life extremely difficult for Jeremy Corbyn. While the election result and the continuing civil war inside the Conservatives have silenced many of Corbyn's critics for now, it would be a mistake to imagine either that Corbyn is going to have an easy path to power or that he is now the undisputed darling of the media. However, it would also be a mistake to imagine that a polished and professional PR strategy, let alone a return to more centrist politics, would have been sufficient to fend off his enemies and to assure Labour's electoral success. Labour's prospects and the future of the left to which these are so intimately connected depend not on the skills of another Alistair Campbell but on the ability of Labour Party members and activists more broadly to nurture an effective social movement that can truly articulate the concerns and hopes of millions of British people. That would be a story no media outlet could afford to ignore.

NOTES

1. There is a list of anti-Corbyn headlines in *The Guardian* at theguardian. fivefilters.org.
2. James Curran, letter to *The Guardian*, 12 June 2017.

3. Gary Younge, 'Journalists' lack of curiosity about Corbyn was professional malpractice', *Prospect*, July 2017.

4. Media Reform Coalition *Corbyn's first week: Negative agenda-setting in the press*. Media Reform Coalition, 2015, p2.

5. Bart Cammaerts, Brooks DeCillia, Joao Carlos Magalhaes and Cesar Jimenez-Martinez, *Journalistic Representations of Jeremy Corbyn in the British Press: From Watchdog to Attackdog*, London School of Economics: London, 2016, p2.

6. James Walsh, 'Why Labour voters are turning towards Jeremy Corbyn', *The Guardian*, 24 July 2015.

7. Quoted in Rowena Mason, 'BBC may have shown bias against Corbyn, says former Trust Chair', *The Guardian*, 12 May 2016.

8. Justin Schlosberg, *Should He Stay or Should He Go? Television and Online News Coverage of the Labour Party in Crisis*, Media Reform Coalition, 2016, p15.

9. *Ibid*. p16.

10. Stephen Cushion, 'Were broadcasters biased against Jeremy Corbyn? It's the details that count', *New Statesman*, 21 June 2017.

11. Paul Myerscough, 'Corbyn in the media', *London Review of Books*, 22 October 2015, p9.

12. Peter Oborne, 'Is the British press really so feral?', *British Journalism Review*, Vol. 23 No. 3, 2012, p61.

13. Gaby Hinsliff, 'The media don't hate Jeremy Corbyn. It's more complicated than that', *The Guardian*, 3 June 2016.

14. *Ibid*.

15. Owen Jones, 'A strategy for Jeremy Corbyn's leadership to succeed', www.medium.com, 18 September 2016.

16. Helen Lewis, 'The echo chamber of social media is luring the left into cosy delusion and dangerous insularity', *New Statesman*, 22 July 2016.

17. Dominic Ponsford, 'Political columnists eat humble pie and apologise over dire election predictions for Corbyn and Labour', *Press Gazette*, 12 June 2017.

18. Quoted in William Turvill and David Knowles, 'Jeremy Corbyn starts Labour leadership by attacking "abusive", "cut-off" media and blanking Sky News reporter', *Press Gazette*, 14 September 2015.

19. Quoted in Ben Chacko and Luke James, 'Don't fight me, fight the Tories', *Morning Star*, 21 December 2015.

20. Quoted in Rowena Mason, 'Corbyn: Labour must use social media to fight rightwing press attacks', *The Guardian*, 3 May 2015.

21. James Stewart, 'How Corbyn cut through: Exclusive interview with a senior Labour strategist', www.theconversation.com, 15 June 2017; Monica Kaminska *et al*, 'Social media and news sources during the 2017 UK General Election', www.oii.ox.ac.uk, 5 June 2017.

22. Quoted in Rowena Mason, *ibid*.

23. Dieter Rucht, 'Protest movements and their media usages' in Bart Cammaerts, Alice Mattoni and Patrick McCurdy (eds), *Mediation and Protest Movement,* Intellect: Bristol, 2013, pp249-268.

24. Frantz Fanon, *A Dying Colonialism*, Penguin: London, 1970, p93.

25. Steve Topple, 'Pro-Corbyn campaign by the public has sent the mainstream media into a hissy fit', www.thecanary.co.uk, 1 August 2016.

26. Stephen Cushion, Allaina Kilby, Richard Thomas, Marina Morani and Richard Sambrook, 'Newspapers, impartiality and television news', *Journalism Studies*, 28 April 2016.

27. Centre for Research in Communication and Culture, '82 per cent circulation advantage in favour of Brexit as *The Sun* declares', Loughborough University, www.lboro.ac.uk/research/crcc/, 14 June 2016.

28. Stephen Cushion, *ibid*.

29. Seumas Milne, 'Jeremy Corbyn's victory has already transformed politics', *The Guardian*, 16 September 2015.

30. Tanya Gold, 'Why we must politicise the tragedy of Grenfell Tower', *New Statesman*, 16 June 2017.

Mind the Labour Gap

Hilary Wainwright

Jeremy Corbyn leading Labour from the radical left, Jeremy Corbyn on his way to winning the next general election – *Oh Jeremy Corbyn!* The chant wells up spontaneously but along with a stubborn question: what about transforming the Labour Party? To do so the Corbyn momentum (sic) will need to be sustained not just over one joyous summer but during a possible four-year wait until the next general election. And for a process of transformation that support will need to be deepened too.

The work of Ralph Miliband, author of the classic text on the Labour Party *Parliamentary Socialism*, first published in 1961, still provides the best guide to why such a transformation is needed and the problems it will face.[1]

The Labour Party remains fundamentally the 'parliamentarist' party Miliband described: it is more dogmatic about parliament than about socialism. And in Miliband's analysis, the membership has no effective power to change this. A relatively successful election campaign – such as Corbyn's – is not, in Miliband's analysis, proof of anything very radical; it's the one moment when the parliamentary party appreciates (indeed positively *needs*) all those radical, energetic members whom they normally despise. Richard Crossman famously described (and Miliband quoted in support of his argument) the role of the party's extra-parliamentary membership as follows:

> In order to maintain the enthusiasm of party militants to do the organising work for which the Conservative Party pays a vast army of workers, a constitution was created which apparently created full party democracy while excluding these members from effective power.[2]

How much has really changed in the almost six decades since Crossman wrote those words?

The moderating influence of the trade unions, especially the leadership, is important to this analysis. It was they who, in the past (for example against Tony Benn), after an initial show of support in the last instance provided the 'stabilising' bulwark of the structural, lasting power of parliamentarism. True, currently there are key trade unions which support Corbyn in response to the pressures of a membership radicalised by austerity, but how sustainable is this likely to be in the long term?

Another crucial factor is the founding feature of both Labourism and parliamentarianism alike: a deference to the British state. As Miliband points out in *Parliamentary Socialism,* the party's founding manifesto, 'Labour and the New Social Order', contained virtually no commitment to constitutional reforms that would democratise the British state. Instead, it was fervent in its reassurance that the manifesto's policies of public ownership and redistribution would be carried out by means of parliamentary government, Westminster style, with its unwritten constitution, royal prerogative and a centralised executive, preservation of the United Kingdom and all. Corbyn did not sing the national anthem, for sure, and will never fawn in the presence of royalty, but where is his radicalism in relation to electoral reform and institutions of genuine, democratic decentralisation and popular participation?

We need to engage with these kinds of questions because, to be strategically effective, we need to address even at the highpoint of our enthusiasm and excitement, the problems we face in carrying through the logic of Corbyn's victories, to transform the Labour Party itself.

WINNING FROM THE LEFT

The appeal of Jeremy Corbyn's straightforward, humane, calm and encouraging leadership, combined with John McDonnell's unrelenting opposition to austerity, has proved dramatic. It's been an appeal strengthened rather than weakened by Corbyn's ability to withstand the bullying by fellow MPs showing a contemptuous disregard for party members. This, plus Momentum's social media organising, facilitated a grassroots-driven general election campaign that produced the first example, beyond the extraordinary circumstances of the years immediately following the Second World War, of Labour Party electoral success – though not yet victory – on the basis of an appeal from the left. (And even in 1945, it was not the party leadership but the activists and the voters who were on the left.)

At the same time as turning the Tory tabloids into paper tigers, this electoral success from the left removes one important sustaining shibboleth of centre-left parliamentarianism: the insistence – an article of faith, really – that because of the peculiarities of the British electoral and party system, Labour can only win elections by moving to the centre, to attract the 'floating voters in the marginals' and that accordingly, given the importance of unity against the Conservatives (in a two party system), the left in the party and the trade unions alike have always moderated their demands and subordinated themselves to the imperatives of unity and electoral success, on the terms set by the Parliamentary Labour Party (PLP). This has meant a prohibition on politicised industrial struggles, on any questioning of our nuclear defence policy, or of the British state in all its imperial and martial feigning of 'greatness'. Corbyn, attacked with all the possible and most extreme demonising taboos ever thrown at a party leader, broke this imprisoning cycle.

It is true that the party's election manifesto made compromises on defence, to be consistent with party policy as it is. In response to the Manchester terrorist attack, however, when campaigning resumed, Corbyn treated the electorate as adults and addressed not just the attack – which he of course condemned as we all do – but the causes of it. He pointed out that after sixteen years of the disastrous 'war on terror' Britain is still subject to terrorist attacks; and he connected these attacks to the failures of British foreign policy, among other reasons.

As Andrew Murray, seconded from Unite to be a member of the inner core of the election campaign team, commented:

> This was a courageous thing for him to do. It would have been far easier to simply condemn and leave it at that. But that would have not been levelling with the public. He said there should be a serious debate, with everything on the table … that there is a connection between British foreign policy this century and the continuation of terror attacks in Britain. In so far as no party-political leader has dared make this linkage publicly since 2001, we can say that Rubicon has been crossed.[3]

I would add that Corbyn's statement now opens the way for developing an alternative to traditional notions of national defence, shaped by entrenched mentalities of empire and a special Anglo-American relationship.

THATCHER'S DESTRUCTION OF TRADE UNION CORPORATISM

In Miliband's analysis, parliamentarianism was reinforced by a corporate and sectional trade unionism concerned with bargaining over workplace issues, while delegating wider political issues of welfare, taxation, industrial policy, macroeconomic policy and foreign policy to the Parliamentary Labour Party. Here Miliband's concept of 'Labourism', complementary to 'parliamentarianism', was the idea of the Labour Party as an instrument for a sectoral, corporate understanding of the interests of organised labour, reflecting 'the growing integration of the trade unions into the framework of modern capitalism'.[4]

Miliband understood that a sustained integration of the trade unions into capitalism was a condition of the Labour Party's power structure, ensuring that the union leaderships would accept the confines of parliamentarianism and Labourism. This in turn requires stable corporatist relationships of political economy, whereby the trade unions are acquiescent and integrated at the factory, company and government level as 'partners', effectively locked into permanent institutional subordination. After Thatcher's sustained attack on the trade unions, left virtually untouched by Blairism too, such conditions do not hold in the UK and this, together with other newer forms of 'popular insubordination' lead to the breakdown of the PLP/trade union leadership alliance at the apex of Labour's power structure. Corbyn's victory in the 2015 Labour leadership election owed a lot to the pent-up anger of trade union members, not only in the long aftermath of Thatcherism but in response to Blair's continuation of too many Thatcherite policies. Some trade union leaders, such as Len McCluskey, general secretary of Unite, either shared this anger, or as with Dave Prentis at UNISON, could not hold it back from determining their union's decision in both leadership elections.

Furthermore, under Ed Miliband's regime as party leader, the centralising grip that Blair and Mandelson had imposed in their obsession with control, was somewhat loosened – so that a few left-wingers got through the net of parliamentary selection. Moreover, the rules of leadership elections were changed so that individual trade union members (rather than each union voting as a block) and party supporters could vote for the leader. This released the expression of membership anger – rather than giving a 'moderate' membership a voice against an 'unrepresentative' leadership as the Blairites advising Miliband had hoped.

As the militant dynamics of trade unionism were blocked by anti-trade union laws, the pent-up anger of trade union and other activists found a new political expression, through their support for Jeremy Corbyn. During the 2015 leadership election campaign almost 100,000 trade union members directly signed up to join the Labour Party while even more signed up as registered supporters. Under such dynamic and volatile conditions, the reproduction of the formations of labourism the party had become used to, could no longer be guaranteed.

TOWARDS A TRANSFORMATIVE PARTY?

Together, these two arguments: the collapse of an important pillar of right wing parliamentarianism and the breaking of the conditions for the reproduction of labourism are important. But they don't yet indicate whether Labour can become a truly transformative left party, as distinct from simply a better version of a traditional social democratic party. One that would lead a reforming government, backed by radicalised trade unions and associated social and protest movements, prepared to confront the vested interests of capital protected by the inherited institutions of the British state.

BREAKING FROM OLD POLARISATIONS

To better understand the divisions that have arisen so sharply in the Labour Party since Jeremy Corbyn's election as leader in 2015, we need to start from the fact that historically debate, creative thinking and experimental practice on the left has been distorted by hermetically sealed polarisations, usually framed by the right. Post-1917, this was framed as between Bolshevik insurrection and liberal, Burkean parliamentarianism (with its taboo on effective accountability of parliamentary representatives to constituency parties or trade unions-the extra-parliamentary organisations of labour) and then during the Cold War from the late 1940s and its prolonged after life under Blair, between the command economy (Stalinism and a planned economy, original Clause 4 style) and a private 'free' market economy.

This distorting polarisation weakened the influence on Labour Party debates about co-operative, syndicalist and emancipatory traditions which have always been present on the British left and could be consistent with a radical, participatory and transitional role for representative democracy, enabling the direct expression and recognition of transformative civic initiatives and a social economy against the capitalist private profit driven market.[5] Moreover, the dominance of Cold War thinking in mainstream politics and media tended to freeze progressive debates about processes of social change. This desensitised the response of both Labour and those of the wider public, to struggles and initiatives that, in their practice, went beyond the traditional dichotomies of market versus state.

After the financial crisis of 2008, movements rose in revolt against neoliberalism and the complicity of the whole political class in its attacks on working and would-be working people. Significantly, they turned in disgust against the corruption of the political system, to creating directly positive solutions of their own. This emphasis on the direct creation of civic sources of power – building on traditions going back to 1968 and the rebellions of the 1970s and developing not in counter-position but in alliance with radical initiatives to gain governmental or municipal office, provide the basis of overcoming these debilitating polarisations. The movement in support of Jeremy Corbyn was in many ways our British version of the Indignados.[6]

For, once he was on the Labour leadership election ballot paper, Corbyn became a powerful magnet for the kind of discontent expressed by the 'movements of the squares' in Greece and the Indignados in Spain: discontent which, within the specifics of the British context, had at its core an angry reaction to Tony Blair's New Labour government with its continuation of Thatcher's agenda of deregulation, privatisation and austerity.[7]

The diverse energies of the movement that lifted Jeremy Corbyn to the party leadership came as much, if not more, from outside the Labour Party as from inside. Environmental campaigners and direct-action groups, those radicalised by their own precarity, by growing inequality, austerity and the 2008 financial crash, and by the mounting threat to the survival of the planetary ecological system, joined with thousands of trade union members angered by government cuts and their consequences for public services, local government and the lives and prospects for young people, and deeply disillusioned by Labour after the experiences of Tony Blair.

The initiatives of many of these social movements and struggles were more than protests; like those in southern Europe. Out of their resistance, they developed forms of practice that tried to prefigure in the here and now, the values and social relations of the future society for which they worked. Housing co-operatives, social enterprises and co-operatives for renewable energy, centres to support women facing violence, micro enterprises producing sustainable forms of agriculture and food, a huge variety of cultural and knowledge-sharing initiatives facilitated by the new tools generated by the revolution in information and communication technologies. These experiences point to two distinctions that enable us to understand the emergence of initiatives of this prefigurative kind. These, I would argue, provide stimuli to imagine and tools to experiment, towards a Labour Party of a new type.[8] This is a possibility opened up, but not guaranteed by, both the movement stimulated by Corbyn's leadership and consolidated through Momentum as a movement active in a variety of extra-parliamentary initiatives as well as in highly effective electioneering. Openings are increased by the earthquakes generated Corbyn's success, producing deep cracks in the established institutions of British, including Labour, politics.

FROM STATE VERSUS MARKET TO SOCIAL VERSUS PROFIT DRIVEN

A key tool for rethinking Labour politics involves a radical move away from the conventional classification of the economy into the market, the state and some notional 'third sector'. Instead, drawing on the work of radical, ecological civil economist Robin Murray, the key divide is increasingly between those parts of the economy that are driven by social goals (the social economy) and those which are subject to the imperatives of capital accumulation.[9]

We need, Murray argues, to understand the social economy as a hybrid of several sub-economies, all distinct in how they are financed, and to understand who has access to their outputs and on what terms, what kinds of social relations are involved, how any surplus is distributed and what kind of economic discipline is exerted to achieve their social goals. The sub-economies consist of the household, governed by relations of reciprocity; the state, funded by taxes and governed in theory by democratically decided social goals; and that section of the market which involves the exchange of equivalents – those few areas of the market (between small social or co-operative businesses) not yet dominated by capitalist enterprises.

They are all in different ways in conflict and in tension with the profit/capital accumulation driven economy and are all vulnerable to being dominated by its imperatives. But there is nothing intrinsic to the state, grant or household economies that drives them towards capital accumulation. As economies, they are oriented to their own social goals; each can operate in the market, in pursuit of these goals without necessarily being drawn into the vortex of accumulation. Many of the lasting, though always precarious, alternatives created by social movements over the past decade (and in fact, with ups and downs, in the decades since 1968) can be understood in this way.

But if we are to understand the sense in which these civil initiatives (including those stimulated or supported by trade unions) are a foundation of a new politics and with it, a transformed Labour Party, we need to overcome the nineteenth century liberal distinction between politics and economics. We need, therefore, to go further than Robin Murray's analysis of the civil economy and understand these prefigurative initiatives as an assertion of power, but power of a distinct kind.

POWER AS DOMINATION VERSUS POWER AS TRANS-FORMATIVE CAPACITY

Here we need to distinguish between on the one hand 'power over,' which could also be described as 'power-as-domination' involving an asymmetry between those with power and those over whom power is exercised. Historically, social democratic parties have been built around, at best, a benevolent version of the understanding of power-as-domination. Their strategies have been based on winning the power to govern and then steering the state apparatus to meet what they identify as the needs of the people. It is a paternalistic political methodology. On the other hand, is 'power to', or 'power-as-transformative-capacity'. This is the power discovered by social movements of students, radical workers, environmentally conscious technologists and feminists as they moved beyond protest to proposing and directly creating practical, pre-figurative solutions.

The notion of power-as-transformative-capacity emerged out of widespread frustration at the workings of power-as-domination exercised by political parties of the traditional left. The distinctive feature of the rebellions of the 1960s and 1970s was that students, workers, insubordinate women and others took power into their own hands, discovering through collective action that they had capacities of their own to bring about change; and that through rebellion, they had leverage because the power of their oppressors depended on their complicity. These were not simply movements of pressure, demanding with extra militancy that the governing party do something on their behalf. Their approach was more directly transformative. For example, women took action directly to change their relations with men, with each other and with public services; workers took militant action in their workplaces not only to improve their working conditions but also to extend control over the purpose of their labour; and community groups squatted in empty buildings, occupied land against speculation and campaigned for alternative land-use policies for the wellbeing of their communities. They no longer focused primarily on the parliamentary politics of representation.

A common theme of these rebellions involved overturning conventional deference to authority and the forms of knowledge that those in authority deployed as their source of legitimacy. The other side of the movements' rejection of these forms of authority was a pervasive and self-confident assertion of their own practical and sometimes tacit knowledge, as well as their collaborative capacity, against the claims of those in authority to know 'what is best' or 'what needs to be done'. Along with this self-confidence in their transformative abilities went inventiveness about the forms of organisation that would build that capacity. While acknowledging the mixed and uneven legacy of the 1960s and 1970s, a distinctive feature of the radical movements of those years, was their tendency to emphasise and value the sharing of different kinds of knowledge, practical and experiential as well as theoretical and historical. In their refusal to defer to authority, such movements broke the unspoken bond between knowledge and authority that underpinned the post-war settlement – the paternalistic idea that those in power know what is best for the mass of people.

The uncertain, experimental process of democratising knowledge tends, in practice, to involve instead an emphasis on decentralised and networked organisations sharing and developing knowledge horizontally, and breaking from models that presume an expert leadership and a more-or-less ignorant membership (the model described by Robert Michels in his study of social democratic political parties and his hypothesis of 'the iron law of oligarchy').[10]

The radically democratic approaches to knowledge pioneered in the 1960s and 1970s (most notably by feminists but also by networks of workplace, community organisations, and critical technologists) laid organisational and cultural foundations that have underpinned many civic movements ever since, from the alter-globalisation movement of the late 1990s through to Occupy and the Indignados.

Yet what has also become very clear in developing new institutions through social and labour movements is that the autonomy of non-state sources of power tends to be precarious and difficult to sustain, however transformative and creative they can periodically be. This repeatedly has raised the question of how far, and under what conditions, power-as-domination (essentially, in this context, having control over state institutions, national and municipal) can be a resource for power-as-transformative-capacity. It is important to recognise that although there is a sharp distinction between these two types of power, they are not necessarily or invariably counter-posed.[11] We therefore need to probe further into both concepts of power, and then into what new forms of institutions of representation could enable the two to best combine for purposes of transformation, revitalising forms of representation in the process. How, for example, could power-as-domination be a resource for power-as-transformative-capacity, as distinct from weakening or overwhelming forms of social power originally autonomous from the state? And what kinds of transformative capacity are strategically relevant to bring about change, with resources from power-as-domination?

Moreover, civic sources of power cannot automatically be assumed to be transformative or strategically significant. Under what conditions, if any, could institutions of representative democracy provide a framework or platform through which these two kinds of power could combine in a process of social transformation?

THE CORBYN TURN

All this might seem a long way from the Labour Party; focused almost exclusively on electoral politics, excessively deferential towards state power, and overly defensive about the party's trade union links. But in another sense, this approach continues, in contemporary form, traditions embedded in the party's origins. These traditions gave us the original Clause 4, the party's famous commitment not only to common ownership but also to the 'popular administration and control of each industry and service' and 'to secure for the workers by hand or by brain the full fruits of their industry and the most equitable distribution thereof'. Note here the emphasis on 'workers by hand and by brain', and that it refers explicitly not to state or public administration and control but to 'popular administration and control'. Surely an implication of this is that in the preparation for gaining power, the type of party leadership needed is one that not only prepares its shadow cabinet for managing the affairs of state, but also that leads the party to engage in a process of empowering and building the capacity of its members and supporters, the labour movement and its social allies, for the process of 'popular administration and control of every industry and service'.

Much to the stunned surprise of those forces hostile to him, in the Parliamentary Labour Party and in the liberal media as well as in the right-wing media – in *The Guardian* as well as in the *Daily Mail* – Corbyn, given the focus and publicity of a general election campaign, unleashed a suppressed radicalisation arising from the experience of over a decade of austerity. A section of the PLP and the previously entirely hostile party apparatus will always be impressed by the ability to win votes – winning elections was always one aspect of parliamentarianism – and with this success Corbyn for now has secured their support. Another less responsive, more entrenched, dimension of parliamentarianism however is a deference to the British state, the union, the queen in parliament and with it the power of private capital as organised through the City of London. These ideological Blairites, committed to the British state and to the free market – whose ideal world would be run by Hillary Clinton, Emmanuel Macron and Tony Blair – will continue to organise to ensure that Corbyn will never be prime minister. The problem for them is that in the past they have always been the electorally successful part of the Labour Party and therefore hegemonic within the party which after all is united by a desire to defeat the Tories and form a government, however much left and right differ about what they want a Labour government to do.

As I have argued, the distinctive feature of Jeremy Corbyn's leadership, understandably not anticipated by Ralph Miliband's influential analysis is that it has begun to break with the assumption that the only way to win elections is by what Miliband called 'parliamentarism' with its deference to the British state. Corbyn has shown that – after decades of neoliberal economics – it is possible to win from the left. This provides him with a hegemonic window in the party and greater legitimacy in wider society. Exactly how this will be followed through remains unclear but hopeful: what an electorally successful left party, aiming for a radical transformation of the capitalist state, involves in practice is uncertain, but the negative lessons of Greece warn harshly against any separation from the radical social movements from whence such parties came, and on whose transformative power they depend to achieve the changes they promised and for which they won support.

By way of a strategic conclusion, then, I would suggest the debates in the Labour Party – and indeed the broader discussions and alliances on the left which will become increasingly important – can most productively be framed not by the traditional categories inherited from the Cold War, of left equalling more state and right equalling more market, but between those who uphold the existing institutions of the British state with its separation of parliamentary politics from struggles and alternatives of civil society, with all their political ramifications, versus those who are rooted in those struggles which they see as the basis of a new productive and participatory politics. A Labour Party that is no longer divided along these old lines, although for some those will remain, but more importantly in permanent creative tension with refounded and renewed forms of representative and party democracy in common cause with those who share that ambition inside and outside of parliament,

NOTES

1. Ralph Milband, *Parliamentary Socialism: A Study in the Politics of Labour,* Merlin Press: London, 2009.
2. Richard Crossman, 'Introduction' to Walter Bagehot, *The English Constitution,* Harper Collins: London, 1988.

3. Andrew Murray, '#GE2017: Lessons for the Stop the War movement', www.stopwar.org.uk, 3 July 2017.
4. Ralph Miliband, *ibid.*
5. See Stephen Yeo, *New Views of Co-operation,* Routledge: London, 1988.
6. In Scotland, it took the form of a radically democratic movement for Scottish independence around the 2013 referendum. This was led by an alliance of Greens, social movements, trade unions, and radical NGOs, and was supported by many of the most influential Scottish intellectuals and cultural figures.
7. See Alex Nunns, *The Candidate*, OR Books: New York, 2015.
8. For a more elaboration of these arguments see Hilary Wainwright, 'Radicalising the party movement relationship: From Ralph Miliband to Jeremy Corbyn and beyond' in Leo Panitch and Greg Albo (eds), *Socialist Register 2017: Rethinking Revolution*, Merlin Press: London, 2016.
9. See for example Robin Murray, 'Global Civil Society and the Rise of the Economy' in Mark Kaldor (ed.) *Global Civil Society*, Palgrave Macmillan: London, 2012.
10. Robert Michels, *Political Parties: A Sociological Study of the Oligarchical Tendencies of Modern Democracy*, Simon & Schuster: London, 1997.
11. My analysis here differs from that of John Holloway for example who also makes a distinction between 'power over' and 'power to' but within a different theoretical and political framework.

The Authenticity of Hope

Eliane Glaser

It has become commonplace over the last two decades to claim that we live in a post-ideological era. In the wake of the EU referendum and the election of Donald Trump, it seemed as if politics was becoming polarised once again, as right-wing populists channelled the public's suppressed desire for ideological commitment by giving the impression of saying what they really think. But in fact they perpetuate the departure from explicit democratic contestation, and their focus is not idealism but 'authenticity'. In the new era defined by Brexit and Trump, the old divisions between left and right, rich and poor, seem to give way to a confected and highly corrosive opposition between 'the people' and 'the elites'.

In this schema, those without university degrees are pitched against those with them; the working class against the middle class; 'patriots' against internationalists; and natives against immigrants. The class conflict between a blue-collar voter in Hull and an investment banker free to live and work between London, Zurich and Shanghai thus becomes a dramatised conflict between that Hull voter and a lecturer on a zero-hours contract teaching at Middlesex University, or between the same voter and an asylum seeker who has been given temporary housing. The claims of the 99 per cent against those of the 1 per cent are replaced by an attack on those who would speak for the working poor or for the already-squeezed middle class. Benefits claimants are placed outside legitimate discourse; the super-rich are exempt from scrutiny.

As quickly as that new era was established, however, everything changed again with Jeremy Corbyn's spectacular success in the 2017 general election. Along with the waning appeal of Marine le Pen in France, and the politically-inflected anger following the Grenfell

Tower fire, it suddenly seemed that right-wing populism was not hegemonic after all. This set of circumstances has created a moment in which the future character of our politics hangs in the balance. It remains to be seen whether a reinvigorated left-wing Labour Party will continue to make electoral gains, and whether it will have an opportunity soon to do so, or whether the Conservatives will remain in power in the long term, combining scorched-earth modernisation with 1950s nostalgia, and the protection of financial and corporate interests with the co-option of 'ordinary working-class people'.

If Corbyn's Labour Party retains its strong position, it is also open to question whether we will see a full-blown return to the contest of ideologies rooted in economic interests, or whether the fault-line will be between right-wing and left-wing populisms. If populism remains prevalent, the defining opposition will be between the people and the system, which is a poor substitute for agonism. It is in this context that Corbyn will continue to be defined as embodying elements of both populism and elitism. It is only by foregrounding the ideological content of his programme that public support for Corbyn and what he represents will be sustained.

ILLUSORY ALLIANCES

The political era ushered in by the events of 2016 produced a series of imaginary and deeply unhelpful associations. Right-wing politicians, the right-wing press and finance capital forged a spurious alliance with working-class voters in order to lend their iniquitous policies the air of equality and popularity, and to silence reasoned, left-wing objections. They recruited a left-wing critique of financial and corporate power and converted it into a toxic anti-intellectualism, a vicious and bullying attack on 'experts', professionals, thinkers, writers and journalists. Those who analyse, uphold the rule of law and hold power to account were framed as 'enemies of the people'. In a further act of co-option, the right merged the left's critique of global capitalism with an opposition to immigration and supra-national bodies such as the EU.

The defining categories of right and left, rich and poor are still there, and still real – albeit refracted by complexities of identity. But in 2016 they became overwhelmingly obscured by these new artificial divisions and alliances. Right-wing populism takes kernels of truth – the neoliberalism of the EU, the atrophying and profession-alisation of parliamentary democracy, the strain on public services – and uses these to construct a through-the-looking-glass world where everything is turned on its head. Right-wing populism is like a cancer: it takes the healthy left-wing antibodies that should be fighting inequality and injustice, and it turns them against the body politic itself.

This political landscape came to define the ways in which Jeremy Corbyn was framed in political discourse and in the media. It was a landscape that was fundamentally false, toxic and confused, and it proved highly damaging both to Corbyn and to the broader cause of left-wing politics. Both terms, 'populism' and 'elite', which have been used so widely in the current political conversation, are ambiguous and inadequate. Yet the representation of Corbyn has until recently been organised around these two poles. He has been framed – ambivalently – as both populist and elite. This contradictory representation reveals that Corbyn is a paradoxical and ambiguous figure in the public imagination. However, equally it reveals that the highly resonant yet oddly mercurial categories of elitism and populism have turned our already degraded political culture into a hall of mirrors, full of codes and inverted archetypes, where reality is the opposite of appearance, nobody says what they really mean, and everything turns out in the worst possible way. Hope has emerged in the altered political mood following the 2017 general election, but it is likely that the categories of populism and elitism will continue to inflect our political culture. The left needs to reframe its alliances along the lines of economics and ideology if it is to make further gains.

THE POPULIST DISRUPTION

Populism is disrupting established political systems across the world, but it is a much misunderstood term, and it is also used to mean many different things. In essence populism invokes a pure, morally virtuous and unified people defined in opposition to an 'other'. In the case of right-wing populism, this 'other' is twofold. Right-wing populism kicks down as well as up. It rejects immigrants and foreigners and blames them for 'ordinary' people's problems. But it also vilifies the political 'establishment' which is accused of favouring and mollycod-dling new arrivals. Instead of regarding politics as a democratic theatre of opposition in which the interests of the poor are pitted against those of the rich, right-wing populism and its version of anti-elitism diverts public anger away from financial and corporate elites and turns it not only onto academics, journalists and other middle-class intellectuals, but also onto the political system itself. According to this narrative, politicians – particularly on the left – represent a kind of statist, patronising authority. In this way, the response to economic inequality becomes an attack on the very people who work to eradicate that injustice.

Left-wing populism's antagonised 'other' is the financial and corporate interests that corrupt and distort the political system, what Podemos calls '*la casta*': the merging of political and economic elites. Building on the work of the political theorists Ernesto Laclau and Chantal Mouffe, left-wing populists deploy the notion of the 'empty signifier', a pragmatic coalition of interests that unite against this dominant political/economic power. As Ernesto Laclau put it:

> One has to discursively construct the enemy – the oligarchy, big money, capitalism, globalisation, and so on – and for the same reason, the identity of the claimers is transformed in this process of universalisation of both the aims and the enemy ... once we move beyond a certain point, what were requests *within* institutions became claims addressed *to* institutions, and at some stage they became claims *against* the institutional order. When this process has overflown the institutional apparatuses beyond a certain limit, we start having the people of populism.[1]

There is a pragmatic utility to this approach, but a left-wing populism – like all populisms – is inherently problematic. It imagines 'the people' as falsely unified and lacking ideological divisions based on differing economic interests. The political system is currently dominated by financial interests, but this is not by definition always the case; yet populism tends to throw the baby of democracy out with the bathwater of its current state. This serves the purpose of highlighting the failings of a democratic system that has become corrupt and unrepresentative, but it does not in itself posit any firm ideas of a positive system that would better represent people. In fact, it encourages the current move towards anti-politics and depoliticisation by downplaying ideological difference and calling on people to reject government, democratic institutions and the state. A popular left politics – as distinct from left populism – retains a belief in the formal structure of democracy, seeking to succeed within it by advocating a vision compelling enough to encourage people to vote for it.

In part because of a lack of clear ideological direction, left-wing populism has faltered where right-wing populism has become increasingly dominant around the world. Right-wing populism denounces the political system while quietly taking it over. It then undermines the system from the inside, eroding representation and state support, while consolidating executive control. The neoliberal right is both anti-ideological and covertly intensely ideological; it works to subordinate the political system to 'the markets', and is utterly committed to the pursuit of partisan hegemony. In left-wing and right-wing populism alike, the strategically useful critique of the neoliberal distortion of democracy blurs into a critique of democracy itself.

Brexit provided the perfect storm for this populist transformation, with the EU referendum pitched against parliament. 'The people' were figured in opposition to politicians as 'the elite'. The fact that politics happens to be dominated by corporate interests and finance capital, and the fact that so many MPs are middle-class career politicians are contingent realities, but they became reasons to junk representative democracy entirely. The phrase 'political elite' is itself a composite phrase, signifying two contradictory elements: on the one hand, it signals the MPs who read PPE at Oxford and are looking forward to at some point exiting through the revolving door into a lucrative job at McKinsey or PWC. But on the other it signals the political system. It is important to distinguish between the two.

THE ROOTS OF DECLINE

The seeds of this counterproductive state of affairs were of course planted way before Brexit. As working-class communities have been hit by de-industrialisation, they have lost the civic infrastructure and local political networks which used to provide the building blocks for their national political representation. Politics has become a career option for a very narrow, and generally privileged, demographic. At the same time, there has been a rift between the metropolitan middle-class left and a more socially conservative working class living in smaller towns, coastal and rural areas. Since they do not share the same economic interests, alliances between these two groups were once built determinedly and systematically. Those alliances have now largely broken down, exacerbated by the fact that the communities themselves are more divided. However this rift, though real, is over-stated in the right-wing media. It is a dramatised conflict that depends on the real opponent, the 1 per cent, being kept out of the picture.

A vicious circle is thus established where working-class communi-ties have a quieter voice, aside from the ventriloquism of right-wing tabloids; where the background and life experience of many Labour MPs becomes ever more detached from that of working-class voters; where those communities vote against their own interests; and where left-wingers who question the rationality of doing so are accused of regarding those voters as 'stupid'. They are not stupid, but they are misinformed by the right-wing press and led to vote against their own best interests; and it is surely wrong to assume those voters hold opin-ions which are somehow 'natural' and thus their genesis and merits cannot be questioned. It is also the case that many disaffected voters are aware that right-wing politicians will betray them, but the power of the right is now so great that those voters with no other alternative exercise the only power they have left, which is to punish the left for moving to the right.

Left-wing parties are told repeatedly by politicians and the media that they need to move to the right in order to get elected; then they duly move to the right, and lose anyway, to an even more right-wing party. These parties are warned that ordinary people are intrinsically Conservative, and then blamed for losing touch with their heartlands. In the Labour Party, the right of the party have such an ingrained belief that no left-wing candidate could ever have mass appeal, that they refused to believe the evidence of their own eyes: the surge in Labour Party membership; the mass rallies; the pre-election shift in the opinion polls. Not even Corbyn's evident popularity could persuade them of his popularity. But that vicious circle has been broken – at least for now.

THE APPEAL OF CORBYN

Commentators generally ascribe Jeremy Corbyn's popularity to his authenticity – his down-to-earth style. He wears a rumpled suit and no tie; he talks well to 'ordinary people'. What is emphasised less often is his clear articulation of left-wing ideology. In this sense, Corbyn represents a return to Old Labour and the politics of the mid-twentieth century: the politics of left against right. It is the popularity of Corbyn's ideas that attracted hundreds of thousands of new members to the party, and Labour's opinion poll ratings jumped after the appearance of his unashamedly strident manifesto. After the Conservatives did relatively badly in the election, the diagnostic consensus was that Theresa May was a shambles, and they had fought the worst campaign ever. Although there were failings in the Tory campaign, this narrative was a blatant rewriting of history that served to downplay the ideological appeal of what Labour had to offer.

Combined with his non-populist ideological expression, Corbyn has employed, or has benefitted from, campaigns which some describe as 'populist', but which are perhaps better described as 'mass engagement'. He has been bolstered by Momentum, which helped to connect Labour Party election campaigning with a broader mass support of new-wave activists. Momentum is itself a divided formation: it is split between old-style vanguard socialism and newer, more participatory forms. It has elements both from the top-down and the bottom-up. These internal conflicts have caused it to fracture, but Momentum's core appeal resides in the fact that it is a grassroots political campaigning organisation rather than a classically populist movement. Mobilising around a target seats strategy for the 2017 general election campaign, Momentum applied 'big organising' techniques such as 'barnstorm' meetings and face to face conversations, which had helped to mobilise huge support for Bernie Sanders in a short space of time.[2] Momentum's online mobilising initiatives like 'My Nearest Marginal' were strategic interventions designed to increase support for a mainstream party; they were innovative, but not strictly populist.

Corbyn's use of more purely populist strategies, however, is less admirable. His practice of reading out questions from 'ordinary people' at PMQs, his preference for not wearing a tie, and his non-slick rhetorical style signals a non-alignment with professionalised politics and the Westminster 'machine'. These strategies can be effective, but they have been employed by neoliberal politicians from Tony Blair to Nigel Farage: they are the trappings of 'authenticity', which, without ideological content, can be easily co-opted by the other side.

Even more troubling are Corbyn's attempts at full-blown populism; positioning himself as representing 'the people' against the Westminster 'elite'. This was more effective when Corbyn was as an insurgent figure pitched against an oppositional PLP, but it has become damaging in its recruitment to the cause of generalised anti-politics. Corbyn declares that:

> I've spent over forty years in politics campaigning for a better way of doing things, standing up for people, taking on the establishment. ... Every day I see the political system letting down the people of this country; how decisions made in Westminster are making people's lives harder.[3]

Here, there is a problematic slippage between neoliberal governments and the political system itself, particularly when he adds 'People didn't trust politicians and they didn't trust the European Union'.[4] Speaking to the Fabian Society in January 2017, Corbyn pledged to make a 'complete break' with a 'rigged system' that serves the elites.[5] He is right about the rigging, but what does a 'complete break' mean? At around the same time, Corbyn's inner circle set out to 'relaunch' him as a left-wing Trump. This last ploy was rightly derided by many as gimmicky and unprincipled.

Jeremy Corbyn's image is in fact unstable and ambiguous. The very characteristics that cast him as an anti-Westminster-elite populist – his professorial appearance, his bicycle – are the very characteristics which signal to right-wing populists that he *is* a member of the elite. The fact that he has been an MP for decades and is in this sense a member of the political establishment, the fact that he is an old-style socialist, and that he represents a mainly middle-class constituency, causes his representation to flip from populist to elitist. Former Labour MP Tom Harris has described the problem of Corbyn's Labour Party as 'just too out of touch with its roots, too metropolitan, too Emily Thornberry to connect with working-class voters'.[6] Or, as Rachel Sylvester puts it, the real problem with Labour is that it is 'turning into one big Islington dinner party offering vegan lasagne to people who prefer beef'.[7] These are caricatures but they have a resonance which even after 8 June cannot be lightly dismissed.

The Corbyn supporters who have joined the Labour Party since 2015 are regularly represented as young, middle-class students or graduates.[8] Labour's relative success in the 2017 general election was widely put down to middle-class support: students and their families were 'rallying' to Corbyn, we were told, on the strength of his pledge to abolish tuition fees. 'The route to a sustainable Labour victory', declared Labour MP Phil Wilson in the wake of the election, 'will not be found by travelling only the middle-class streets of Kensington and the campuses of our university towns'.[9] Yet as Owen Jones has pointed out, working-class support for Labour increased in the 2017 election.[10] The Labour Party had lost touch with those communities not simply because too many of its MPs were drawn from an increasingly narrow social base, but because in the process it had moved to the right.

This ubiquitous framing of Corbyn and his supporters as elite conceals a number of problematic implications. First, characterisations coming from the right of the Labour Party are indistinguishable from those of Conservatives and their tabloid supporters. Second, they carry a disturbing anti-intellectualism and anti-cosmopolitanism. Third, they strengthen the pernicious notion that 'liberals' dominate the political establishment – a lie that was also propagated in Trump's campaign. The reality of course is the opposite: it is neoliberalism that, by and large, has been dominant over the last four decades. Fourth, it is a covertly political intervention masked as objective analysis. The injunction that Labour must appeal to working-class voters sounds progressive, but it is not. Because it always assumes that working-class voters are fundamentally to the right of Corbyn, and that Labour should accordingly shift rightwards. This assumption has dogged Labour for decades. But the 2017 election largely revealed it to be false.

When he is at his best, the appeal of Corbyn is his authenticity; but an authenticity of ideological substance, not hick anti-Westminster style. He says what he thinks, not in the Trumpian manner of raising hell at a Washington fundraiser, but in the sense of being explicit about his beliefs and his analysis of what is wrong with Britain. Corbyn found his mojo when he turned away from populism and towards the combination of rhetorical sincerity and co-ordinated grassroots campaigning that were the hallmarks of the Sanders campaign. Corbyn was quoted at an election event in Peterborough: 'Elections are, yes, about knocking on doors and talking to voters', he said, 'but they are also about framing the debate'.[11] This is key to his success.

THE LIMITATIONS OF 'LISTENING'

Ever since the focus-group, polling and the question of 'what comes up on the doorstep' began to dominate political culture, political opinions have been increasingly regarded as born, not made: politicians simply have to find out what they are and then appeal to them with a policy 'offer', and polling companies attempt to divine what this should be in the run-up to elections. According to an implicit assumption held by the right-wing press and many amongst Corbyn's most critical Labour MPs, the political views held by working-class people are particularly natural and inherent. The shock of the EU referendum result was interpreted by many as a sign that Labour had lost touch with its working-class voter base. The prescribed remedy was to go out there and 'listen' to communities outside the south-east.

Politicians routinely claim that they are not motivated by ideology, but by what 'really matters' to 'ordinary people'. But this simply drives ideological motivation underground and narrows the bandwidth of clear political alternatives that people actually crave. Ideology is created in a two-way street between politicians setting out their position and constituents asserting their concerns. But too often the pattern has been for the tabloids to make policy by falsely purporting to represent the views of the people, and then politicians have simply followed this rather than setting out what they believe. To simply agree that whatever voters say is acceptable is the death of politics. Opinions are both formed and open to challenge.

2017 cast this predicament in a different light, by revealing that popular opinion is not necessarily conservative, and that the right-wing tabloids are not as hegemonic as they previously seemed. The spaces for change where the left can make headway is thus now more open than it has been for decades. However, the question remains whether the left can make the most of this opportunity.

FINDING THE ROUTE TO A COMMON CAUSE

It is vital that the broken connections between the middle- and working-class left are mended for the Labour Party, and the left in general, to have a future. The experience of working-class communities has to be fed into Labour policy. The problem of inequality has to be a key element of its message. Labour needs to find ways to address the predicament of post-industrial regions. And they need to find ways to diversify their members and MPs and ensure they are drawn from a broader demographic base. But it is not enough just to admonish cosmopolitan leftists to 'listen'. The social and institutional structures that used to bring people from different backgrounds together have been dismantled or become highly segregated. A permanent conversation between a left now made up of so many different social backgrounds needs to take place, not in the abstract, but to shape both co-operation and change, on all sides. And this needs to contribute to a process Corbyn himself has foregrounded for Labour: as well as listening, we need to advocate for left-wing politics – to take a lead, set out a platform of beliefs and seek to persuade. For a long time, Labour even shied away from using the words 'left' or 'socialism'. The task now is to come up with an explicit ideological narrative to both reuse those words and give them popular substance.

In the quest for authenticity, our political culture has been reduced to a futile opposition between 'ordinary people' whose opinions cannot be questioned, and 'out of touch' politicians whose notable character-istics are not who their policies actually benefit, but who they are as people – what school did they go to, how many kitchens do they have. Under the guise of anti-elitism, we ended up with anti-politics.

The left needs to be careful to not return to this simplistic framing of people versus elite. We must stop co-opting the right-wing framing of those in authority and those who know things as elitist. As the Grenfell disaster revealed, we need experts, and we need central co-ordination with people qualified to take charge. We must distin-guish between political office and the kind of person who is occupying that office.

Corbyn is ultimately a composite and ambiguous figure in relation to the terms of populism and elitism, which in turn reveals the limi-tations and chimerical nature of these now clichéd terms. As well as figure-heading an ostensibly populist left based on grassroots and social media mobilisation, he is also a creature of the old political system. This ambiguity represents a confusion among his supporters about political institutions and about political temporality and progress. On the one hand, the political system is perceived to be a 'dinosaur', the establish-ment as the embodiment of an obsolete and crumbling order that must be replaced by something fresh and new. But on the other hand neolib-eralism has distorted and corrupted the political system and political institutions over the last four decades, so that what people are thirsting for is actually a return to an older model of doing politics when parties were divided along clear ideological lines, setting out a clear platform of explicit principles for voters to choose between. And this means that the left needs to ask what elements of the political system need simply rescuing from the grip of financial and corporate dominance, and what elements need reinventing from scratch.

Decades of disaffection, detachment, ossification and neoliberal domination have caused the left to disparage representative democracy in favour of social movements, typified by Occupy, and dominated by what Nick Srnicek and Alex Williams have dubbed 'folk-political thinking': 'the festishisation of local spaces, immediate actions, transient gestures, and particularisms of all kinds'.[12] The problem with this version of left populism – as with all versions of populism – is that it prevents political actors from advocating for mainstream politics as a transformative force. Corbyn's electoral success forces a rethink. It means not writing off the state as a post-war relic, and instead regarding it as both a protective structure and a vehicle of radical change. It requires us to recognise that while the Labour Party needs to connect with grassroots social movements and the 'left behind', it also needs clear ideological leadership. Above all, it asserts the primacy of politics over anti-politics, prompting an unfashionable question for those on the social movementist left who had more or less given up on party and state, as symbolic of an old and decrepit Labourism: if Corbyn became prime minister, would we need to junk the old system after all?

NOTES

1. Ernesto Laclau, 'Why constructing the people is the main task of Radical Politics', *Critical Inquiry*, Vol. 32 No. 4, 2006, pp654-655. See also Ernesto Laclau, *On Populist Reason*, Verso: London, 2007; Íñigo Errejón and Chantal Mouffe, *Podemos: In The Name of the People*, Lawrence & Wishart: London, 2016.
2. See Becky Bond and Zack Exley, *Rules for Revolutionaries : How Big Organizing Can Change Everything*, Chelsea Green Publishing: Chelsea, VT, 2016.
3. Jeremy Corbyn, 'New Year Message', www.labour.org.uk/, 30 December 2016.
4. Jeremy Corbyn, *ibid*.
5. Jeremy Corbyn, 'Speech to the Fabian New Year Conference', www.labourlist.org, 13 January 2017.
6. Tom Harris 'Labour is just too out of touch with its roots', *Evening Standard*, 14 February 2017.
7. Rachel Sylvester, 'Labour Arrogance is Destroying the Party', *The Times*, 14 June 2016.

8. See Rajeev Syal, 'Disproportionate number of Labour's new members are wealthy city dwellers', *The Guardian*, 21 January 2016.

9. Phil Wilson, 'Labour's purpose', www.fabians.org.uk, 4th July 2017. See also John Gray, 'Labour's populism for the middle classes', *New Statesman*, 18 June 2017, and Peter Wilby, 'Corbyn's bung to the middle class', *New Statesman*, 2 June 2017.

10. See Owen Jones, 'Armageddon hasn't happened – so the Labour right needs a rethink', *The Guardian*, 6 July 2017.

11. See Dan Roberts, 'Ridiculed, reviled, resurgent … Is Corbyn's campaign beginning to #feeltheBern?' *The Guardian*, 30 May 2017.

12. Nick Srnicek and Alex Williams, *Inventing the Future: Postcapitalism and a World Without Work,* Verso: London, 2016, p.3.

Generation Grime

Monique Charles

Generation Grime came out in full support of Labour in the June 2017 general election. YouGov described the impact of age in their authoritative post-election survey as 'the new dividing line in British politics. The starkest way to show this is to note that, amongst first time voters (those aged eighteen and nineteen), Labour was forty-seven percentage points ahead (of the Tories)'.[1] And this lead wasn't much reduced amongst twenty to twenty-four year-olds either: 40 per cent.

These younger voters had a significant impact on the outcome of the election. This is impossible to account for without tracing the interesting and evolving relationship between grime and politics in the overall context of the changing interaction between British music and politics over the past forty years. This has been characterised primarily by race and class via music and politics, and today, more than any other political leader most of us can remember, Jeremy Corbyn has come to both represent and articulate it.

Grime is a genre of music that emerged at the turn of the twenty-first century in inner-city London neighbourhoods.[2] At its early stages, the sound was most often likened to US hip-hop and rap owing to MCs spitting (rapping) with British accents over instrumental beats. Its sound includes the juxtapositions of intensely heavy baselines,[3] and a vastness of space which is both futuristic and 'non-musical'. Grime has a lo-fi sound quality which David Machin describes as a merging of sounds within a song where sounds are absorbed by other sounds.[4] To paraphrase, lo-fi sounds are not clear or distinctively heard (like hi-fi sounds). The sounds are not separate from one another, but form part of a multilayered cacophony of sounds that give a sense of depth, closeness, space and movement (e.g. panning sound) all at the same time. Grime also generally has a fast tempo with an average ranging between 136 and 140 beats per minute.[5] Early on, the use of the PlayStation in music-making contributed to grime's gritty sound.[6] Grime 'officially' became 'labelled' its own defined sound in 2002 with More Fire Crew's crossover British chart-topper 'Oi'.[7]

For those in the know, grime is connected, sonically and culturally, to its musical predecessors, which include music from the British underground scene such as garage and jungle, in addition to Jamaican dancehall, electronic/experimental music and punk rock. The grime 'sound' has developed as the genre grew into itself, eventually being acknowledged as its own genre of music by the MOBO (Music of Black Origin) Awards in 2015 and iTunes in 2016. However, grime has always been more than music. It is a culture, and its broader cultural significance, alongside its involvement in the 2017 election, helps to explain why young people voting Labour became so significant.

Grime, originating as a predominantly black British musical form, appealed to young people irrespective of race or ethnicity. The common ground in its appeal was the connection to their collective class-based oppression and British cultural references.[8] Richard Bramwell describes this process: 'There was a moment in which the grime aesthetic socialised the subjective feelings of a generation of working-class youth in London'.[9] Bramwell found engaging in grime in live performance settings to be cathartic, and that grime enabled 'a collective resistance to the stigmatisation of the working class' and the 'construct[ion of] oppositional identities'.[10] It assisted those taking part to make sense of their lives in a wider social context.

Whilst racism remains pervasive, it impacts Generation Grime in different ways. We now live in a time of diverse multicultures, particularly in the inner cities, which over a period of time have developed into what have been called 'new urban ethnicities'.[11]

Sociologist Les Back uses this term to propose that such areas are 'not mixing heritages; but making a new heritage',[12] which he describes as 'neighbourhood nationalism', whereby location is not strictly tied to race per se, but to a commitment to an area and length of time lived in the area.

> … new ethnicities are produced in part through a productive tension between global and local influences. This way of framing ethnicity

can be seen as radically different from the situational model prevalent within anthropology and the sociology of race relations, for it avoids the tendency to define ethnicity in primordial ways and acknowledges the simultaneously local and trans-local nature of identity formation.[13]

Simon Jones dates the beginnings of this back to the 1960s. Living in such multicultural locations has had what he calls a communalising effect, which has strengthened over time.[14] Contemporarily, location, particularly postcode, identifies who belongs: insiders and outsiders.[15]

ROCKING AGAINST RACISM

The idea of interracial unity promoted through music started forty years ago, with the musical-political organisation Rock Against Racism (RAR) in response to Eric Clapton's endorsement of Enoch Powell's racist outburst at his Birmingham Odeon concert in August 1976:

> Stop Britain from becoming a black colony. Get the foreigners out. Get the wogs out. Get the coons out. Keep Britain white. I used to be into dope, now I'm into racism. It's much heavier, man. Fucking wogs, man. Fucking Saudis taking over London. Bastard wogs. Britain is becoming overcrowded and Enoch will stop it and send them all back.

It was Clapton's tirade which prompted Red Saunders and friends to write an open letter to the *New Musical Express* which, in effect, founded RAR:

> When we read about Eric Clapton's Birmingham concert when he urged support for Enoch Powell, we nearly puked. Come on Eric ... you've been taking too much of the *Daily Express* stuff and you know you can't handle it. Own up. Half your music is black. You're rock music's biggest colonist. You're a good musician but where would you be without blues and R&B?
>   You've got to fight the racist poison otherwise you degenerate into the sewer with the rats and the money men who ripped off rock culture with their cheque books ... We want to organise a rank and

file movement against the racist poison music. We urge support for Rock Against Racism.

P.S. Who shot the Sheriff, Eric? It sure as hell wasn't you![16]

Unlike the working-class National Front sympathisers of the 1970s that RAR was up against, the white working class who experience hardship in contemporary multicultural settings are less likely to blame their non-white neighbours. This kind of class unity is a relatively recent, to some extent generational, turn away from the previous popularity of the British National Party and Ukip in the 2010 and 2015 general elections. On both, these parties' votes were accompanied by a more generalised rise in popular versions of xenophobic and anti-immigration attitudes.

Grime is a working-class scene. It originates amongst the very people and places government legislation has hit the hardest with its austerity measures over the last fifteen years. The bedroom tax, special measures and underfunded schools, the abolition of the Education Maintenance Allowance, tuition fee rises, zero-hours contracts, dwindling prospects of becoming a homeowner, increased job insecurity. Those young people able to vote in 2017 voted in response to their lived experience, the government's disregard of their future, and the disconnection they felt from a Conservative Party that hardly recognised them, couldn't relate to their lives and knew little about the localities they called home.

In these ways, nothing very much has changed since the Thatcher governments of 1979-90. Under Thatcher, the political climate lead to increased racial attacks, frozen wages, cuts to the public sector and soaring prices. In response, the short-lived 2-Tone musical and cultural era, 1979-81, worked to build on RAR's ideas of challenging racism and promoting racial unity. This was a musical movement that also faced down sexism and unemployment while favouring a generalised anti-Thatcher and pro-nuclear disarmament politics. This was followed in 1985 by a collective of politically-oriented musicians and creatives who, with the Labour Party, launched Red Wedge to increase youth engagement and encourage first-time voters. Anti-racism was the initial focus, but Red Wedge also adopted a class focus over time. The push was on for a fairer world. But it didn't last.[17]

In the intervening three decades, we haven't seen anything similar. During this period, the authorities problematised black and working-class youth under the NEET (Not in Education, Employment or Training) category,[18] through the implementation of ASBOs, dispersal orders and social exclusion initiatives.[19] Anyone falling into the NEET category was seen as a problem, including enterprising grime artists. From the political class to the mainstream media, there was little or no appreciation that via grime, young people affected by these issues were promoting their concerns via a collective response; issues that were of course intimately linked with government policy.

Finally, in 2017, Generation Grime were acknowledged in the political arena, when grime artists, such as AJ Tracey and Novelist, and rapper Akala, voiced public support for Jeremy Corbyn. AJ Tracey appeared in a Labour campaign video and singer Rag n Bone Man spoke to Channel 4 news about voting Corbyn. This was compounded by renewed interest in Stormzy's liking of Jeremy Corbyn's 'energy' in 2016 and JME's interview with Jeremy Corbyn. The latter had a significant impact on his social media supporters, despite him not personally endorsing Corbyn. This is when grime not only became understood as political, but also, consciously or not, when it connected with that earlier punk energy of RAR, the multicultural appeal of 2-Tone and the party politics of Red Wedge.

THE ORGANIC INTELLECTUALS OF GRIME

Artists in the grime scene are what the social theorist Antonio Gramsci once called organic intellectuals.[20] They are amongst those who have close ties with their communities and express class identities and aspirations. Writing of a similar musical-political movement, hip-hop, Nelson George describes the use of music as 'a way of announcing one's existence to the world'.[21] Organic intellectuals are the ones who expose private troubles. They are powerful because they connect individualised frustration to a collective experience. In the contemporary moment, organic intellectuals are often found at the margins of the music industry,[22] and this is where grime artists were primarily located until some learnt how to navigate the commercial/underground music industry barrier. In doing so, they managed to maintain their integrity in the scene while enjoying commercial success. That success however, gives artists an extra modicum of agency both inside the scene and the communities they are immediately connected to, but also outside of them. They are the voices of the communities they are a part of. Crucially, they are central to the scene not outsiders; instead they have come up through it with the respect of their peers. Of particular importance to the scene is the crew, 'the collective of friends'. This gathering together to share resources to make music, for camaraderie and in some cases for protection from outsiders, is a microcosm of the collectivity of those involved more widely in the scene. Whilst the lyrical content in much of grime may not be obviously political, the lived realities and hardships that are described certainly are. This time around, the artists who are leading a popular political movement are from working-class backgrounds. They exist at the intersections of race and class.

Jeremy Corbyn's understanding of racism, poverty and homelessness struck a chord with Generation Grime. This group has experienced policies that effectively quarantined their life chances. Corbyn returns politics to a representation of their collective experience via a narrative of fairness, social justice and the redistribution of wealth.

Stormzy has touched on the reasons for Corbyn's appeal: 'I saw some sick picture of him from back in the day when he was campaigning about anti-apartheid and I thought, "Yeah, I like your energy"'.[23] Grime artists' endorsement of Corbyn is from the bottom up, unlike the Blair/Britpop relationship. The grime endorsement is led by those who are themselves marginalised, not those who have had a degree of privilege now speaking out against injustice on others' behalf. As a result, those involved have a sense of political agency much greater than simply providing a musical backdrop to an election campaign.

PEOPLE POWERED

Grime artists are unsung heroes. They use their position as organic intellectuals to engage with formal politics and push for change *with* the collective, *for* the collective. Although Labour did not win the election, this was a moment in history that has injected new energy into politics and political engagement amongst young people.

The 2017 election gave Generation Grime the opportunity to realise their political power, and significantly gave opportunities to use it. Through social media particularly, grime artists made significant contributions toward galvanising Generation Grime into political action through the use of hashtags such as #Grime4Corbyn. This became a key moment where young people felt they could do something to influence both British society and their own futures. The innovative use of technology, new organising techniques and training programmes inspired by the Bernie Sanders campaign, the chant 'Oh, Jeremy Corbyn' and viral social media content enabled social media clicks and shares to be transformed into political action. These tactics were fluid enough to reach out to young people in ways no political party in this country had encountered before.

Corbyn has capitalised on this moment, making himself highly visible in the immediate aftermath of the vote. He spoke on Glastonbury Festival's Pyramid stage. Here he promoted the idea of unity, positioning multiracial unity in direct opposition to Trump's building walls to keep 'others', primarily Mexicans, out of the USA. He spoke about housing, the environment and racism. Corbyn's speech was both measured and charismatic – that's his style – showing a real connection to how his supporters were feeling in the current climate, making politics relevant and accessible.

GRENFELL

In response to the Grenfell fire disaster, Simon Cowell released a charity cover version of Simon and Garfunkel's classic 'Bridge over Troubled Water', led by a Stormzy intro. Stormzy's lyrics highlight the connectivity between communities that live in racialised and classed spaces – those new urban ethnicities. In his lyrics in the introductory portion of the song, he demonstrates a sense of connectedness to those who perished in the fire. He acknowledges that there is a real possibility that his own family members, or he himself could have been in that situation as a result of living in high rise tower blocks. This human connection to the tragedy is poignant. It speaks to those who live in these kinds of buildings, where such a tragedy could very much be a reality, especially since testing on other blocks across the country since Grenfell found that many were fitted with flammable cladding attached to the exterior of their buildings. Stormzy empathises with the realities and felt moved to do something, to be part of the solution. The Grenfell Tower fire is the new political catalyst for those people marginalised and horrified by neoliberalism, a tragedy that encourages them to continue pushing for social change.

Stormzy also used his own Glastonbury performance to pay tribute to the Grenfell victims and to demand answers from the government. A collective of grime artists organised a fundraising event for the survivors of the fire using the hashtag #Grime4Grenfell. Local grime artist Piki Saku and rap artist Akala used live broadcasting opportunities to challenge the government. They provided social analysis on why the fire took place and questioned how it was handled by the authorities while highlighting the community spirit of the area.

Hip-hop and grime artist Lowkey, another local, filmed an interview with a friend who was a survivor of the fire. This gave his friend a voice, but also gave viewers a first-hand account of what happened. Lowkey emphasised that neoliberalism cost the lives of the poor and racialised; he questioned who should be held accountable, and drew attention to government malpractice in the treatment of survivors, particularly regarding rehousing. He called for justice, and significantly, political mobilisation. Another local grime MC, AJ Tracey, highlighted the lack of response from both local and central government, the area's gentrification and the racism that underlies this. He specifically mentioned Corbyn's proactive response to Grenfell and declared that this kind of open engagement with community in the wake of the tragedy was why people voted for him on 8 June 2017, and argued that this is why people continue to have faith in him to become the next prime minister.

Significantly, and unlike previous pop and politics collaborations for social change, Corbyn engages directly with both musicians and the communities they come from. Red Wedge sought to be the go-between for the youth and politicians and thus to generate youth interest in politics. Blair instead sought an aesthetic: 'Cool Britannia'. Corbyn rejects both approaches; rather, he works directly with and for communities himself. He has been doing this for decades as a dedicated campaigner and it is this authenticity which appeals to the youth, to marginalised communities and to others who have concerns about our current government. He fights for fairness. His use of social media ensures he has direct access to the public and makes himself accountable. He attempts to engage with people in the 'everyday', to be relevant.

Corbyn's sentiments regarding the Grenfell tragedy stood in stark contrast to those of the Conservative government and demonstrated that his politics resonated with those affected. He visited the victims and the area. He used social media to speak out against the tragedy in the context of social stratification, and against the lack of support for Grenfell survivors from the authorities. He made the public aware that he was contacting the government to push for survivors to be included in the public inquiry. People who had felt ignored for too long now feel listened to.

OOOHHHH JEH-REH-MI CORBYN

Corbyn is actively engaging with young people and popular culture. This strategy, however, is Blairesque. Tony Blair was very active with pop culture and popstars in the lead-up to the general election in 1997, when he attended the Q Awards and the music industry BPI annual meeting. Britpop was seen as a reconnection with British rock and roll of the 1960s, and was accepted into the mainstream rather than being treated as an alternative to it, a counter culture. Many Britpop musicians enjoyed and made full use of the money, culture, fashion and media opportunities their mainstream income afforded them. This union of pop and politics was strategic on the part of Blair's campaign.[24] While the Labour Party sought to control the dynamic, they did not want the political organising that Red Wedge was allowed to pursue in the early years of Neil Kinnock's Labour leadership, and there are plenty in the party who remain suspicious of an autonomous socio-cultural movement, such as that which #Grime4Corbyn could yet become for, but not of, Labour.

In his book *Walls Come Tumbling Down*, author Daniel Rachel makes this key point: 'Red Wedge was teaching the Labour party how to listen'.[25] Corbyn has adopted this tradition by engaging with Generation Grime on its own terms. Grime, now attractive to the middle classes, straddles the mainstream versus counterculture divide. However, grime artists also remain connected to real community issues. Grime does not get particularly caught up in celebrity for the purposes of marketing or conspicuous consumption.[26] This is another feature of grime and its origins. It is, and remains, contrary to the upwardly mobile, aspirational lifestyle of its immediate predecessor, UK garage. Grime is primarily an underground genre, much 'harsher, grittier, [it reflects] the world as it [is] rather than a varnished, romanticised version of the truth'.[27] It is the voice of those 'left behind'. It reflects the economic hardships of the areas it came from and emerging artists openly declare in lyrical content an oppositional worldview as its ethos.

To paraphrase the founder of modern sociology, C. Wright Mills, grime has become the public issue of collective private troubles. This is the voice of those hardest hit in response to political decisions made by government. Although there remains a desire for economic success and security, this is not a culture founded on hyper-individualism. The success achieved by those in the scene, for one, is viewed as a success for all, for the 'endz'. Individual achievement produces collective pride. Grime's success is collective. This collectivism contributes to one's sense of identity and culture. It also congeals the successful individual with the collective, the 'endz'. The collective experience of hardship, and navigating it, fosters community. It was an enterprising ingenuity that created and expanded the scene to begin with. Grime has gone it alone, but as they see someone, Jeremy Corbyn, who appears to recognise their realities, artists are encouraging people to use proper channels to express their political concerns, alongside the agency they have had to develop as a result of previous governments' marginalising policies, an agency to self-organise.

Thus, grime's potential is somewhere between the aesthetic of Blair's incorporation of Britpop and the day-to-day grassroots political organising of the Red Wedge tours. This is neither an attempt to make Corbyn cool nor to 'sex up' the party with a decent soundtrack. It's something different; we're just not quite sure what, yet.

Both the general election and Labour's response to the Grenfell tragedy could be the start of an ongoing dialogue and sustained political engagement amongst not just young people but older, equally disillusioned, voters too. In this process, grime artists remain very much connected to their communities; they are organising, albeit in sporadic, informal, even anarchic ways, that sit uneasily with the traditional Labour Party methods. The shift grime is making may be the space for more overtly political lyrical content and imagery in artistic expression, for both established and emerging artists. Labour will need to listen if it is to remain tuned into the obvious potential. Listen, but not seek to take over.

Generation Grime's actions in 2017 made everyone sit up and take notice. But can Labour learn lessons from it? Grenfell made public the devastating impact of neoliberal agendas. Now there is the possibility of a government that will govern #forthemanynotthefew. To achieve this, Generation Grime wants a *relatable* leader. Labour's 2017 manifesto suggests it is beginning to understand the pressures of existing policy on the working classes. They share concerns about homelessness, education and the National Health Service. Jeremy Corbyn is viewed as someone who promotes the issues that young people see as improving their life chances: the abolition of tuition fees, extra funding for the NHS, increasing the number of new homes, scrapping the bedroom tax and income thresholds for spouses of migrants, whilst asking the more wealthy to pay more tax, for a fairer more inclusive country. Seeing the outcome of this general election, Generation Grime has begun to realise its political power. We want to push forward, led by Corbyn, but shoulder to shoulder with him as an equal, for a fairer Britain, built by effective local organising and sustained community engagement.

NOTES

1. YouGov, 'How Britain voted at the 2017 General Election', www.yougov. uk, 13 June 2017.
2. See Monique Charles, 'Grime Central! Subterranean Ground-In Grit Engulfing Manicured Mainstream Spaces' in Kehinde Andrews and Lisa Palmer (eds), *Blackness in Britain*, Routledge: London, 2016, pp89-101.
3. See Paul Sullivan, *Remixology: Tracing the Dub Diaspora*, Reaktion Books: London, 2013; Julian Henriques, *Sonic Bodies: Reggae Sound Systems, Performance Techniques and Ways of Knowing*, Continuum: New York, 2011; Lloyd Bradley, *Sounds like London: 100 Years of Black Music in the Capital*. Serpent's Tail: London, 2012.
4. David Machin, *Analysing Popular Music: Image, Sound, Text*, Sage: Newcastle, 2010.
5. *The South Bank Show*, 'Grime, Bow and How UK Hip-hop Found its Voice', Sky Arts. 18 May 2012.
6. See, for example, Andrew Missingham, *Why console-games are bigger than rock 'n' roll: What the music sector needs to know and how it can get a piece of the action*, Youth Music Organisation: London, 2007. Paul Lester, *Bonkers: The Story of Dizzee Rascal*, Omnibus Press: London, 2010.
7. Simon Reynolds, *Bring the Noise*, Faber and Faber: London, 2007.
8. See Richard Bramwell, *UK Hip-Hop Grime and the City: The Aesthetics and Ethics of London's Rap Scenes*, Routledge: London, 2015.
9. Bramwell, *ibid.*, p33.
10. Bramwell, *ibid.*, p75.
11. See Les Back, *New Ethnicities and Urban Culture*, UCL Press: London, 1996.

12. Back, *ibid.,* p52.
13. Back, *ibid.,* p4.
14. Simon Jones, *Black Culture White Youth,* Palgrave MacMillan: Basingstoke, 1988, pp127-128.
15. Ben Gidley, 'Youth Culture and Ethnicity: Emerging Youth Interculture in South London', in Paul Hodkinson and Wolfgang Deicke (eds), *Youth Cultures: Scenes, Subcultures and Tribes,* Routledge: London, 2009, pp145-160.
16. See Roger Huddle and Red Saunders, *Reminiscences of RAR: Rocking against Racism 1976-82,* Redwords, 2016.
17. See Daniel Rachel, *Walls Come Tumbling Down: The Music and Politics of Rock against Racism, 2-Tone and Red Wedge,* Picador: London, 2016.
18. Joy White, *Urban Music and Entrepreneurship: Beats, Rhymes and Young People's Enterprise (Routledge Advances in Sociology),* Routledge: London, 2016.
19. Chris Shannahan, 'Excluded Urban Youth and Religious Discourse in the Trans-local City Theoretical Framework', Dept. of Theology and Religion, University of Birmingham, 2009.
20. Katina Stapleton, 'From the Margins to Mainstream: the Political Power of Hip-Hop', *Media, Culture and Society,* Vol. 20 No. 2, April 1998, pp219-234.
21. Nelson George, *Hip Hop America*, Penguin: London, 1999, pp14.
22. See Barry Stoller, 'Music, Marxism, and the hype about D.I.Y. ("Do-It-Yourself")', *Monthly Review,* Vol. 49 No. 7, 1998, pp34-43; George Maher, 'Brechtian Hip Hop: Didactics and Self production in Post-Gangsta Political Mixtapes', *Journal of Black Studies,* Vol. 36, 2005, pp129-160.
23. Quoted in Sam Wolfson, 'Stormzy: "My man Corbyn! I dig what he says"', *The Guardian,* 21 May 2016.
24. See John Harris, *The Last Party: Britpop, Blair and the Demise of English Rock,* Fourth Estate: London, 2003.
25. Rachel, *ibid.,* pxxiv.
26. See Thorstein Veblen, *Conspicuous Consumption: Unproduction Consumption of Goods Is Honourable,* Penguin: London, 2006.
27. Lester, *ibid.,* p26.

A Progressive Majority

Sue Goss

During the 2017 general election campaign, Jeremy Corbyn managed to achieve three very important things: he mobilised young people to vote, brought sensible social democratic policies back onto the agenda and he shook off his public image of incompetence. Indeed, by facing down the accusations of a hysterical right-wing press, he has managed to look authentic and honourable when before he seemed to many in the Labour Party, and beyond, to be culpably naïve. Corbyn seems to have found his political feet. The campaign played to his strengths. Because of the extended television and radio coverage, the electorate got to see more of him and liked what they saw. There seems to be much to admire. He appears to have integrity, authenticity and commitment and lives an austere lifestyle. He has tirelessly campaigned against injustice and inequality, upholding many unpopular causes. He has stamina and he has courage. Even his initial reticence when persuaded to enter the leadership campaign was disarming:

> If I can promote some causes and debate by doing this, then good. That's why I'm doing it.[1]

He has many years of political experience and campaigning from which to draw reflection and analysis – not simply as an MP, but as a trade union official, a district health authority member, a local councillor, a party agent and organiser. He has a hinterland: he is a keen gardener and cook, he reads Shelley and Okri. His strong values help him to survive the onslaught of the media. He is not vain or selfish, in a political world consumed by vanity and a monstrous collective self-importance.

These things matter, because politics is emotional as much as it is rational, and Corbyn's matter-of-fact ordinariness amongst the spin drew many people new to politics to support him. And campaigning suits him too – the rallies and the walkabouts – he doesn't need to be choreographed. He is interested in people. No one doubts the genuineness with which he immediately went to meet community groups and victims of the Grenville Tower fire and the same again after the murderous assault on the Finsbury Park Mosque in his own constituency.

For many of us who have been active on the left of politics for the past thirty years, Corbyn has been a fixture, part of a small group of MPs from the fringes of Labour, clinging on through the Blair years without compromising their principles. His struggles have been against war; against nuclear power, miscarriages of justice such as the Guildford Four and Birmingham Six, and the misuse of international power. Throughout, he has kept faith with an internationalist socialism, a quasi-marxist economic analysis and a campaigning politics that seemed out-of-date in the world of global social media – reminiscent of the romance of the cyclostyled leaflet, the hand-written poster and the embroidered trades union banner.

In his first year as leader, Corbyn looked as if he would be destroyed by a Labour machine built for a very different sort of leader – for the brash energetic self-confidence of Blair – an aggressive 'telling' machine that centralised power in the leader's office and spent every waking hour trying to control and direct a new 24-hour media. It brought out the worst of Corbyn's leadership; with inexperienced speech writers parcelling up complex ideas into soundbites and slogans, trying to 'fix the news story', launching half-baked policies like products, struggling to mask the reality of confusion with a 'strong narrative'.

And now? The opportunity for oppositional MPs and their backers to organise against him has fallen away, for the moment at any rate, while MPs from the centre left who were previously critical have come forward to say they were wrong. The Labour Party is attempting to reunite yet it remains unclear just how much has really changed.

AN ALTERNATIVE ELECTORAL STRATEGY?

The nineteenth and twentieth century thesis that voting was an expression of class interest was tested to destruction by Thatcher in the 1970s, when working class voters deserted the Labour Party of poor and badly managed public services for her aggressive, chauvinistic social conservatism. After three successive defeats, Labour recognised the need to create a competent, efficient state, and Tony Blair's 1997 landslide was won through an authoritarian appeal to social conservatives – 'tough on crime, tough on the causes of crime' – combined with renewed funding for more efficient public services, and a relaxed, deregulatory approach to business. Since then, the orthodoxy has been that a winning left-of-centre strategy needs to connect an economically radical and socially conservative working class, with an economically conservative but socially radical middle class. For Blairites with long memories, therefore, any shift of Labour to the left risks this fragile coalition, and a return to the fringes of political life.

But a lot has changed. The crash and resulting austerity seemed, at first, not to influence voting patterns, but now everything has become uncertain. Populist parties from left and right are emerging in Europe and overturning established parties. Unpredictable results are becoming so commonplace they're almost predictable. The Brexit vote woke young people up to the cost of leaving politics to the older generation. The Westminster establishment, like many other establishments across Europe, has been shown to be out-of-date and out-of-touch.

In these circumstances, Jeremy Corbyn and John McDonnell hypothesised an alternative electoral strategy, whereby Labour could attract support to radical economic policies if they could be heard by the electorate. They need not pander to the right-wing press if instead they attracted the left-of-centre voters who had abandoned Labour. Central to this was activating the vast swathes of young people who traditionally don't vote.

It's easy to forget that Labour lost the 2017 election. And it's important to notice what else happened. Jeremy Corbyn wasn't an electoral asset everywhere. For all the people for whom he has been an inspiration, there are many others who are sceptical, or downright hostile. Where Labour won in 2017, it was often due to the effectiveness of a local campaign on the ground, adapted to the particularities of their circumstances, rather than due to a national message.

THE LABOUR OF MANY DIFFERENT TRIBES

John Harris has pointed out that what we are seeing is the emergence not of a single 'Corbynist' Labour but different versions of Labour in different parts of the country.[2] So we can see, alongside Corbyn supporters, a northern, pragmatic, more authoritarian urban Labour articulated by Andy Burnham; a more intimate, community-led version characterised by Lisa Nandy in Wigan; the maverick, disquieting moral challenge from Jon Cruddas in East London; a cool, modern, tolerant, diverse and business friendly Labour led by Sadiq Khan; and a collaborative, tactically minded and plural Labour in parts of the home counties. These different 'Labours' can be seen as competing and colliding or they can be seen as adaptive responses to different local circumstances and different electorates, capable of building a wider and broader alliance than any single, centralised 'version'.

The truth is that Labour has always been an alliance. From its beginnings as the Labour Representation Committee in 1906, Labour was a federation of many organisations attempting social change – the trade unions, local movements and left of centre parties – with the narrow aim of building an electoral alliance. The early Labour Party in the 1920s was a place where the idea of an 'alliance' was a live part of local meetings, with delegates from unions, from the Co-operative Society, Women's Co-operative Guild, the Independent Labour Party and from time to time the Communist Party.[3] Labour has always represented a wide spectrum of political and social views – and has always existed in conversation with Liberalism, and with activists to its left. Labour wins elections when it emerges with a compelling narrative that is drawn from a deeper and wider engagement with the rest of society and with tacit or active liberal support.

'BORROWED' VOTES

Labour tribalists, celebrating a return to two party politics, fail to appreciate that in the 2017 election, supporters of other parties 'lent' their votes to Labour, either to express opposition to Brexit, or to stop the Tories gaining a majority. These votes can't be taken for granted, and may move away as fast as they came.

The election was characterised by a huge effort to create tactical voting, campaigns and websites such as More United and Best 4 Britain – tactical vote and vote swap sites – all had an impact. The Progressive Alliance went beyond simply encouraging tactical voting, with parties at grassroots level beginning to work together. Groups such as Sussex Progressives had been working across parties for a long time, and building up strong relationships and mutual trust. The generous and far-sighted decision of the Green Party to stand down candidates with little chance of winning in some key marginal seats was an act of real political leadership – and not without cost. Greens made an important collaborative gesture and got little or no thanks, and the scope for long-term relationships has been damaged by the short-sightedness of Labour nationally on the issue. The Progressive Alliance can claim victories for progressive candidates in a number of important seats, but a progressive majority could have been in sight if cooperation had succeeded elsewhere. Worse, the Labour machine has reacted with vicious speed to punish those who participated in local alliances. Three members of the Labour Party who developed a powerful cross-party alliance in South-West Surrey have been expelled from the party. Such a closed and ungracious mindset must change if anything resembling a different kind of politics is to be achieved.

We have an archaic electoral system unfit for the twenty-first century; it creates extraordinary unfairness in party representation. Despite the existence of six major parties on the British mainland and six more in Northern Ireland, the system unjustly allows the electoral dominance of two main parties. And while the two major parties believe that it is in their interests to maintain a system biased towards them, the reality is that majority governments are becoming rarer. The Greens and the Liberal Democrats are denied parliamentary representation that would match their share of the vote so Labour and Conservatives can pile up majorities of tens of thousands. In safe constituencies too many votes are wasted, and we are then left with the prospect of a hung parliament minus the mindset of long-term thinking that could turn these into genuine coalition governments.

Over the past thirty years the differences to be reconciled have been widening – between an affluent and conservative older population, a poor but adventurous younger population, between settled immigrants and new arrivals, between those in the high skill high wage economy and those trapped on benefits or in the gig economy. The *New Statesman* has characterised this as the growth of a 'Divided Britain' cataloguing new electoral divisions based on age, education, ethnicity, home-ownership, city versus country, and open versus closed cultures.[4]

Labour has traditionally won more support from the BAME population, from public sector workers and from women. But in June 2017, the biggest split in voting was based not on class but on age. According to *The Sunday Times*, 67 per cent of 18-24-year-olds voted Labour while 60 per cent of over 65-year-olds voted Conservative. Besides these differences in UK voting patterns there are national differences; Welsh Labour is a very different creature to Corbyn's Labour, and Scottish Labour made little headway against the SNP, picking up seats mainly because the Conservative vote increased.

Voters no longer see an automatic alignment between their own interests and any particular party – they begin to look for a story that includes them, and move tactically between parties in response to different and sometimes conflicting messages.

While Labour spoke, for the first time, to young people and seemed to be championing their cause, there is no reason to believe that their votes will necessarily stick. The year before the 2017 general election research for the Fabian Society suggested that only 5 million voters now consider themselves as 'loyal Labour voters'.[5] Despite the increased Labour vote there is no way of judging the longevity of any such new Labour loyalty. In these circumstances Labour would do well to remember that switch voters can switch again.

HOW TO LOSE MEMBERS AND NOT INFLUENCE PEOPLE

Labour currently has the highest membership of any left of centre European party at around 500,000. But at the same time this still represents only about 1 per cent of the UK electorate. And many of these new members have already found the traditional Labour Party organisation a boring and excluding place. It is the very dullness of the mechanisms of Labour politics that entrenches the most tribal of activists at the heart of the machine.

And even within the new arrivals, the differences are as great as the similarities. Alongside those who have joined to take part in politics for the first time, there are returnees from the different tribes of the left, which have to rub along, sometimes uncomfortably, with the more creative, energetic and demanding arrivals. This is even more a problem in Momentum, a movement supportive of Corbynism within the party. Lewis Basset from Lambeth Momentum describes two strands: Labourism, steeped in the traditions and ideology of the British labour movement (many of whom left the party and have returned); and Movementism, activists who had previously spurned party politics in favour of the innovative and exciting campaigns like Occupy, UK Uncut and Climate Camp.[6] Laura Catriona Murray describes a third stand too, the remnants of a Leninist left:

> While dyed in the wool Trotskyists are not the majority in Momentum, they are a vocal, disruptive and over-bearing minority who have won themselves key positions in the regional committees, national committees and even the steering committee.[7]

Murray goes on to give what must be one of the most vivid descriptions of the impact such groups have on meetings:

> Unrepresentative local groups elect delegates – usually either the loudest and bolshiest person in the room or the person with the most free time to dedicate to activism – and propose pointless motions on policies which Momentum can't implement, by way of it not being a political party, which are then thrashed out between people who have significant experience in long, boring meetings and take pleasure in angrily arguing for their own narrow and exclusionary political ideology.[8]

It is this ungracious, tin-eared dimension of left politics, by no means restricted to Trotskyists, that most threatens the possibility of a successful democratic socialist movement.

A RETURN TO VALUES?

A return to values is essential if we are to challenge a free market 'common sense' which argues that there are no alternatives to the widening inequalities of modern capitalism. Values help us define the sort of society we want to live in, and enable us to describe the changes we want to see.

But while there are important values that most Labour Party members agree on, this agreement could also be extended to many people from other parties. Labour and the Liberal Democrats share a commitment to human rights and civil liberties; Labour and the Greens share a commitment to helping the vulnerable, and to protecting the environment, Labour and the SNP and Plaid Cymru share beliefs about protecting social provision from the market and redistributing wealth. The differences come when different parties make judgements about how to trade off these values, not from the values themselves.

Collaborative movements make this explicit, setting out values under which activists from all left of centre parties and those from no party can work together. Local progressive alliances are creating a cross-party conversation around values such as equality, economic justice, democracy, environmentalism and internationalism.[9]

All of these could also be described as the sort of values that lie at the heart of Corbynism; but neither he nor Labour has a monopoly on them. The new young activists are attracted not so much to a party but to ideas, and, for the moment, to the party leader who best represents those ideas. Rather than narrowing the scope for any alliance, we need to widen it.

There are too few voices on the left, not too many. We need many more interpretations, ways of framing and reframing the problems we face, mapping out possible solutions. The goal must be to recreate a common sense of the left that can explain society first to itself and then, crucially, in conversation with others. This is a mode of organisation that is as much about listening as talking.

We need access to outsider voices, critical thinking, challenge and open dialogue. We need to share information widely and remove any hierarchy of information – so that we all know what there is to be known and can help to build solutions. We need to 'track weak signals' while listening to the lone voices telling us things we don't enjoy hearing.[10]

For Labour that means not looking just at policies (that's the easy bit), but examining the way we organise, the way we treat each other, the way we think and the assumptions we make. Crucially, this means changing how we behave. It means treating people with different views from our own with respect and generosity, and being actively curious about the reasons for their support for Ukip, the Conservatives, SNP, Plaid Cymru, Greens and other parties. The 'kinder politics' that Corbyn promised on his election as leader never quite arrived, but it is needed more urgently than ever. This isn't an optional extra, but rather an essential prerequisite for a learning party. Without humility, generosity and open minds, change is impossible. It means that the shouty, finger-pointing politics of some on the Labour left, and the vicious manoeuvring from some on the Labour right, both spell disaster for the party's aspirations after the election of 2017.

THE PROGRESSIVE ALLIANCE IS IN IT FOR THE LONG HAUL

The Progressive Alliance initiative purposefully shared this perspective rather than simply stitching up deals between opposition parties to put forward a single challenger to Tory incumbent MPs. The aim was to create a shared political space in which to learn as well as co-operate in elections. If left of centre politics is to win support from the majority of people in the UK (which must be surely what our politics aims to do) then we need to show how across all aspects of our lives a collaborative, redistributive, moderate, less selfish, less exploitative way of life could offer the safety, nurture and opportunity that most of us crave.

We need to model a practical future society, in which many millions of people, all with very different lives, can see a place for themselves and a way to thrive. What is the UK's place in the world, post-Brexit, and how do we balance the needs of communities for stability and belonging with the need to attract energetic workers from across the globe? What should affordable health and social care look like in the twenty-first century? What is the economic strategy for the future? Political parties need to work together not just to swap votes, but more importantly to exchange ideas. That means working across the spectrum of parties in the UK, but also looking to parties, movements, institutions and thinkers across Europe and beyond.

What is needed now is not soundbites and crass policy initiatives, but a serious dialogue involving all the institutions that stand outside the pure market – the universities, the trades unions, schools, the NHS, the BBC, the voluntary and community sector, local government, residents groups, youth and student organisations. It needs to engage the energy of local communities, and local government, to find solutions that work at local level. We need blogs and podcasts and TED-type-talks, videos to share thinking and ideas – engaging broadcasters and serious journalists across the spectrum. Think-tanks, academic foundations and charitable organisations have a crucial role, as do the third sector and the socially-focussed parts of the private sector. As the numbers of employee-owned and community businesses grow, there is scope for public and social entrepreneurs to work together to find different solutions.

As in previous successful social movements, the arts will be vital – through comedy, drama and music – projecting possibilities to a far wider audience than politics on its own can reach. An open, generous, curious and creative left working across party boundaries would create a sparky, imaginative exchange of ideas.

There will be disagreements and they should be welcomed, encouraging exploration with a willingness to pursue the 'weak trails' that might lead to something. Conversation needs to be respectful, welcoming dissent – living with the discomfort of the tensions and conflicts between parties – not trying to bully each other into accepting our point of view. This openness is already starting to happen at a civil society level. Sadly, it is the political parties and their leaders that are lagging behind.

IS THERE A SOCIAL DEMOCRATIC FUTURE?

The demands on Jeremy Corbyn's leadership have only just begun. Far harder than leading a campaign, is leading a party, a movement, and possibly, a government. There are some steps that he could take that would make a social democratic future for the UK more likely.

Jeremy Corbyn should encourage the party to draw on the skills of those practiced in alliance building and facilitation – to turn Labour outwards, engaging local parties in a process of change – helping them to use the resources of the new members to transform the way they work and think; using meeting designs such as open space and world café to create an environment where a narrow group of aggressive ideologues cannot dominate; modelling and supporting openness and curiosity – and rethinking the way the party works at all levels.

He could commit the party to the introduction of proportional representation in the next Labour manifesto. This would allow for the emergence of different party-political, and other voices while reflecting the reality of electoral choices that remain more than the sum of two parties.

He could signal a serious engagement with academics and experts, city leaders and community entrepreneurs, across the whole spectrum of the centre left to plan and deliver an ambitious process of political debate and discussion – working both across parties and beyond the boundaries of these parties to generate evidence and ideas. A new political project has to face the disparate experiences, the different identities and the difficult lives of many ordinary people. What is needed is work on what the theorists Ernesto Laclau and Chantal

Mouffe once called a 'logic of equivalence', which translates those different experiences into a common search for a better life. [11]

Finally, and perhaps hardest of all, the alliance at the core of the Labour Party needs to be rebuilt. This means using difference as the starting point for enquiry rather than entrenching division, sparking a creative conversation that starts from somewhere else and forges new solutions, turning the current sterile inner-party warfare into an active learning process. After all, Corbyn spent his life building relationships with people from very different communities across the globe, and forging alliances even when his own party didn't support him. For him, a generosity towards divergent ideas should make sense. The use of party discipline, whipping votes, sacking ministers who won't toe a temporary and tactical party line, expelling members for working across party boundaries – these are all part of the obsolete machine politics.

Success will not be the triumph of one 'version' of Labour over the others, and the elimination of internal opposition and debate. Success will start with changing how politics works. The 'isms' we need will include humanism and socialism and pluralism rather than seeking to sum everything up by adding the latest 'ism' to the name of one man. Leaders require the courage to challenge the orthodoxies of their own supporters, and to reach out to those with the creative ideas for the future, even if they have been opponents. It is, as Corbyn himself acknowledged at Glastonbury in June 2017, about building bridges, not walls.

NOTES

1. Jeremy Corbyn interviewed by Simon Hattenstone, *The Guardian*, 17 June 2015.
2. John Harris 'A Labour Party of the future is beginning to emerge', *The Guardian*, 29 September 2016.
3. Sue Goss, *Local Labour and Local Government*, Edinburgh University Press: Edinburgh, 1988, p16.
4. *New Statesman*, 'Divided Britain', 6-12 January 2017. See articles by Stephen Bush, Helen Lewis, Jonn Elledge, Tristram Hunt, Rob Ford and George Eaton.
5. Andrew Harrop, *Stuck: How Labour Is Too Weak to Win and Too Strong to Die*, Fabian Society, 2017, p4.
6. Lewis Bassett, 'From Movementism to Labourism', www.opendemocracy.net, 28 November 2016.

7. Laura Catriona Murray, *Momentum v Inertia*, www.medium.com, 5 December 2016.
8. Laura Catriona Murray, *ibid*.
9. See www.sussexprogressives.com.
10. See Margaret Heffernan, *Wilful Blindness*, Simon and Schuster: London, 2012.
11. Ernesto Laclau and Chantal Mouffe, *Hegemony and Socialist Strategy*, Verso: London, 1985.

Class Politics and the Revenge
of the Future

Phil Burton-Cartledge

The reversal in Labour's polling prior to the 2017 general election was as steep and sudden as it was spectacular. More than a bland affair of Labour pursuing a better share of the votes and capturing more seats than were forecast, Jeremy Corbyn's electoral performance was an insurgency that not only shook a seemingly unassailable and complacent Conservative Party to its core, it represented a revolution against decades of received wisdom about electoral politics. The view that a left-wing programme is something to be hidden under a bushel while party elites triangulate a coalition via an anaemic programme of technocratic management has been thoroughly debunked. Against the dogmatic insistence that Labour's electoral success lies through the centre, the left's strategy proved that politics is malleable and can be redefined under certain circumstances by challenging the consensus.

Politicians, commentators, political scientists and sociologists were caught out by the result as much as anybody, especially as polling companies reported varying figures throughout the campaign. We need a hypothesis to explain what happened. It would be a mistake to put too much stress on the events that defined the campaign without an analysis of what was happening in the background.

This is not as straightforward as it seems; the election threw up some disarming results. If it was a matter of simply recreating a new 'old' Labour for the twenty-first century to appeal to working-class people, it is difficult to explain how constituencies like Kensington and Canterbury were taken and dozens of Conservative seats went from safe to marginal. Similarly, how does that explain the loss of a handful of working-class seats? In my native Stoke-on-Trent, Labour conceded one seat to the Tories and witnessed a decline in the majorities in the two it retained.[1] Yet the northern apocalypse forecast in Labour's non-metropolitan seats did not materialise either, despite the repeated arguments from pundits and academics, that Corbynism is a movement of the middle class.[2]

Corbynism needs to be understood as a haphazard upwelling, full of fits and starts, of underlying changes to class relationships and of the crisis of capitalism across North America and Western Europe. But it is not a mechanical expression. Corbynism comes stamped with the circumstances of Corbyn's long history on the left of the party. The horizons of the movement, as well as the party's future electoral prospects, are tied to Corbynism's ability to speak to, address, and articulate the new class politics. In effect, the movement has to understand itself and become conscious of its origins, position and the interests it is pulling together. This essential task of self-clarification assists with identifying its political limits, as well as the positioning of its opponents and enemies. In short, Corbynism expresses a Labour Party in the throes of political and social recomposition. Ultimately, how Corbynism pushes this process along will determine its success or failure, and therefore the fate of left-wing and socialist politics in Britain for the foreseeable future.

CRISIS CAPITALISM

David Cameron fought the 2010 and 2015 general elections by blaming the recession on Labour 'profligacy'. He argued that the cuts to the public sector he implemented were therefore justified, in terms of shrinking the deficit and striking a new balance between private and state-owned sectors, even though this favoured, of course, the private sector.

Despite this turn to deficit determinism, the promised economic uptick from cutting public sector jobs, winding up or privatising agencies and services, and taking money from the pockets of social security recipients did not materialise. Senior Conservatives repeatedly and disproportionately talked up a jobs miracle that actually saw relatively well-paid, secure jobs in the civil service and local authorities replaced by an explosion of low-paid, insecure, part-time and short-term work, and registered self-employment. The overall picture was of shallow shrinkage and modest growth, a performance short of Treasury projections. This has continued post-Cameron, despite Theresa May's retreat from this approach at the rhetorical level. Therefore, there is some debate over how much the shallow growth seen since the stock market crash is a resolution of long-term trends, as opposed to the consequence of the episodic policies adopted by the Conservatives. Some refer to the absence of a 'courageous' or an 'entrepreneurial' state as the root of stagnation.[3] Others suggest that mounting inequality is choking off social mobility and opportunities for many, hampering entrepreneurial talent, holding down wages and therefore depressing consumer markets.[4] And there is also the argument that capitalism is undergoing decomposition: the inflation crisis of the 1970s found its resolution in the credit bubbles of the following decades, which ultimately culminated in the crash. Yet capital's weak institutional base – after decades of defunding and privatisation – means policy makers are trapped within horizons bounded by the sorts of policies that strongly contributed to the crisis in the first place.[5]

Perhaps the most radical argument is the one that places the transformation of class struggle at its heart. In his book *Postcapitalism*, Paul Mason makes this case, via an interpretation of capitalism in terms of advancing and receding long cycles of capitalist development, or Kondratiev Waves. He notes:

> a long wave takes off because large amounts of cheap capital have been accumulated, centralised and mobilised in the financial system, usually accompanied by a rise in the supply of money, which is needed to fund the investment boom. Grandiose investments are begun – canals and factories in the late-eighteenth century, railways and urban infrastructures in the mid-nineteenth century. New technology is deployed and new business models created, leading to a struggle for new markets – which stimulates the intensification of wars, as rivalries over colonial settlements increase. New social groups associated with the rising industries and technologies clash with the old elites, producing social unrest.[6]

In the rising of the wave, economic downturns are brief as the most productive tend to operate in the most profitable sectors of the economy, and therefore suck in most capital. The wave crests when a market saturation point is reached, before a declinist tendency asserts itself. Markets are glutted and profitable opportunities are fewer.

Playing the stock market promises quick returns, which can touch off short-lived credit booms, and recessions grow in length and depth before whole sections of capital, physical and financial, crumple and liquidate in a depression.

Paul Mason believes there have been four such waves since the advent of industrial capitalism in the mid to late eighteenth century. These more or less correspond with: the initial wave of industrialisation; the application of steam and the advent of the railway; the emergence of heavy industry, steel, and the internal combustion engine; and latterly atomic energy, computers, telecommunications and information technology. The latter was fully underway by the end the Second World War and was then prolonged by Keynesian interventionism and state-led industrial activism. Like the preceding waves, knowledge, business practice, and technology were revolutionised. However, once it tipped over into its neoliberal phase, capital increasingly cannibalised the structures and institutions that allowed it to accumulate in the first place. Massive privatisation projects and the subordination of public services to market discipline witnessed capital drain from productive investment, in favour of short-term returns on money and property markets. Like all previous waves, it too crested, broke, and petered out. The 2008 crash signalled its end.

According to Paul Mason, the problem is that this fourth wave has passed into history but the next wave is struggling to be born. The primary reason he gives is the state of class struggle in neoliberal societies. A key (if not *the* key) driver of innovation is exploitation of the workforce. For capital to be profitable, it must secure a greater share of social wealth. In Marx's critique of capitalist economics, profit lies in surplus value, the difference between the value a worker produces for an employer and the value of the wage or the salary they receive in return. It follows that the employer – capital – has an interest in keeping the wage bill low, while introducing new measures to enhance the productivity of labour, and therefore yielding more surplus value and realising more profit. Meanwhile, workers, as human beings, have an interest in capturing as much of the value generated by their labour power as possible, while resisting speed-ups, management interference and intimidation of workers, the extension of the working day without compensation, and so on. It follows that where workers are collectively organised and are capable of enforcing their demands at work, the employers do not have the capacity to appropriate a greater share of the value produced. There are two ways around this problem. If worker consciousness and militancy is high, a government can enforce the right of capital to the greatest share of the surplus, by pursuing naked class war policies and breaking unions. Or, capital can innovate its way out of the problem by introducing more machinery that does the workers' jobs for them.

Neoliberalism, as a doctrine of economics and politics, is the result of the first of these approaches and has been implemented over the last forty years by governments of ostensibly different political hues. The problem is, for Paul Mason, that the success of the neoliberal offensive has slain the trade union dragon and given capital the whip hand. However, in an irony of history, weak labour movements and low levels of worker militancy mean firms do not innovate anywhere to capture surplus value. In Britain, because capital's share of surplus value is not threatened by a strong workers' movement, rather than investing in the research, design and implementation of new software and robotics to replace workers, it makes sense to simply employ more people. The absence of class conflict therefore dampens innovation in the process of production. Capital's victory in the class wars of the 1980s has hampered its ability to grow further.

Another issue is structural: commodities have undergone a profound transformation. Increasingly, markets are about the production of information, knowledge and services for profit, and this presents capital with another problem. For instance, in material commodity production, the worker produces x amount of goods in return for a wage. The value over and above this is unrealised within the commodity itself. The commodities go on sale and the employer receives a return on their investment – surplus value is realised – when they are sold. Out of this, rent, loans, tax, future investment and profits are allocated. If this circuit of capital breaks down because a substantial amount of goods go unsold, surplus value is not realised and a loss is made, often imperilling the investor. The emergence of information production as an increasingly important sector results in information commodities that are infinitely reproducible with next to no labour time required. A video game may have consumed thousands of hours of programming and a significant capital outlay, but – provided the copy protection is cracked – it can be duplicated. Hence the product can circulate, but a significant proportion of the surplus value remains stuck in stasis.

Therefore, the combined effect of the balance of the class struggle and the structure of knowledge production presents capitalism with a significant challenge. The technological basis is present for a further wave of capitalist development, but the efficient use of it by capital, along with little impetus to extend this to existing production, is proving to be a logjam.

Does Corbynism provide answers to the impasse? The explicit anti-austerity thrust of Corbyn's message promises remedy to the neoliberal policies that have exacerbated the situation. Some ways to address some of the problems of British capitalism (an epitome of these tendencies) might include: a more proactive role for the state; wage growth policies to jumpstart consumer markets; a new role for trade unions and collective bargaining; and a lifelong education service people can dip in and out of throughout their careers. However, Corbynism is more than a technocratic project. As an expression of an emerging class politics, it must fix capitalism by *changing capitalism*. This project is inseparable from organising and making conscious the new working class of which the movement is an expression.

THE NEW WORKING CLASS

In their *Empire* trilogy,[7] Michael Hardt and Antonio Negri argue that the switch from material to immaterial labour marks a watershed moment in capitalism's history. They therefore suggest that class politics requires rethinking for two key reasons, identified as follows.

Firstly, from about the 1970s onwards, as capital subsumed society to its logic, greater proportions of workers were drawn into jobs that had the object of reproducing capitalism as a socio-economic system. This increasing mass of workers producing services and care coincided with the growing stress on information and knowledge, and constituted the emergence of immaterial labour as an important facet of social life. This set a disruptive tone in the relationship between capital and labour, because the key force in this type of production is the brain. Traditionally, the subordination of labour to capital requires that the latter possesses the knowledge of the production process, and workers come to employers without tools or training. Accomplished in the early twentieth century, deskilling workers and management storing knowledge of production, allowed workers to be easily replaceable.[8] This was, and remains, a strategy of control, albeit an increasingly obsolete one. In the new 'cognitive capitalism' discussed above, because capital does not own the brains of the workers, the production of information commodities always produces a surplus of knowledge, which is retained by the worker and can be put to other, non-commercial purposes.

Secondly, the production of information and social relations requires new collaborative forms of working. For example, workplace cooperation was previously mediated by the pace of machinery and the hierarchy of management. Increasingly, this is giving way to self-organising networks that enable the fulfilment of tasks. As these networks self-organise, they draw deep from the well of social knowledge that exists outside of the employer/employee relationship. The tendency, therefore, is for workers to approach the workplace and mobilise their intellect, ideas, tools and networks that are constituted independently of it. Software houses, for example, may depend on a loyal core of programmers but require additional workers on a job-by-job basis: they do not provide training and knowledge of programming is something acquired outside the workplace. Likewise, an Uber driver enters into a relationship in which the car, knowledge and driving skills were acquired independently of, but are mobilised by, the firm.

This has a number of consequences. In particular immaterial labour is more exploitative than other forms of work. As Hardt and Negri note, 'When our ideas and our affects, our emotions, are put to work, for instance, and when they thus become subject in a new way to the command of the boss, we often experience new and intense forms of violation or alienation'.[9] The exploitative relation of employment, usually hiding behind wages and salaries, is forced out into the open. At the lower-paid end of the new job market, the bogus 'self-employment' of Uber and Deliveroo workers, to name two, allows them to see the revenue their labour power generates and how much of that is appropriated by the company. Similarly, 'consultants' identify large savings for organisations, or help an employer to acquire lucrative contracts, and here surplus value – actual and latent – is extracted right in front of the employee's eyes. This is accompanied by disposability. With a pool of pre-trained workers, capital can theoretically take its pick. The spread of zero hours contracts, for example, presents the naked reality of the power imbalance between capital and labour. In all cases, a generalisation of precarity appears to be the case.

Yet both immaterial labour and the emergence of what Negri terms the 'socialised worker' also offer new political opportunities.[10] The independence and self-organisation required by this form of labour continually add to the store of social knowledge, both in know-how and in consciousness of capital's exploitative relationships. We can therefore start speaking of the 'socialised worker' in terms of a rising class, as it becomes an increasingly hegemonic notion of what it is to be 'a worker', while we simultaneously regard it as a networked collective, possessing a growing capacity to reorganise the social order as it sees fit.

What could this new class politics look like? Hardt and Negri identify a number of features we might expect to see attending Corbynism if their theory works as an interpretative frame.

In the first place, given the distance between the socialised worker and what Negri terms the 'mass worker' (i.e. the previous hegemonic ideal, as typified by the manual worker employed in large enterprises and integrated into the post-war compromise via trade unions), one would expect the impulse for a new radicalism *not* to come through the organisations of the established labour movement.

Secondly, forms of resistance to capital and its policies would be carried by networks without any clear centre – a vision far from what you might term 'Fordist radicalism', and the concordant view that the workers' movement would be organised as a weapon with the revolutionary party as its spearhead.

Thirdly, Hardt and Negri argue that, along with the development of the socialised worker in the production of the prerequisites of capital's existence, there has been a shift toward 'biopolitics'. The work of Michel Foucault, who spent his career looking at how institutions and hegemonic knowledge (discourse) creates subjects, suggests there are certain classifications that define how human beings behave. In a set of studies on medicine, the prison and sexuality,[11] Foucault explored how discourses of expertise defined and introduced methods of control, to ensure people who entered these institutions or came under the specialist's eye were disciplined into behaving correctly. This inaugurated a politics of the body, where people were forced by rules, violence and the threat of violence, and in some cases medical intervention, to submit to the prescriptions of how a patient, a prisoner, a homosexual should behave. In sum, these amount to methods (or technologies) of micro, individual-level governance of human bodies. Hardt and Negri suggest that these processes of creating officially-sanctioned persons of a certain 'type' are so integrated into Western cultures that they are largely imperceptible. We merely accept that we, as individuals, have to act in certain ways in particular institutional settings. And yet these remain key methods of social control for managing populations.

Pierre Dardot and Christian Laval have built on this approach, and argue neoliberalism is more than a particular form of economic theory and policy, but is a mode of governance as well.[12] By accident and design, a range of institutions address us as self-reliant entrepreneurial individuals. This sensibility of creating and recreating one's self as an entrepreneur mobilises different forms of capital (cultural and social in addition to economic). This is enforced by institutions which have been set up to treat you as a particular kind of subject. It is a calcu-lating mindset, in which every situation is approached through costs and benefits, and success is interpreted in terms of the metrics that the individual or the institution/culture imposes upon it. At work, one's performance is managed with reference to metrics. In leisure time, we are exhorted to follow a healthy life bound by metrics of calories burned, heart rates and steps on the pedometer. Free time is filled with the accumulation of objects and experiences. Social media has its own attention economy governed by numbers of followers, reach of one's posts, and it offers metrics that work as crude conversions of your sum total of social and cultural capital. It is no coincidence then that private life has seen itself stripped back to abstract numbers and subject to logics of accumulation, while the crude means/end ration-alities of neoliberalism have run amok at work and in wider culture.[13]

This colonisation of the mind reiterates the importance of the body, of biopolitics. If we are expected to act in particular ways, then what we do with our bodies is absolutely an object of politics. Unsurprisingly the substance of body politics is a key feature of not just leftist radi-calism, but a key battleground of all politics today, almost fifty years after the emergence of the women's and sexual liberation movements. In addition to bodies, identity has become fundamental as well. By colonising the mind and attempting to frame the process of cognition, capital tries to survive in the age of networked, socialised labour, but at every step its attempts to frame subjectivity are contested to the point where symbolism and language are stakes in the struggle.

LABOURISM AND CORBYNISM

In many ways, the Labour Party is an unlikely vehicle for this new class politics. Far from networked and decentralised, the party is terrifyingly hierarchical and bureaucratic, and instead of being at the cutting edge of radical politics, the party has historically had problematic relationships with transformative socialism. It is also significant that the last period of Labour government deepened the neoliberal consensus.

Yet, despite this, the Labour Party is the only mass party of the left in this country, via sheer weight of numbers and tendencies, and, as such, it has always had a certain openness within it. It remains a party that is fundamentally class-oriented in both conception and operation, and it does seek to represent all those who have to work for a wage or a salary. Furthermore, even when it has also always been a mainstay of establishment politics, it has been a repository of hope for millions of people.

The unwitting moment in its transformation was Ed Miliband's initiatives, largely with the backing of Progress and the Labour right, to replace block affiliations of trade unions with an opt-in supporter status for members, and to introduce the then-celebrated, more recently reviled, £3 fee for individual supporters. Ostensibly designed to curb the clout wielded by trade unions around internal elections, it was hoped that this reform would dilute their influence yet further. Ironically, a studied exorcism of the old Labour phantoms opened a window for wider frustrations and hopes to condense around a left-wing candidate.

When Corbyn announced his 2015 candidacy, he set out a simple but straightforward political message: a programme of cuts and war are not the way forward, alternatives to the status quo of almost forty years are possible, and we should be aiming for a more equal, more tolerant society. This was in stark contrast to the other 2015 leadership candidates who offered platforms based entirely around the received template of centre-left politics. Corbyn's message, combined with the fact that he was largely unknown to the public-at-large allowed him to become a canvas for the projection of political idealism. His call attracted large numbers of existing activists involved in extra-parliamentary politics outside the Labour Party, and thus largely outflanked the established candidates – whose supporters controlled the party bureaucracy – by swamping them with hundreds of thousands of new members and registered supporters.[14] The campaign activated a mass of atomised individuals, members and activists, who were isolated but for the connections established between them via social media. They had experienced and felt the deleterious consequences of decades of neoliberalism, from the erosion of workplace rights to the erosion of free time, from the retreat of social security to greater precarity. These sentiments multiplied among networked workers, were shared in Facebook statuses, in tweets ripping into *Question Time* guests, and were found in blog posts about parenting, mental health, gender identity and more. While highly individuated by neoliberal culture in and out of work, Corbyn's brand of left politics spoke to socialised workers and provided a frame for their collective interests. He may have been derided as a fossil from the 1970s, but it just so happened that his politics were the most modern because he spoke to the grievances that had been crowded out of establishment politics, and he offered an alternative to them.

It should be remembered that, in many ways, this was accidental. Indeed, Corbyn has been called the accidental leader.[15] Just prior to the launch of the campaign, there was little sense the Labour left was standing on the threshold of something politically big. As Alex Nunns has noted,[16] Jeremy Corbyn became the left's standard bearer in the 2015 leadership contest because it was his turn, although there was little enthusiasm, his milieu was small, he had little representation in Parliament, and was pretty much excluded from mainstream political debate. Nevertheless, while Corbyn did make it onto the ballot paper with minutes to spare, it was almost as if the general population had been waiting for him.

Hardt and Negri have linked the networked resistance adopted by the socialised worker to the subjectivities necessary for immaterial labour. They argue that distributed networks are appropriate for all kinds of activism, because all points of the chain are capable of becoming conscious and articulating new (resistance-focused) forms of subjectivity and being. Networked activists, whether veteran or entirely fresh, swarmed into the party and have swollen it to well over half a million members. Yet because the basis of Corbyn's support is his ideas and how they speak to radicalised networks, his support does not relate to him in simple command terms. This constitutes an important strength, but also a limit of Corbynism. The support for it is self-activating and self-organising, as Hardt and Negri lead us to expect; different parts of the network are active in doorstep campaigning, constituency party activity, the dissemination of pro-Corbyn media, work with Momentum, and so on. Identification with the Labour leader is based on ideas and the extent to which he embodies them or allows an opening for further, radical ideas. For as long as Corbyn does not compromise on key policies to appease internal and external critics, his position will remain strong. However, as the relation is one of moral authority, exercising hands-on leadership of Corbynism as a movement, is difficult to the point of impossibility. It makes it very easy for opponents to attack Corbynism on the basis of the cranks, misogynists and anti-Semites who, for whatever reason, have hitched themselves to Corbyn's bandwagon. In an age of social media, the means simply do not exist for effectively shutting these groups down.

After Jeremy Corbyn's election and re-election as Labour leader, the 2017 general election represented the second phase of Corbynism. If the first eighteen months of leadership were about establishing and consolidating the revolution in the Labour Party, the election, naturally, saw Corbyn turn outwards. A diffuse but networked feeling of something-not-being-quite-right was met by a strong campaign of plain messaging that differed markedly from the hubristic tone and chaotic agenda set by the Conservatives.

Unsurprisingly, given how immaterial labour and the socialised worker cut through traditional measurements of class, the final result of almost 13 million votes showed Corbynism's capacity to range across occupational groups, from the low-paid and insecure to the relatively privileged professional. Neither was it surprising that younger voters were more receptive to Corbynism: they not only face disproportionate material deprivation and disadvantage, but are increasingly socialised into subjectivities and (networked) practices that ready them for life as part of the general population. The often noted 'age effect' is actually a cohort class effect,[17] and is partly powered by the divide between the promises cognitive capitalism offers and its reality. Corbyn's success is far from being simply about the pledge to abolish tuition fees, as even the Conservatives belatedly acknowledged.[18]

THE LIMITATIONS OF CORBYNISM

Hardt and Negri emphasise the international and cosmopolitan character of the multitude (their catch-all term for the mass of people in all their complexity) and specifically critique the politics of nationalism as deleterious. Clearly, a component of those who voted to remain in the EU, particularly the young, were motivated less by a love for the European Union as an entity and more by its representing an (imperfect) instantiation of internationalism and tolerance. Corbynism itself is internationalist and opposed to nationalism and racism, therefore it must foreground those values whatever position it adopts on the specifics of Brexit.

Regardless of the character Brexit assumes, if Britain finds itself outside the Single Market and Customs Union there will be sweeping political repercussions. Post-Brexit then is likely to be a volatile period for party politics. Advocating a position that is set to put the livelihoods of workers, whether socialised or not, at risk is a dangerous prospect for Corbynism, even if Labour's Brexit is couched in terms of freedom from neoliberal EU rules on state ownership and the protection of markets.

However, there is another limitation on Corbynism. While the socialised worker is its base, and immaterial labour is transforming work and class beyond those directly employed or working in cognitive roles, not all parts of the multitude *are* socialised workers. The flipside of the age breakdown is that older voters, who are less likely to be either socialised workers or networked in the same way as younger cohorts, are still disposed to support the Conservatives. This group are mostly composed of retirees and are proving most resilient to Corbynism. There are a number of reasons for this, such as the tendency for 'security issues' and their proxies to become more salient as one gives up work and relies on a pension. These voters are also more likely to consume the 'old media', which has persistently framed Corbynism in hostile terms. It is important, therefore, that Labour makes inroads into this bedrock of voters; doing so will make it more difficult for the Conservatives to recover and will help to protect Corbynism against electoral shifts, especially post-Brexit, that may shake loose some of Labour's softer support.

TRANSFORMATION TIME

Corbynism at its best represents the return of a class politics 'from below', a new class politics appropriate to the ways in which the nature of the commodity has been reconfigured, along with work and the limits of neoliberalism. Corbynism should therefore be read as the first flush of a rising class of workers struggling into collective consciousness. As such, Corbynism itself can only be transitory but nevertheless has the potential to define politics not just for the next few years, but for a generation, if not a century. This requires a number of objectives if we are to seize that prize.

Corbynism must overcome the anti-intellectual legacy of Labourism to try and understand the position it is in, its relationship to the political economy of global capital, and crucially its expression of the views of the general collective of voters.

It must ensure its policy agenda not only reflects the interests of its class base but actively encourages the reproduction of more socialised workers. Labour's commitment to lifelong education, of industrial strategies, of tackling precarity and rebuilding the public sector are definitely policies that point in this direction.

It must continue to politically organise as many people as possible. Participation in the Labour Party and its transformation, from bureaucratic vote catcher to a democratic movement able to win elections, means a programme of democratisation that empowers and encourages.

Corbynism must exercise an informed vigilance over its limitations as a class project. Class struggle produces tensions and antagonisms with declining strata and class fractions as well as positions tied indissociably to capital.

And finally, it must expressly articulate its vision of the good life, of what a cognitive socialism looks like and of the measures that can be put into place to bring this about. Corbynism therefore is a dialogue, a great feedback loop that draws from the thoughts and talent of all to remould and remake the social.

Corbynism represents a breakthrough moment. It has changed politics because it represents the cutting edge of social change, but this is a wave of change, incomplete and still with a long way to run. 2017 is the start of this process, not its end.

NOTES

1. Stoke-on-Trent Central increased its Labour majority to 3897 from the 2620 scored at the by-election in February 2017, but the proportion of that margin declined from 12.4 per cent to 11.8 per cent. In Stoke-on-Trent North, between 2015 and this year, the Labour majority declined from 4836 to 2359, or 12.5 per cent to 5.6 per cent.
2. See Joe Watts, 'Jeremy Corbyn is "out of touch" and an "election loser" among working class voters, poll finds', *The Independent*, 23 September

2016. For an academic account of the working-class 'problem', see Robert Ford and Matthew Goodwin, *Revolt on the Right: Explaining Support for the Radical Right in Britain*, Routledge: London, 2014.

3. Richard Murphy, *The Courageous State*, Searching Finance, 2011.

4. Thomas Piketty, *Capital in the Twenty-First Century*, Harvard University Press: Cambridge, 2014.

5. Wolfgang Streeck, *How Will Capitalism End? Essays on a Failing System*, Verso: London, 2016.

6. Paul Mason, *Postcapitalism*, Allen Lane: London, 2015, pp37-8.

7. Michael Hardt and Antonio Negri, *Empire*, Harvard University Press: Cambridge, 2000; Michael Hardt and Antonio Negri, *Multitude*, Penguin: London, 2004; Michael Hardt and Antonio Negri, *Commonwealth*, Harvard University Press: Cambridge, 2009.

8. See Harry Braverman, *Labor and Monopoly Capital*, Monthly Review Press: New York, 1974.

9. Hardt and Negri, 2004, pp65-6.

10. See Antonio Negri, *Reflections on Empire*, Polity Press: Cambridge, 2008.

11. Michel Foucault, *The Birth of the Clinic*, Routledge: London, 2003; *Discipline and Punish: The Birth of the Prison*, Penguin: Harmondsworth, 1991; *The History of Sexuality: The Will to Knowledge*, Penguin: Harmondsworth, 1998.

12. Pierre Dardot and Christian Laval, *The New Way of the World: On Neoliberal Society*, Verso: London, 2013.

13. Phil Burton-Cartledge, 'After Neoliberalism', www. averypublicsociologist.blogspot.co.uk, 24 August 2016.

14. See Alex Nunns, *The Candidate: Jeremy Corbyn's Improbable Path to Power*, OR Books: New York, 2016.

15. Tom Quinn, 'Jeremy Corbyn: The Accidental Labour Leader?' www.psa.ac.uk/insight-plus/blog, 7 September 2015

16. Nunns, *ibid*.

17. For voter breakdown figures by demographics, including age, see 'How The Voters Voted in the 2017 election', *Ipsos MORI Estimates*, June 2017.

18. Nicholas Mazzei, 'Changing the Party to Attract the Youth Vote', www. conservativehome.com, 2 June 2017.

No More Racing to the Bottom

Maya Goodfellow

'No one seriously concerned with political strategies in the current situation can now afford to ignore the "swing to the right"', observed Stuart Hall in January 1979.[1] What was then a 'swing' – in the months before Margaret Thatcher's election as prime minister – subsequently solidified into a decisive restructuring of UK politics in the following decades, moving the centre ground firmly to the right. After the end of the Blair-Brown governments, Hall reminded us that New Labour largely abided by the Thatcherite neoliberal agenda.[2] Tony Blair himself said his task was 'to build on some of the things she [Thatcher] had done rather than reverse them'.[3]

In recent years, the disastrous effects of this project have become painfully evident: standards of living have plummeted, inequality has steadily grown and political disenfranchisement has proliferated. To escape blame and stifle dissent, mainstream parties, as well as their outliers Ukip and before them the British National Party, have focused popular discontent on migration. Politicians have blamed immigration for low wages, lack of affordable housing, community collapse and Britons' sense of powerlessness. The danger embodied in such inflammatory politics shouldn't be underestimated.

But in the 2017 snap election there was a monumental shift in British politics. Jeremy Corbyn, a leader derided even by many of his own MPs as unfit for the job, successfully took on the status quo. Labour under Corbyn did what these MPs, former Labour leaders, critics and commentators had warned them not to do for years: they tacked to the left. The party began to offer an alternative to the long-protected neoliberal consensus. And this proved immensely popular. Labour did not win a majority, nor did it become the largest party, but it proved that the analysis coming from large swathes of the commentariat – including from some on the left – to be largely shallow. It bucked a trend that had been occurring across large parts of Europe: while the French, Greek, Dutch and other traditional social-democratic parties performed poorly in elections, Labour secured 40 per cent of the vote, turned former safe Tory seats into marginals and won seats in Scotland, a place where just two years prior they had faced near-annihilation.

Yet Hall would encourage us to examine in full the specificity of the current political conjuncture. On the question of immigration, Labour remains troubled and troubling. While Corbyn's Labour have not regurgitated xenophobic bile in the same way previous versions of the party did, they have struggled to break free from long-held prejudices that shape anti-migrant politics. If the Labour Party is to be a force for transformative change, it must confidently take on the so-called migration 'debate'.

Commentators and politicians from Trevor Phillips to Yvette Cooper constantly tell us that we need to have an 'honest debate' about migration. They claim anti-migrant sentiment is a response to the left consistently shutting down talk of immigration. This suggestion is as ironic as it is absurd: in the 2015 general election, Labour sold mugs stamped with the words 'controls on immigration'. The problem is not that politicians have shied away from discussing immigration but that this debate has been woefully ill-informed. Labour's challenge to the disastrous status quo must address the issue of immigration head on, and that means decisively rejecting anti-migrant politics in all its forms.

ANTI-MIGRANT POLITICS

On the afternoon of 16 June 2016, exactly one week before the EU referendum, pro-refugee Labour MP Jo Cox was shot and stabbed to death outside a library in her constituency. Her murderer was white supremacist neo-Nazi, Thomas Mair, who in court gave his name as 'death to traitors, freedom for Britain'. Just hours before Cox's murder Nigel Farage, at the time Ukip leader, stood proudly in front of a billboard that read 'Breaking Point'. Pictured under these inflammatory words was a queue of people, who were predominantly people of colour. The message was obvious enough: these people were a threat to the stability of the nation. Eight days later, in a self-congratulatory speech infused with imperial nostalgia, Farage declared that the Leave Campaign had won the referendum 'without a single bullet being fired'.[4]

The vicious and often racist rhetoric that characterised the referendum debate translated into other violent actions, too. While the white-supremacist, anti-migrant beliefs that drove Mair to murder Jo Cox were quietly swept into the wings of the political stage, migrants and British-born people of colour were attacked on the street and told to 'go home' as Britain witnessed a fivefold increase in hate crimes following the referendum.[5] Leading right-wing politicians didn't so much as blink.

Much of the anti-migrant sentiment that flourished in the days, months and years before the 2016 EU referendum was the product of seeds planted long ago in the UK. Xenophobia is no new beast in this country; successive left and right governments have demonised migrants and asylum seekers. More recently, this has taken on a distinctly Islamophobic tone, as aggressive anti-Muslim politics intensified during the war on terror. But the referendum was set specifically against a backdrop of heightened hysteria over migration. Politicians, aided by substantial sections of the media, lambasted migrants as simultaneously benefit claimants and job thieves. A supposed 'migrant crisis' was used to sow fears about outsiders threatening the UK through both their presence and their assumed criminality. The terminology of the 'wholesale' movement of people helped to construct migrants and refugees as the threatening 'other'. This rhetoric buttressed a preposterous belief that Europe was at the forefront of housing people escaping war and oppression, when the vast majority of refugees actually live in countries outside of Europe, including Turkey, Lebanon, Kenya and Pakistan. A life-altering tragedy for people forced to leave their homes was turned into a 'crisis' for Europeans.

Politicians who trade primarily in xenophobia wielded anti-migrant messages to help create and exacerbate public fear of the 'other'. David Cameron's own adviser, David Korski, admitted his researchers couldn't find suitable evidence that migration put pressure on communities – which is a popular but factually incorrect adage used by politicians.[6] No matter the inaccuracy of the argument, xenophobic politics gave the impression that migrants (regardless of generation), refugees and asylum seekers were undesirable, and Muslims were the ultimate enemy. Anti-migrant politics was and continues to be a tissue of lies that sells the public a narrow story about what 'the nation' should be.

Many of these fears over migration stemmed originally from a 'new racism', a term first coined by academic Martin Barker. 'It is a theory that I shall call biological, or better, pseudo-biological culturalism', explained Barker in 1981:

> Nations on this view are not built out of politics and economics, but out of human nature. It is in our biology, our instincts, to defend our way of life, traditions and customs against outsiders – not because they are inferior, but because they are part of different cultures.[7]

As Barker suggests, the biological essentialism of an earlier kind of 'scientific racism' has largely been abandoned. Instead, there is a focus on cultural incompatibility between people of colour and migrants with 'civilised' UK society. This form of racism relies on the mischaracterisation of racial discrimination; treating the discourse of cultural difference as entirely separate from racism. In this illogical line of thinking, migration is and always has been a threat to the supposed cultural cohesion of British society.

THE LEFT'S RESPONSE

The active emboldening of bigoted views, racist sentiment and white supremacist thinking did not appear to prompt a rethink among a considerable number of Labour MPs, who had for some time been openly flirting with and at times even encouraging anti-migrant feeling.[8] Instead, they grossly misunderstood the situation and encouraged calls for migration to be curbed. Rachel Reeves, for instance, predicted 'riots' would break out in her constituency if migration was not reduced, buying into the Powellesque idea that immigrants were ultimately incompatible with the country and would be damaging to existing society.[9]

One of the most alarming, yet entirely predictable, versions of this kind of politics following the EU referendum (and after the 2017 general election too) has been a recurrent fixation on the 'white working class', a mythical block of people who are all assumed to hold the same views. Labour MPs such as Stephen Kinnock suggested these people must be prioritised above the party's alleged emphasis on 'diversity'.[10] This narrative is lazy and disturbing; it erases the experiences of working-class people of colour and implicitly suggests that their poverty and disenfranchisement are somehow acceptable. Working-class people of all races and genders are struggling in poverty, dealing with the sharp end of rampant capitalism and ideologically-driven austerity policies. The rewards reaped from whiteness are few and far between if you are poor. However, white people do escape the racism that shapes the lives of working-class people of colour, which for working-class women of colour is compounded by sexism. Likewise, the sexism that underlies economic relations and shapes society does not have a significant impact on working-class men in the way that it does on women.

The call to focus on the 'white working class' is often paired with voices from across the party demanding that Labour abandons 'identity politics'. This is code for a belief that demanding equality for women, people of colour, migrants and other marginalised people alienates anyone who falls outside of these groups. Instead of trying to tackle these forms of discrimination deeply embedded in society, those denouncing 'identity politics' wanted to pander to them.

This works on the basis of ignoring that whiteness is a socially-constructed racial category because, as academic Gloria Wekker has explained, it is not seen as a 'racialised/ethnicised positioning at all'. 'Within the realm of ethnicity', Wekker notes, 'being white is passed off as such a natural, invisible category that its significance has not been a research theme'.[11] Whiteness works in insidious ways and places white people's experience as central. When Labour MPs position the 'white working class' at the forefront of the political conversation while rejecting identity politics, they implicitly reinforce the notion that whiteness equates to superiority and signal that they can compete with right-wing ethno-nationalism in wanting to reinforce the racial hierarchy and put white people first. The white working class narrative erases people of colour from analysis and divides up a group that could be united – although to achieve solidarity in this group, it is equally necessary to address racism and sexism; economic change alone will not lead to their eradication.[12]

IMAGINING A POPULAR PRO-MIGRATION, ANTI-RACIST POLITICS

Jeremy Corbyn's leadership election seemed to signal a challenge to these anti-migrant tendencies. Corbyn has been committed to anti-racism throughout his time in parliament: during the New Labour years he was part of a group of backbenchers – which also included current shadow home secretary Diane Abbott – who consistently opposed New Labour's draconian asylum policies. When he became the favourite to win the leadership, an iconic picture circulated on social media: a young Corbyn in 1984, escorted down the street by two police officers with a sign around his neck that read 'Defend the right to demonstrate against apartheid. Join this picket'. It was a picture that signified a politician with convictions, who took racism and xenophobia seriously.

In the 2015 leadership contest, Corbyn stood on a platform that promised honest politics. 'What will Labour do about immigration?' was a regular question in the scores of hustings that were held up and down the country. His three opponents – Andy Burnham, Yvette Cooper and Liz Kendall – answered with the kind of veiled anti-migrant sentiments that had become fashionable in the Ed Miliband era. Corbyn, in contrast, was unashamedly pro-migration. Rejecting the idea that the UK needed stronger immigration controls, he said Labour should campaign on the basis of solidarity and emphasised the need for entire communities to work together. On becoming leader, his first act was to speak at a pro-refugee demonstration in London, a largely symbolic move, but one that appeared to signal he would not personally or politically kowtow to the anti-refugee sentiment that the right had stirred up, aided by left-liberal opinion.

Individuals alone can't be tasked with bringing about a whole sea of change in Labour, particularly when the rest of the party is either moving the other way or doesn't know which direction to take. Yet it's significant that under Corbyn, Diane Abbott was made shadow home secretary in the October 2016 shadow cabinet reshuffle. This was a clever move. Abbott, who was the country's first black woman MP, is a strong migration advocate and has a sharp intellect. She also understands far better than most how race and racism operate in the UK. In fact, Abbott has spoken out about the vicious racism she has personally received on social media. 'I receive racist and sexist abuse online on a daily basis. I have had rape threats, death threats', she wrote in February 2017, 'The death threats include an EDL-affiliated account with the tag "burn Diane Abbott".[13] This racist abuse stretches beyond visceral online comments. The way Abbott is treated by certain parliamentary colleagues (including some in the Labour Party) and journalists is a product of the subtle forms of racism that pervade UK society; her abilities are constantly questioned and she is regularly the subject of ridicule.[14] Perhaps unsurprisingly, her important appointment to such a prominent position seemed to go largely unnoticed by people who had previously and loudly called for a better gender balance in Corbyn's shadow cabinet. The level of attacks directed at Abbott became particularly intense during the 2017 campaign; the Conservatives ceaselessly used dog-whistle politics to imply she wasn't fit to be home secretary and people sent her torrents of racist and sexist abuse online, which included death and rape threats.[15]

But for all the promise, Labour under Corbyn hasn't fully delivered on the bold declarations he made about migration in those heady days of summer 2015. In the 2017 snap general election, the party offered a mixed message. Corbyn maintained staunch opposition to scapegoating migrants, and an early leaked version of the party's manifesto recognised the 'historic contribution of immigrants and the children of immigrants to our society and economy'.[16] Unlike the 2015 election, Labour didn't stoke xenophobia by carving 'controls on immigration' into an eight-foot-six stone tablet. Nor did it embrace the Blue Labour agenda of race, family and patriotism. Corbyn was also steadfast in his refusal to set a target for reducing migration. The party had long been warned that if they didn't mimic the right's rhetoric on immigration, they would be doomed. This did not come to pass. While Theresa May centred her policies almost entirely around xenophobia, Labour offered, in contrast, a radical agenda, promised economic investment and an opportunity for change, which appealed to people from a range of socio-economic backgrounds.

Yet the party's welcome rhetorical shift was not universal and did not directly translate into policy. The final, published version of the party's election manifesto said Labour would 'replace income thresholds with a prohibition on recourse to public funds',[17] which hardly sent out a positive message on migration. This would deny people access to state support if needed and it reinforces a notion that migrants don't truly belong in the UK. And significantly, the party pledged to end Freedom of Movement. This policy was nowhere to be found in the leaked manifesto but a week later it was there in the party's official offering. This was no small shift and while triangulating on immigration might have appealed to some, it will undermine efforts to put an end to the scapegoating of migrants. Some pro-migrant voices in Labour reluctantly saw this as a halfway measure.

None of this is to say freedom of movement within the EU should be uncritically celebrated. There are credible criticisms to be made of a Europe that allows free movement across its member states but builds walls laced with barbed wire along its continental border. The racism embodied in the Schengen Agreement is evident, and white migrants are often afforded a level of solidarity to which migrants of colour are not privy. The appalling discrimination, treatment and imprisonment of those people who fall into the latter category has long been normalised. However these are not the debates being had in Brexit Britain. But Labour needs to challenge xenophobic border policies for all migrants, including calling for an end to immigration detention centres and everyday border policing in schools and hospitals.

CORBYNISM VS RACISM

Labour needs to be bold on migration, and how they do so is a critical question. Many in the party, and the UK more broadly, are susceptible to pandering to anti-migrant sentiments and reinforcing racialised notions of the nation. In fact, the left is by no means immune from taking these dangerous paths. Sections of the party believe entrenched prejudices are too difficult to challenge, and shy away from conversations about race and migration. Meanwhile, others argue Labour must listen to and tacitly agree with fears over immigration – always understood through the disingenuous prism of 'legitimate concerns' – instead of using evidence to argue that migration has, in fact, not made the country worse. Making oneself heard in this din is itself a challenge. Pondering what to say and do is another question altogether, a dual problem that embodies at least some of Corbyn's woes. On race and immigration Labour's left tend to tick many of the correct boxes, but this needs to translate into a popular, powerful and transformative movement that is rooted in specific anti-racist policies and pro-migration messages.

Globally, the far right have helped to further normalise mainstream aggressive racism and xenophobia, bringing it into mainstream political discourse. From Donald Trump to Marine Le Pen and Geert Wilders, far-right politicians are either in power or heavily influencing debate with their xenophobic rhetoric. This has been deemed a victory for 'populism', a term regularly bandied about and assumed to be synonymous with far-right, anti-migrant politics. While the resurgence of far-right politics led many to believe the left should shift (further to) the right in order to win support, Corbyn's Labour showed in June 2017 that this was not true.

It's arguably unhelpful to view Corbyn's Labour through the lens of populism. This term is now used regularly in media analysis with little robust probing of what it means. For my purposes, it is perhaps more useful to think about anti-elite politics. In the contemporary UK, this anti-elitism broadly has two forms. Both direct blame towards a country's corporate, media and political elite who have undermined and sold out 'the people'. But one has a much narrower, racialised version of what (and who) constitutes 'the people'.[18] When they speak about uniting 'the people' and disingenuously promise to make the country better for them, far-right politicians mean only those that 'matter': the people who are constructed and counted as human beings within the extremely limited, racist definition of the population. In the US and UK this functions on the basis of privileging white identity – the same form of politics that underpins discussion of 'the white working class' – and is imbued with nostalgia for empire.[19]

But another form of anti-elite politics has the potential to advocate for a broader understanding of 'the people', explicitly including people of colour, migrants and white people. This is what Corbyn's Labour needs to build upon. There's no reason for a popular left-wing project to be anti-immigrant or buy into white nationalist framing – particularly when elites, not migrants, traded away peoples' rights (in this case anyone outside the wealthy) to give power to big businesses. While Labour is now adamantly anti-austerity, they have not yet attempted to fully shift the framing of migration in an equally dramatic way.

In a climate of sustained xenophobia and longing for empire, some find it impossible to imagine such a plausible challenge to the narrow, racist version of right-wing politics. Left-wing commentators and politicians are fond of proclaiming that the left has lost the argument on migration; that facts will no longer be sufficient to influence views. They argue that hard statistics have proven insufficient to persuade people of the left's arguments on migration but they have simultaneously failed to unpick how these prejudices have been constructed.

People are angry about poor housing, low pay, lack of jobs, growing inequality, political disenfranchisement and few prospects for the country's young people: these are the outcomes of the global capitalist system. Racism and the demonisation of migrants is intimately connected with this. Drawing on the country's imperial past, politicians channel certain Britons' belief that it is in their economic interests to reduce immigration. In doing so they win consent for the exploitative economic system by focusing blame on the 'other'.

However, it is reductionist to boil anti-migration sentiment entirely down to economic anxiety. There are people on the left urging Labour to abandon 'identity politics' and focus more attention on economic failure. But both can and must be done: the party's past unwillingness to challenge the economic order had nothing to do with privileging the discourse of equality instead. Creating a fairer economic system will not automatically solve racism and xenophobia; prejudice cannot always be understood as a by-product of economics. There are broader issues of national belonging and identity at play, which are rooted in racism and ideas of an idealised whiteness. It is no coincidence that in the weeks after the EU referendum, people of colour – regardless of where they were born – were told they were unwelcome in the UK. The racial element of the Brexit vote has been overlooked and speaks to a much deeper problem of a racialised interpretation of 'the UK'.

It is possible and necessary for Labour as a movement to make combatting anti-migrant politics a central part of their alternative vision of the country. The party needs to be part of a project that reimagines the 'us' that both defines the nation and stretches beyond national boundaries to form a global movement. In this respect, as a first step, Labour must define the country as heterogeneous and unite the people against the elite. This would require grassroots, democratic engagement at a community level; shining a light on the countless workplaces where migrants and British-born people live and work side-by-side and unite to demand better pay, rights and living conditions. The politics of individualisation has become commonplace in British discourse, but it is not a product of human nature. To revitalise the ethos of collectivism, Labour has been right to argue migration does not make the country worse off. They should continue to explain that the reason behind growing inequality is the broken economic and political system, which favours big business over people, and an unorganised, largely unionised labour force separated along artificial national lines. The politics of divide-and-rule must be revealed and rejected.

Yet, Labour should also show how the current migration debate ignores the broader context within which people around the world, as well as in the UK, are being exploited. Although people migrate for many different reasons, when over one billion people live on less than a dollar a day, large-scale migration is inevitable. And as the ravaging effects of climate change take shape, people across large parts of the world will be forced to leave their homes to survive. From global exploitation to environmental destruction, these are problems left-wing parties across the world should be uniting to face.

2017 proved the power of Labour's grassroots movement, which has ballooned in size thanks to the party's shift to the left. Hundreds of thousands of activists targeted seats up and down the country, helping to deliver Labour one of the most impressive election results in UK history. Labour must develop a national pro-migrant message and pair this with bottom-up campaigning. If this movement robustly, actively and practically challenges widely-accepted stereotypes that people who were born abroad and people of colour born in the UK are a problem, while contextualising the cause of these dangerously-mistaken ideas, then it can begin to erode prejudice. Here, Paul Gilroy's notion of conviviality might be helpful:

> the processes of cohabitation and interaction that have made multi-culture an ordinary feature of social life in Britain's urban areas and in postcolonial cities elsewhere … The radical openness that brings conviviality alive makes a nonsense of closed, fixed, and reified identity and turns attention toward the always unpredictable mechanisms of identification.[20]

Labour should champion this form of interaction and openness through grassroots initiatives that challenge misconceptions about migration and the very idea of fixed identities and culture. Building anti-racism into the centre of local Labour activism – as many are seeking to do – can increase interactions between different peoples through popular campaigns and collective struggles, all while questioning the misinformation and prejudice upon which anti-migrant politics is built.

Venomous anti-migrant rhetoric courses through the veins of British politics. Even if the number of migrants coming to this country were reduced, right-wing politicians would still wield anti-immigrant arguments to play divide-and-rule and distract the people from their own disastrous politics. This is their race to the bottom. As the country negotiates to leave the European Union, Labour must take the sting out of this deeply dangerous xenophobia with a pro-migration message if the party is to be any kind of force for transformative change.

There is a rich history of anti-racist, pro-migrant activism from which Labour can learn in order to help transform the debate about migration and belonging in this country. Some believe that racialised hurdles are insurmountable, but they can be challenged with a politics that highlights humanity, actively combats prejudice, shows that the country's national story is one of migration and brings people together through collective struggle across the country. Real change is about more than ticking boxes: anti-racist politics must be at the heart of any challenge to neoliberalism if it is to be effective. To borrow from Stuart Hall, 'If we are correct about the depth of the rightward turn, then our interventions need to be pertinent, decisive and effective'.[21] Such is the case for an anti-racist, pro-migrant Labour party.

NOTES

1. Stuart Hall, 'The Great Moving Right Show', *Marxism Today*, January 1979, p14.
2. Stuart Hall, 'The March of the Neoliberals', *The Guardian*, 12 September 2011.
3. 'Tony Blair: "My job was to build on some Thatcher policies"', *BBC News*, 8 April 2013.
4. Heather Saul, 'Brexit: Nigel Farage branded "shameful" for claiming victory "without a single bullet being fired"', *The Independent*, 24 June 2016.
5. Nazia Parvee and Harriet Sherwood, 'Police log fivefold rise in race-hate complaints since Brexit result', *The Guardian*, 30 June 2016.
6. David Korski, 'Why we lost the Brexit vote', *Politico*, 24 October 2016.
7. Martin Barker, *The New Racism: Conservative and the Ideology of the Tribe*, Junction Books: Toronto, 1981, pp23-24.
8. Helen Pidd, 'Immigrants must not lead "parallel lives" in UK, says Chuka Umunna', *The Guardian*, 25 September 2016.
9. Caroline Mortimer, 'Labour MP Rachel Reeves: Riots could sweep streets

of Britain if immigration is not curbed after Brexit', *The Independent*, 28 September 2016.

10. Ned Simons. 'Labour must stop "obsessing" about diversity, says Stephen Kinnock', *Huffington Post*, 22 November 2016.

11. Gloria Wekker, *White Innocence: Paradoxes of Colonialism and Race*, Duke University Press: Chapel Hill, 2016, p2, p22.

12. Omar Khan and Faiza Shaheen (eds), 'Minority Report: Race and Class in Post-Brexit Britain', www.runnymedetrust.org, March 2017.

13. Diane Abbott, 'I fought racism and misogyny to become an MP. The fight is getting harder', *The Guardian*, 14 February 2017.

14. Maya Goodfellow, 'Misogynoir: How social media abuse exposes long-standing prejudices against black women', *New Statesman*, 27 February 2017.

15. Diane Abbott, 'Diane Abbott's powerful speech describing "mindless" online abuse', *The Guardian*, 12 July 2017.

16. 'Manifesto: For the many not the few', *BBC*, www.bbc.co.uk, 11 May 2017, p10.

17. *For the Many Not the Few: The Labour Party Manifesto 2017*, p28.

18. Michael Kazin, 'Trump and American Populism: Old Whine, New Bottles', *Foreign Affairs*, 6 October 2016.

19. Nadine El-Enany, 'Brexit as Nostalgia for Empire', *Critical Legal Thinking*, 19 June 2016.

20. Paul Gilroy, *Postcolonial Melancholia*, Columbia University Press, 2004, pxv.

21. Stuart Hall, 1979, *ibid.*

Lessons from Syriza

Marina Prentoulis

Syriza and Jeremy Corbyn's Labour Party, while different and set in different national contexts, can each be usefully understood as responses to the 2008 financial crisis, and the subsequent questioning of the neoliberal consensus. Most importantly, they each highlight the urgent need to leave behind the neoliberal turn embraced by most social-democratic parties in the 1990s – including Britain's New Labour and Greece's Pasok (Panhellenic Socialist Movement) – and to find a left alternative that is appropriate for the twenty-first century. Both New Labour and Pasok gave in to the governing logic of neoliberalism when they were in power: they moved away from traditional social-democratic measures, glorified individualism and abandoned collectivism; and they embraced laissez faire economics, deregulation and privatisation. But neither party had anything approaching an adequate response to the financial crisis, and this left voters in both countries searching for alternatives.

Any successful alternative to the neoliberal consensus will have to be based on the forging of creative links between grassroots initiatives and new (or transformed) political parties, so that they can work together to win elections and secure transnational alliances. These issues have been, and will be, addressed differently in the Greek and British national contexts. Here I focus on three main areas where a comparison may be useful: the question of how to reconnect politically with 'the people' in a context of post-democracy; the nature of relationships between movements and parties; and the negotiations of each country with the EU.

POST-DEMOCRACY AND THE PEOPLE

After the financial crisis, and as Syriza (alongside Podemos in Spain) began to emerge as the leading political force against the neoliberal consensus in Europe, the term 'Pasokification' gained prominence in European left political discourse.[1] This term referred to the total electoral annihilation of Pasok in Greece after 2010, and came also to signify the wider collapse of other European social-democratic parties. Each country's social-democratic party has a different history, and Pasok is no exception. It is a party that has changed considerably over time – from its promising formation in the 1970s to its later dismal collapse. In the 1980s, the ideological and electoral leadership of Pasok was rooted in a convincing narrative: the party was seen as representing the 'people', and as making a serious attempt to transform and democratise the Greek state. Its success rested on a broad base and the organisational structures of a mass party rooted in the key socio-political movements of the time – which were demanding change and the renewal of Greek democracy. In the years that followed, however, the change Pasok had in mind shifted dramatically: it began to focus on a programme of modernisation and Europeanisation – and these were processes that took a particular form within the Greek context. By the 2000s, fully immersed as it was in electoral politics, and now solidly incorporated into the Greek state and establishment, Pasok became too willing to form alliances and follow policies that had little relationship to the demands of its own social base. And the structure of the party meant that the grassroots had little say in the formulation of policies and programmes, or the selection of electoral candidates. This lack of participatory structures, which led to the marginalisation of the party's membership, played a decisive role in Pasok's dramatic demise.

As a result of this shift away from popular politics, Pasok has effectively been replaced on the left by Syriza, whereas in Britain the party of social democracy is very much still alive, particularly since the 2017 general election. But in spite of these differences, Corbyn's election as Labour leader in 2015 entailed a broadly similar promise to that of Syriza: the renewed party would seek to bring an end to the exclusion of 'the people' from the decision-making process, both at party and national level. The success of both Syriza and Labour under Corbyn's leadership was thus a challenge to what some scholars have described as the post-democratic condition: the growing distance between people and governments, and the transformation of 'politics' so that it has become a domain ruled by governments, political experts and elites, all of whom affirm the same neoliberal consensus.[2]

Labour before Corbyn was on a trajectory of decline similar to that of most European social-democratic parties. Tony Blair had been a cheerleader for the social-democratic variant of neoliberalism, and his period in office was characterised by a strong emphasis on governing with the assistance of marketing and public relations methods. (This was by no means a new departure, but the scale and intensive use of these strategies were certainly new under New Labour.[3]) Blair sought to shape and manage debate both within the party and among the electorate through advisory bodies, focus groups and a well-planned communication strategy. Describing Blairism at its height, in 2000, Norman Fairclough wrote:

> Although New Labour constantly initiates 'great debates' and calls for debate and discussion around its policy initiatives (e.g. welfare reform), it seems in broad terms that it sets out to achieve consent not through political dialogue but through managerial methods of promotion and forms of consultation of public opinion (e.g. focus groups) which it can control. The government tends to act like a corporation, treating the public as its consumers rather than its citizens.[4]

Under Blair's leadership, the distance between the grassroots of the party and the leadership became very wide, the party machine was centralised, and marketing became the preferred form of communication with the electorate. Corbynism reflects members' desire to move away from this approach – and instead to close the distance between people and decision-making and shift away from neoliberalism.

Syriza was the answer to a similar demand, though in the first instance at national not party level. The effect of the financial crisis on Greece had been much more severe than in Britain, since the economy was seriously indebted and thus more exposed to the disaster created by global financial markets. In 2010, the then Pasok prime minister George Papandreou announced that, in order to avoid bankruptcy, Greece would become subject to the lending mechanisms of the Troika made up of the European Commission, the European Central Bank and the International Monetary Fund. The series of 'bailouts' that then followed, carried with them catastrophic lending agreements that imposed privatisation, severe austerity measures and threatened labour rights, while still allowing public debt to spiral out of control. The initial announcement of these measures in 2010 came as a shock to a substantial section of the public, who up to that point had been more or less oblivious of the severity of the situation.

The Greek people felt betrayed by Pasok as well as by New Democracy, the party of the right (both parties were in agreement about accepting and implementing the lending agreement-memorandum). They therefore turned to Syriza because of its promise to bring the demands and the grievances of the Greek people back into the decision-making centres. In 2013, at its Founding Congress as a party, Syriza stated that:

> In order to be implemented, this platform needs the active intervention of an already existing mass and militant socio-political movement of democratic subversion. A government of the left cannot prevent destruction and give a popular solution to the problems without the synergy and availability of the Greek people, without the determination of the social majority to support this radical change – politically, socially, and productively – so that the country can take a new path. For this reason, Syriza firmly aims to share the above programmatic goals with the vast majority of the Greek people. For this reason, we have been holding events in workplaces, in the Parliament, in neighbourhoods and big towns, where specific programmatic proposals on specific issues were presented for public consultation and discussion.[5]

The attempt to bring the people back into politics in Greece (and in Spain with Podemos) could broadly be described as a 'populist' left intervention, in that it attempted to bring diverse grievances together and construct a 'people' that would stand up against the established neoliberal consensus. Something similar is at play with Corbynism. Especially after the encouraging results of the 2017 general election, it has become clear that Jeremy Corbyn is fast becoming the signifier under which diverse groups of people – from liberal, cosmopolitan big-city communities to traditional northern heartland Labour constituencies – are able to express their grievances after seven years of austerity.

There is, however, a significant difference between Corbynism and Syriza (at least Syriza before it came into government), namely the way in which they understand the relationship between party, building alliances and grassroots activity. Syriza was founded when a range of groups to the left of the mainstream social-democratic tradition came together, many of them having a strong commitment to the idea of constructing a politics that connected parties to movements (movements that many of Syriza's activists had been part of). The group around Corbyn, on the other hand, although they represent a clear break with neoliberalism, have over a very long period of time accommodated themselves not only to the culture and milieu of the Labour Party but to a particular 'hard left' tendency within the Labour Party, which seems more comfortable with vanguardist forms of socialist orthodoxy: they do not actively seek alliances, and they have little interest in, and experience of social movements. There are precious few examples where Labour, even under Corbyn, has initiated any kind of broadening of Labour Party practice.

MOVEMENTS AND PARTIES

Stuart Hall, writing in 1979 on the challenges facing Labourism *vis-à-vis* Thatcherism, noted that many on the left operated with a simplistic assumption that 'economic factors will be immediately and transparently translated to the political and ideological levels'.[6] And he argued that, as a result, the left was in danger of neglecting the themes and representations that would shape the ways in which an economic crisis would be perceived. The accuracy of this analysis was only too well illustrated by Labour's years in the desert between 1979 and 1997.

The danger now is that the Labour result in the 2017 election will once more reinforce Labour's economism. After seven years of austerity, and with public services at breaking point, the social-democratic manifesto of Corbyn's leadership – pledging support for welfare provision and a reversal of some elements of privatisation – has finally offered an inspiring and hopeful prospect for the future, which is of course to be welcomed. The Thessaloniki programme adopted by Syriza in 2014, which eventually brought Syriza to power, was not dissimilar to Labour's 2017 manifesto (though, of course, Syriza despite being in office has been prevented from implementing its programme and stopping austerity). Labour in office would not be subject to the same pressures as the Syriza government, but there would be a massive press campaign against a Corbyn-led government, and it is not clear whether it has a strong enough narrative to win support for its economic measures.

Syriza depended for its initial success on a radical break between the Greek people and the Greek political establishment (as represented by Pasok and New Democracy). It started gaining support only when the bonds that connected people to the political establishment and the parties that represented it had been loosened. It is often protest movements that announce such a dislocation, and this was the case with the movements of 2011 in Greece (and Spain). The protests were the visible manifestation of the discontent of the people, and in some ways can be seen as the first 'populist' struggles to emerge after the financial crisis: they engaged diverse groups of people in acts of resistance, and galvanised people's aspirations for change. These protests went much further than simply registering dissatisfaction with the political establishment that had subjected them to an agreement that was leading to the collapse of the social fabric of Greece: the multiple acts of resistance and social experimentation associated with the demands of the protesters – particularly the creation of solidarity networks – created an economic, political and social repertoire that was available for subsequent attempts to implement change at the local and national institutional levels, and potentially at the transnational level.

Syriza's narrative was heavily shaped by the broad alliance that came together in these protest movements. It was largely based on groups from political traditions that recognised the importance of linking movements and parties. The largest party in the Syriza coalition that was set up in in 2004, Synaspismos (SYN, the Coalition of Left, Movements and Ecology), was already strongly orientated towards creating links with the movements. For SYN, the role of the left was 'not to guide but to participate in movements and try to influence them, while learning from them'.[7]

In Britain, Labourism has traditionally been seen as representing a particular constellation of social forces, and its aim from its inception was defined as the political representation of the working class. Although this is a mission it has often failed to live up to, especially during the Blair years, it retains strong links with the trade unions. Yet it is less close to civil society movements of other kinds.

No radical movement similar to the Greek and Spanish Indignados materialised in Britain after the financial crisis. Such anti-establishment sentiments were expressed – most obviously in the riots of 2011 and, in a very different register, the Occupy movement – but had little success in effecting change either in the Labour Party or the wider spectrum of civil society.

The riots of August 2011 were set in motion by the police shooting of 29-year-old Mark Duggan in Tottenham. The looting and violence, in the absence of any clear demands, obscured the root causes of these events, and the anger accumulated by communities that had for decades been victimised and excluded from the benefits of globalisation. But the riots revealed the huge divisions that existed within the metropolitan space; and the widespread failure to recognise their political significance only served to further underline the marginalisation of those involved.

The case of Occupy London was very different, in that it was part of a global reaction to the financial crisis and it had a clear anti-establishment character. But although Occupy did signal a wider dissatisfaction with the socio-economic system after the crisis, and to some extent enriched grassroots activity and the political repertoire of a new generation of activists, its demands did not manage to connect with the wider grievances in British society, and at the time attracted little interest from the Labour Party.

Since then, multiple single-issue campaigns – in particular in defence of the NHS and in the various anti-cuts campaigns – have fought against austerity in Britain, but until 2015 none found an adequate expression via party politics. This has only occurred since Jeremy Corbyn's election as Labour leader.

The break made by the Labour Party in voting for Jeremy Corbyn is not a break with the political establishment as such, but with the direction that social-democratic parties have been taking over the past twenty years, in accepting the premises of neoliberalism. Both Syriza (if it had not been forced by Troika to do otherwise) and a Corbyn-led Labour Party are capable of managing the economic crisis in an egalitarian and just manner. The objective, however, should not only be one of management: what is required is a deeper change in society, which can only be achieved by putting together a new historic bloc of forces, and by understanding that this cannot be based on a simplistic politics of class reductionism. What is needed is not simply a desirable electoral outcome – welcome though that may be – but a challenge to the whole neoliberal narrative.

This is the issue that Corbyn's Labour Party still has to reflect upon – and this has become even more urgent after the 2017 election breakthrough. And it is all the more vital given that any possible future Labour government will face difficulties in implementing its programme, given that it is likely to take office in the midst of a recession brought about by the Brexit negotiations. And if Labour should find itself forming a government before these negotiations are concluded, it will have to be able to intervene in the divisions that have emerged from the Brexit referendum – divisions that cut across classes, as well as divisions within classes.

SYRIZA, LABOUR AND THE EUROPEAN UNION

One of the common challenges facing Syriza and Labour, and one they will continue to face in the years to come, is their relationship with the European Union. Syriza's continuing difficulties with the Troika, and the unresolved challenge it faces in dealing with an unsustainable and continually increasing debt, have brought Greek society to its knees, and inaugurated a period of widespread political cynicism and fatigue. The political euphoria after the results of the Greek bailout referendum in July 2015, when the agreement was rejected by 61 per cent of voters, came to an end after the Syriza-ANEL government was forced into signing another bailout agreement, which is due to end in June 2018. But this did not turn Syriza into an anti-European party. Throughout the negotiations, Syriza continued to valiantly maintain that the issues in dispute were not technical economic questions, but were a political matter, thereby implicitly questioning the dominance of technocratic expertise within EU institutions and the Eurozone, as well as the neoliberal logic embedded in this dominance.[8] The demand put forward by the Greek government for a 'political solution' was rejected time and time again, on the grounds of the 'rules' of the EU and the soundness of neoliberal economics. As German finance minister Wolfgange Schäuble put it: 'Athens can vote as many times as it likes in favour of a deal that promises, even in the vaguest terms, to write off some of its colossal debts, but that doesn't mean the rules allow it'.[9]

These negotiations revealed in the most striking way across Europe and beyond that the central EU institutions are dominated by neoliberal ideas, have little consideration for the people of Europe, and have no appetite for relinquishing any of their power in an effort to solve a crisis that had been caused by the structural deficiencies of the Eurozone. They also testified to the severe weakening by neoliberalism of any vision of 'social Europe', not least because of the close causal correlation between the intransigence of the Troika and the wider post-democratic condition. 'Politics' has become little more than a game that is played out between elected governments and elites, who work together towards the maximisation of business interests through structural reforms enabling market competitiveness.[10] It came as no surprise, therefore, that every Eurosceptic group in Britain advocating Brexit (including those within the Labour Party) made extensive use of the Greek case as a justification for returning back to what they imagined to be 'national sovereignty'.

A key factor in the popularity among a large part of the British public of arguments against membership of both the EU and the Eurozone (although Brexiters seem to forget they were not members of that club) was that Europe seemed far too much focused on rules – rules that were not only unknown to the public, but were also unable to offer solutions to EU challenges, from the financial crisis to the refugee crisis. Invoking the 'democratic deficit' of the EU became a well-rehearsed catchphrase, leading nicely to the promise of 'taking back control', especially during the referendum campaign.

The problem with this position is that it fails to recognise that post-democracy is not a phenomenon that exists only in 'Europe'. There is no evidence to suggest that individual countries have somehow escaped its grip. And this view is also based on an extremely simplistic – and voluntaristic – definition of sovereignty. As has become abundantly clear since the referendum vote in Britain, simply ceasing to belong to a specific institution cannot insulate any country from the forces of global capital. In many ways, to focus on an undifferentiated 'Europe', rather than the specific political balance of forces within the EU, is precisely to subscribe to a post-democracy view of the world. What Syriza needed during its negotiations was political allies supporting its position. The reason this was not forthcoming was that the right form the political majority within EU institutions, and the social-democratic parties in any case did not want to support a party that could challenge their own subordination to neoliberal precepts. In other words, the negotiations were a political battle which Syriza lost. The solution for this for Syriza has been to seek new ways of conducting the battle within Europe and building better alliances, not to withdraw from the regional political arena.

Unfortunately, the Corbyn leadership has not managed so far to make any strategic challenge to the dominant political discourses in British politics around Europe. Labour, when it hasn't been divided on the issue, has largely restricted itself to a role on the sidelines during debates on Brexit. This is partly because Brexit realigned British politics along a division between those who voted to leave the EU and those who voted to remain, and it divides both the Conservatives and

Labour down the middle over Brexit. And although the June 2017 general election can be read as a second major expression of national dissent, of a qualitatively different kind, its implications for the politics of Brexit remain unclear.

Both before and after the 2017 election, the Conservatives have continued to define the political terrain around Brexit. The argument over the terms of any future Brexit deal has largely been between different Tory factions, or from within the business community. Labour remains apparently comfortable to go along with Brexit as long as it can promise a social-democratic national outcome after the event. This waiting game has the benefit of not rocking the boat too much for either Labour's remain or leave supporters – or so it is hoped.

The danger is that the Labour leadership appears to be lagging behind popular opinion rather than helping to shape it. Enlightened political leadership – not in the sense of capitulating and giving the public 'what it wants', but, rather, of enabling the public to break free from the currently dominant 'common sense' that is framing debate – requires the ability to foresee and help shape such shifts. Rather than a simple focus on adapting to current public opinion (which is always problematic but is particularly so at times of rapid change), efforts need to be made to influence the development of public opinion in the future. A popular left leadership needs to be able to galvanise the people in support of a more equal, more democratic and more open society.

If it at some point a Labour government should become the driving force of the Brexit negotiations, the weakness of its position on leaving the single market while simultaneously retaining tariff-free access to that market will be revealed to be distinctly lacking. It is clear that there will come a point when Labour will have to have to rethink its position on the contradictions that emerged with the Brexit vote, and find a way to redefine what is the best direction for the country – taking into account that the constituency supporting a retention of free movement and transnational connectivity (economic, political/and or cultural) is cut across by class divides, but not being immobilised by these divisions to the extent that it becomes incapable of strategic leadership.

FROM MOVEMENTS TO CULTURE

In Greece (at least until its second electoral victory in September 2015), the anti-establishment, anti-memoranda discourse of Syriza managed to define the battle-lines of division in Greek society as being between political forces supporting the memoranda and those against. This was a matter not only of offering an economic programme, but also of understanding the cultural terrain on which politics takes place.

The concepts of 'culture' and 'identity politics' have for a long time been taken by some parts of the left as signifying a deviation from class struggle and a distraction from the all-healing power of egalitarian economic policies.[11] But without any understanding of this field of politics, political leadership will struggle to connect with electors, let alone to construct a successful popular alliance that goes beyond the instrumentality of elections. The question of identity and culture is always present, defining who 'we' are and who the 'others' are. Many of the younger voters who supported Labour in their hundreds of thousands at the 2017 election think of themselves as Europeans. They are passionate supporters of a better, egalitarian economic future, but are equally passionate about feminism, cosmopolitanism, the rights of ethnic minorities and the LGBT community, and desire collective responses to the global challenges their generation faces.

Jeremy Corbyn's proposals for averting a 'bargain basement Brexit' and making sure that any Great Repeal Bill is not used to undermine worker protection, are solely grounded in Labour's by-now well-known economic programme: limiting the operation of the market, setting up a national investment bank, increasing public capital spending, investment in infrastructure and so on.[12] But there is little evidence to suggest that this economic programme, no matter how sound it is, will, on its own, be enough to give Labour a sufficient lead to win outright the next election, especially as long as Brexit is looming.

The overwhelming problem for Labour is that the Corbyn leadership remains trapped in a universe where economic and politics do not meet, and its solutions for twenty-first century challenges are still tailored around the left canon of the twentieth century.

Theresa May's attempt to invoke a collective identity with the term 'Global Britain' goes beyond economics, to a sense of a collective 'we', but it is likely to prove unsustainable during the Brexit negotiations. When this endeavour fails, Labour needs to be in a position where it can put forward its own collective vision, both for the country as a whole and for its international relationships, and one that goes beyond merely the economic. This will offer Corbyn a route not only to office, but to power.

NOTES

1. See James Doran, 'Liquidating Labour', www.novaramedia.com, 13 September 2013.
2. See Colin Crouch, *Coping with Post-Democracy*, Fabian Society, 2000.
3. Norman Fairclough, *New Labour, New Language,* Routledge: London and New York, 2000, pvii.
4. *Ibid.*, p12.
5. This congress founded Syriza as a party rather than, as previously, a coalition. The quote is from the Political Resolution that was adopted.
6. Stuart Hall, *Selected Political Writings: The Great Moving Right Show and Other Essays*, Lawrence & Wishart: London, 2017, p173.
7. Myrto Tsakatika and Costas Eleftheriou, 'The radical left's turn towards civil society in Greece: One strategy, two paths', *South European Society and Politics*, Vol. 18 No. 1, 2013, p93.
8. The Greek prime minister Alexis Tsipras characterised the negotiations in his speech of 11 July 2015 as 'an ideological and political battle'.
9. Phillip Inman, 'Greece's debt can be written off – whatever Wolfgang Schäuble says', *The Guardian*, 17 July 2015.
10. See Colin Crouch, *Post-Democracy*, Polity Press: Cambridge, 2004.
11. Lasse Thomassen, 'Identity politics: Everybody does it (and it's ok too)', www.opendemocracy.net, 1 April 2017.
12. Jeremy Corbyn, 'There is an alternative to bargain basement Brexit', *Yorkshire Post*, 29 March 2017.

More for the Many, Less for the Few

Jo Littler

Neoliberal meritocracy presents us with a landscape in which everyone can have the opportunity to climb the ladder of success, if they just put in enough effort to activate their talent. Meritocratic discourse has been used in the service of capitalism for a very long time, but it has been very energetically re-invigorated and revitalised over the past few decades in British politics, in order to provide a persuasive alibi for the expanding wealth and privilege of plutocratic elites and the widening chasm between rich and poor. You don't need redistribution, runs this argument, because everyone, individually, has the opportunity to succeed if only they work hard enough.

Corbynism has offered a significant and tangible challenge to this ideology, and this challenge that has been key to the movement's success thus far. It has involved a dramatic departure from the endorsement of the neoliberal policies that have dominated the previous three decades of Labour and mainstream UK politics. The continual marketisation of the public sector is, at least at the moment, off the Labour Party's official agenda. Neoliberal financialisation and the economic growth of CEO income is no longer implicitly perceived to be intimately connected to social progress. And crucially, Corbynism invokes a politics aimed at redistributing wealth, at lessening inequalities: of providing more for the many and less for the few.

WHAT MERITOCRACY IS AND HOW IT HAS BEEN USED

Today, 'meritocracy' is generally taken to entail the idea that anyone, if they work hard enough, can activate their talent and climb the ladder of social success. It is a powerful discourse which appeals to democratic sentiments, because it appears to emphasise 'fairness' as opposed to the vested interests of a privileged elite (which of course would be, in itself, a very good thing). Meritocracy's mantra of 'equality of opportunity' also speaks to the idea of extending yourself, of personal growth and flourishing, of being able to move beyond where you started in life (also very good things, in theory). We can trace both of these aspects of the ideology of meritocracy back through many different histories and geographies: whether to the French Revolution's idea of the 'free space for all talents', for example, or open entrance exams in the UK civil service.[1]

However, meritocracy has also been, and is increasingly, used to endorse extreme income differentials. The emphasis on talent, flourishing and overcoming difficulties is stressed, while the problems and severe difficulties that come with inequality are downplayed or ignored. This has occurred in lots of different settings: we might consider how the contemporary Singaporean higher education system urges its subjects to work harder to achieve upward social mobility whilst downplaying the problems of the less wealthy, or how narratives of the American Dream have often focused on those consuming their way to an upward social trajectory rather than those stuck at the bottom.[2]

These are all different examples of meritocratic discourse. The idea was expressed before the word came into being in English, but the first recorded use of the term is by the British sociologist Alan Fox, who wrote about trade unions and industrial sociology.[3] In an article in *Socialist Commentary*, a journal which was at that time a more radical version of the *New Statesman*, Fox used the word 'meritocracy' in a completely critical, negative way.[4] Why would you want to give 'a fat bonus' to people who already have so many 'natural endowments'? he asked. That vision, which belongs to 'a certain brand of New Conservatism' will just exacerbate a 'grotesque paradox', will create divisions between the 'blessed and the unblessed', and make for a miserable society. Instead, he argued we should think about how to share our time and money more equitably to produce a happier society. Fox's vision didn't involve everyone doing the same occupation, or abolishing entry criteria for being a doctor, but it did suggest that financial and social rewards should be more evenly distributed, and that those doing uninteresting manual work, for example, should be paid decently and have more leisure time through what he called 'cross-grading'.[5]

The negative value of meritocracy was also assumed in the 1950s by the philosopher Hannah Arendt. In an essay reflecting on 'The Crisis in Education', based on a lecture given in Germany and aiming at a wider audience through its US publication in 1958, she was scathing in her criticism of the British introduction and extension of the grammar school system as an extreme form of educational and social segregation. 'What is aimed at in England is "meritocracy"', she wrote, and 'meritocracy contradicts the principle of equality, of an equalitarian democracy, no less than any other oligarchy'.[6] In the same year, the British social democratic polymath Michael Young, who was involved in setting up a range of inventive progressive initiatives including the Consumers' Association and the Open University, as well as writing Labour's 1945 manifesto, published a gently satirical bestseller called *The Rise of the Meritocracy*.[7] The first half depicted the extension of the democratic franchise in the UK to the (then) present day; the latter half depicted a fictional dystopia with a roaring trade in black-market brainy babies.

But by 1972, Young's friend the American sociologist Daniel Bell suggested that meritocracy could perhaps be used in a more positive fashion, as an engine of the knowledge economy, where money could be generated from ideas.[8] Then, by the early 1980s, it was being used by a range of right-wing think tanks in a wholly celebratory fashion, as a progressive state to aspire to, in tandem with cutting public services (and in some cases to argue for abandoning comprehensive education altogether).

It is no accident that this complete *volte-face* in the perceived value of meritocracy – from term of slander to wholly positive word – occurred during the exacerbation of neoliberal culture from the 1970s. Neoliberalism, and neoliberal meritocracy, involved seismic shifts which were produced through multiple, interconnected realms: through think tanks, through parliamentary politics, through changing economic policies, through mutating the sense of what was normal, possible and desirable in everyday discourse and popular culture. Slashing public funding for socialised forms of provision, and marketising public services, neoliberalism encourages us to believe that we are above all individuals who need to be in a permanent state of competition with each other in order to achieve. In the west or the global north since the 1970s, we have been increasingly incited to position ourselves as independent strivers who brand and promote ourselves, our worth gained not through sharing but through striving to beat others.

Neoliberal meritocracy is therefore characterised firstly by the extension of such individualised forms of competition into everyday life. We have been encouraged to 'free ourselves' by becoming entrepreneurial in every aspect of our being, from our expressive portfolio of career ambitions to our energy requirements and children's choice of schools. Secondly, it has drawn, highly selectively, on the anti-racist, anti-sexist, anti-homophobic social liberation movements of the 1960s and 1970s for its lifeblood. We are told: no matter where we are from, it's up to us. Anyone can make it now! Meanwhile, the ladders that we are encouraged to climb individually get longer and longer, making it much harder for those who cannot draw on existing resources of privilege to climb them, whilst they are simultaneously blamed for their own failure.

MERITOCRACY IN BRITISH POLITICAL DISCOURSE

In the later part of the twentieth century, at the beginning of the time we now think of as 'neoliberal', the idea that social mobility and 'equality of opportunity' should combine with the erosion of some manifestations of vested privilege was promoted by political leaders. Most notoriously, it was given an almighty push under Margaret Thatcher, who sold off key chunks of the Welfare State's family silver (including its telecommunications, gas industry and much of its social housing). Being able to rise up and buy your own individual car and house (rather than be in council housing or use buses) and make lots of money was the motif of the era which birthed the figure of the yuppie and the working-class financial trader in the City. The subsequent prime minister John Major – less plummy in tone than Thatcher and never having been to university, let alone Oxbridge – was slightly more convincing as the subsequent prime ministerial persona peddling a similar discourse.

When New Labour swept to power in 1997, they kept the narrative of a land of equality of opportunity – using the 'm' word with regularity – but widened this idea out in terms of ethnicity, class and sexuality. Now anyone could make it, so the story went, gay or straight, brown or white. The selective and significant provision New Labour made via Sure Start (support for parents and children in deprived areas) and in tackling child poverty was far more progressive than the Conservative governments, and yet it continued the idea that, after the early years, savage individualistic competition was both fair enough and the correct way to run a society. As part of this ideology, shared by the Clintons in the US, New Labour pushed through reforms shredding social provisions by putting them in the hands of corporations, instigating the private finance initiative (PFI) and the public-private partnerships (PPP) that handed a huge amount of power to private business interests and allowed them to profit from prisons and education.

David Cameron perpetuated neoliberal meritocracy but made it more punitive. In the 'Aspiration Nation' it was your own fault if you failed, no matter the privileges that led to such an uneven starting block in the first place. Under the Conservative-Liberal Democrat coalition government even Labour's early years' provision was cut and the privatisations continued apace in, for example, libraries, hospitals and housing. But the increasingly jarring disjunction between the obviously privileged 'chumocracy' of Cameron's privately-educated and often aristocratic cabinet and the 'necessary' cuts of austerity politics increasingly didn't wash with large sections of the population. The 99 per cent were experiencing deprivation and less 'opportunity' on a range of scales, even if many weren't exactly sure who to blame (Brussels? Red tape? Tories? Labour's deficit? Migrants?). This free-floating disillusion in search of a target fed into the Brexit vote ('we'll teach the political class a lesson'), confounding Cameron's expectations and leading to his downfall and the reign of Theresa May. At the beginning of her term, Theresa May promised to level the playing field, giving a first speech promising to release the poor, the non-white, the oppressed women from injustice: 'When it comes to opportunity we won't entrench the advantages of the fortunate few, we will do everything we can to help anybody, whatever your background, to go as far as your talents will take you'.[9] This was a rhetoric of meritocratic equality of opportunity worthy of Blair. But as time wore on it increasingly jarred, for large sections of the public, with the effects of May and chancellor Philip Hammond's actually-existing policies, such as an increasing number of people using food banks, and the manifesto commitment to a 'dementia tax'. This did not sound like levelling the playing field, so much as those who couldn't pay being pushed off it altogether. It is within this context that we need to understand Corbynism's significant success in challenging neoliberal meritocracy.

NEOLIBERAL MERITOCRACY AS COMMON SENSE

The traffic between Westminster politics and popular culture simultaneously takes the form of explicit links between powerful figures and policies, and the more diffuse, less empirically graspable but critically important form of cultural discourse through which ideas of what is 'normal' and 'common sense' circulate. Neoliberal meritocracy, for example, can be seen operating through very particular policies: by, for instance, extending the process of marketising public services by facilitating and encouraging PFI and PPI in the public sector, or introducing 'the bedroom tax' which slashed housing benefit. It also functions through particular appointments, such as telegenic businessman Alan Sugar being installed as first New Labour's, and later the Conservatives', Enterprise Tsar (appointments which also indicate the imbrication of culture and politics, of celebrity and political capital).

The scale and depth of neoliberal meritocracy as 'common sense' in British politics and cultural life is immense. We only have to look at the extent to which, for example, entrepreneurialism has become embedded as an unproblematic and normalised aspirational ideal in education and popular culture. Children are now regularly encouraged at school to be entrepreneurs; they do not very often learn, however, about how to set up co-ops. Newspapers and magazines regularly encourage mothers to be 'mumpreneurs': to solve the problems of inflexible working conditions, an overwork culture and expensive privatised childcare by setting up their own business from home, whilst their child crawls beneath it (the *Daily Mail* offers prizes for the 'Mumpreneur of the Year'). It is no accident that Donald Trump, who translated his media power into political power by fusing it with his vast personal wealth, was the US presenter of the vastly successful TV franchise *The Apprentice*. Encouraging us to laugh at the foibles of contestants, to feel our own superiority, *The Apprentice* popularised the act of competing in a wide range of thrusting business cultures as a glamorous and normal act that anyone could aspire to. It surfed a wider wave of competitive reality TV shows including *X-Factor* and *The Voice*, which dramatise 'meritocratic' competition that anyone could compete in and potentially win.[10]

Entrepreneurialism is popular because it speaks so powerfully to multiple issues: the inflexibility of many modern working cultures, the possibilities of self-realisation, and the possibility of financial success in a precarious and highly stratified world. But it channels such desires through competitive individualism, economic growth and the search for private profit, rather than through co-operation, and inventing new forms of diverse, non-authoritarian forms of social protection (or 'socialism'). These multifaceted imbricated relations of power means that changing neoliberal meritocracy also needs to be tackled on a number of levels: in terms of policy, practitioners and popular common sense.

ASPIRATION FOR ALL

How does Corbynism promise to break with the discourse and social structure of neoliberal meritocracy? Clearly, the 2017 Labour Party manifesto *For the Many, Not the Few* promises forms of social demo-cratic redistribution from an earlier Keynesian moment. Student fees are to be abolished, key functions are to be re-nationalised, privatisa-tion in the public sector is to be radically scaled back and ultimately ended.[11]

The vocabulary and imaginary of Corbynism moves beyond and against neoliberal meritocracy. This is apparent in a recurrent idea popularised early in his term: aspiration for all. 'The most impor-tant message my election offers', Jeremy Corbyn stated after becoming leader, 'is that the party is now unequivocally on (your) side. We understand aspiration and we understand that it is only collectively that our aspirations can be realised'.[12]

Aspiration was, as we have seen, a key term of Cameronism (who made frequent references to Britain being an 'Aspiration Nation') and it was also a key word used in 2016 by the more Blairite candidates for Labour leadership, particularly Liz Kendall.[13] It is a very good example of how a core neoliberal word – aspiration – has been taken up by Corbynism and re-articulated: for 'all' rather than the individual, or, as the election slogan put it, 'for the many, not the few'. Whereas Cameron and Kendall used aspiration to advocate 'equality of oppor-tunity' in the form of individualisation and privatisation, Corbynite 'aspiration for all' involves the public ownership of schools, strength-ening teachers' trade union representation, strengthening workers' rights, and collective success. This work of re-articulating 'merito-cratic feeling' away from individualism and into mutuality has been a key part of Corbynism's successful politics.

Post-election, the right and centre wings of the Parliamentary Labour Party were shocked into silence by a result far better than their doomsaying predicted. It is very noticeable that a recurrent area of criticism from those on the centre or right of Labour is that the manifesto pledges didn't connect enough to working-class poverty, particularly in terms of early years provision, and that the manifesto pledges were either erroneous or grievous mistakes.[14] The accusation that the promise to abolish student fees would be an unfair burden on the working class is regularly made by some centre-left MPs, for example, and a recent editorial by the Blairite faction of the Labour Party, Progress, described the manifesto's pledges disparagingly as 'bungs' (bribes).[15]

These are interesting charges on a number of levels. They are often noticeably middle-class responses to radical, universalist policies, and this anxiety about the working classes can thus ring hollow. These charges can ignore the importance of the party's appeal to the students, and ignore the reports that there were levels of co-ordination among students to mobilise their vote which hadn't been seen for years, and queuing round the block at polling stations near universities. These criticisms are also indicative of a technocratic blindness to the difficulty of cutting through an overwhelmingly right-wing media, and the power of having bold left redistributive policies in order to do so – a strategy which worked extremely well for the Corbynites. It is right to want more for early years; it is right to raise the issue of addressing the cut in tax credits and universal credits; but this regularly ignores the radical effects of socialised redistribution and how the manifesto also factors in, foregrounds and fully costs a boost for early years and Sure Start provision.

The reason why many on Labour's right wing are obsessed by early years provision for children's learning, development and care, is not simply because the early years are important. They undeniably are. But so are middle years and later years. This particular constituency are perpetually focused on early years because the idea of levelling the playing field at the outset of life, and then letting people suffer at the mercy of marketisation for the rest of it, is not only fully compatible with, but is the central tenet, of neoliberal meritocracy. The problem with this is firstly that it is naïve. Creating an oasis of social welfare safety blankets for babies and toddlers whilst letting corporations make a profit out of education and healthcare everywhere else in the social system becomes increasingly difficult as corporations become more powerful. Secondly, this approach individualises and abandons people later on in their lives. We need to have forms of democratic, participatory, diverse, accountable and socialised provision for schoolchildren, for students, for the old, for the disabled, for everyone who needs housing, clean food and drinking water. The Blairite fixation on looking after the children and then creating a fully marketised adult experience where we are individually responsible for our own success simply does not work: to see this we only have to look at Grenfell, at food banks, at the stratospheric scale of personal and household debt.

Corbynism is promising a profound break with neoliberal meritocracy simply by putting socialism across the life course back on the table, and it needs to build on this in a number of ways. Central to neoliberal meritocracy is the idea of competitive individualism and social mobility. Labour needs to foreground and expose the sheer destruction wrought by competitive individualism and its status as a total fallacy. We are all different individuals who are connected to each other in a range of complicated ways: no person is an island; nobody comes into the world completely on their own.[16] At the same time, is it crucial that any critique of individualism is combined with non-authoritarianism, with the idea of flourishing and diversity. Combining messages, politics and policies of mutualism with diversity is critical.

Neoliberal meritocratic language harnesses the idea of equality of opportunity. This formulation has historically been pitted against 'equality of outcome' – the idea of economic redistribution promised by the left. There are two key problems here. The first is that 'equality of outcome', on a rhetorical level, simply does not speak to an everyday sense of wanting to grow and flourish, to extend yourself, to move beyond where you came from. The second is that, whilst 'equality of opportunity' sounds good, it is always used to savage any forms of mutualism, the welfare state and social safety nets. Corbynism therefore needs to combine rhetoric, policy and strategies of redistributing wealth and mutual support with *diversity*, with the sense that people and the environment can be enabled to flourish in a range of ways.

How to do this is, at one level, about the simultaneously strategic and genuine use of rhetoric and image. Ken Loach's general election party political broadcast for Labour, for instance, depicted a wide diversity of Britons existing in a wide range of habitats, and was one powerful example of how this can be done. Foregrounding a more diverse and complex society pushes socialism beyond the authoritarian imaginary, which is what critics are often gesturing towards when they present Corbynism as 'backward-looking'. There are newer experiments in participatory democracy, as well as many longstanding traditions that Corbynism can draw on to this end. They include support for, and the generation of, workers' co-operatives, where the means of production are owned by the workers. (These are not to be confused with the more ambiguous forms of co-operativism that are outside the orbit of workers' control, as Marisol Sandoval points out, of which the Co-operative Bank has become a depressing example.)[17] The work of political economist Robin Murray gives us many guides here, not least on how co-operatives can function in 'Age of Google' when there is a huge potential for synchronising the work of co-operatives and internet platforms.[18] This all entails moving towards a left politics that is very much of the future and is fashioning a twenty-first century socialism.[19]

The forms of co-production encouraged by think-and-do tanks like Compass, in terms of, for instance, how you might have comprehensive schools with greater levels of parental engagement, is also a powerful example here – a long way from the destructive segmented markets of faith, 'free' and grammar schools.[20] Making public libraries centres for community activity, rather than closing them down or selling them to corporations is another example, as is developing the proposals for Universal Basic Income.[21]

Another more controversial means of democratic flourishing exists in relation to Europe. Debates over Brexit obviously constitute a zone which is profoundly overdetermined with meanings, politics and feelings. One of the motivations of those who oppose Brexit is an often fairly vague sense of cosmopolitanism: of simply wanting to be 'part of' Europe, of belonging beyond Little Britain, beyond the nation. Whilst Brexit is 'about' the European Union, with all of that institution's neoliberal power, it is also 'about' people's movement and interconnections and their sense of themselves as part of a larger social geography. It makes sense not to alienate metropolitan cosmopolitans over Brexit, for this cosmopolitanism is progressive; it needs to be connected to and fused with democratic anti-neoliberal socialism. And moving towards more equality necessarily has to involve changing the disproportionate system of voting in our country and moving to the more proportionate electoral system of PR.

Such forms of radical participation, then, combined with the more Keynesian, mid-century policies that Corbynism currently offers

– such as scaling back corporate power in media and banking and nationalizing key industries – has the potential to further enthuse and energise those who need it most. To survive in this new century we do not need cut-throat individuals who want to step on other people's hands whilst they move up the social ladder of an imaginary 'meritocracy', but instead to use and invent ways of sharing the wealth and cultivating social, cultural and environmental diversity. The opposite of neoliberal meritocracy, promising significant forms of wealth redistribution, gives Corbynism immense potential; emphasising diversity, and radical forms of participation, promises to extend it.

NOTES

1. This chapter draws on and summarises some of the work produced in my book: Jo Littler, *Against Meritocracy: Culture, Power and Myths of Mobility*, Routledge: London, 2017.
2. Nadira Talib and Richard Fitzgerald, 'Inequality as meritocracy: The use of the metaphor of diversity and the value of inequality within Singapore's meritocratic education system', *Critical Discourse Studies*, Vol. 12 No. 4, 2015, pp445-462.
3. This is the first use identified so far; I think there will be earlier instances awaiting discovery by a diligent historian.
4. Alan Fox, 'Class and equality', *Socialist Commentary*, May 1956, pp11-13; for context see David Kynaston, *Modernity Britain: Opening the Box, 1957-59*, Bloomsbury: London, 2013.
5. Fox, *ibid*.
6. Hannah Arendt, 'The crisis in education' in *Partisan Review*, Vol. 25 No. 4, 1958, pp493-513; reproduced in Hannah Arendt, *Between Past and Future: Eight Exercises in Political Thought*, Penguin Books: London, 2006, pp176-7.
7. Michael Young, *The Rise of the Meritocracy*, second revised edition, Transaction Publishers: Piscataway, 2004.
8. Daniel Bell, *The Coming of Post-Industrial Society: A Venture in Social Forecasting*, Basic Books: New York, 1972.
9. Theresa May, 'Theresa May's first speech to the nation as Prime Minister – in full', www.independent.co.uk, 13 July 2016.
10. Nick Couldry and Jo Littler, 'Work, power and performance: Analysing the "reality" game of *The Apprentice*', *Cultural Sociology*, Vol. 5 No. 2, 2011, pp263-279.
11. *For the Many, Not the Few: The Labour Party Manifesto 2017*.
12. Jeremy Corbyn, 'Britain can't cut its way to prosperity. We have to build it', *The Guardian*, 13 September 2015.

13. Jeremy Gilbert, 'What hope for Labour and the left? The election, the 80s and "aspiration"', www.opendemocracy.net, 27 July 2015.

14. Andrew Harrop, 'Labour must return to first principles on child poverty', *The Guardian*, 13 July 2017.

15. Progress Editorial, 'A new establishment', www.progressonline.org.uk, 7 July 2017.

16. Jeremy Gilbert, *Common Ground: Democracy and Collectivity in an Age of Individualism,* Pluto Press: London, 2013.

17. Marisol Sandoval, 'What would Rosa do? Co-operatives and radical politics', *Soundings*, Vol. 63, 2016, pp98-111.

18. Robin Murray, *Co-operation in the Age of Google*, Co-operatives UK, 2010; Robin Murray, 'Post-Post-Fordism in the Era of Platforms', *New Formations*, Vol. 84/5, 2015, pp184-208.

19. Mark Fisher and Jeremy Gilbert, *Reclaim Modernity: Beyond Markets Beyond Machines*. Compass, October 2014.

20. Zoe Gannon and Neal Lawson, *Co-Production: The Modernisation of Public Services*, Compass, 2008.

21. Nick Srnicek and Alex Williams, *Inventing the Future: Capitalism and a World Without Work*, Verso: London, 2016.

An Antidote to Pasokification

James Doran

Across Europe, social-democratic parties have been following a road first travelled by Pasok in Greece: implementing austerity policies when entering government, then suffering the same disastrous organisational and electoral consequences. Pasok's leadership effectively split from the majority of its activists and voters. The result was a move from commanding a parliamentary majority, to being a minor player in a conservative-led coalition, and then finally replaced as a party of government by the radical-socialist Syriza.

The result of this 'Pasokification' has been the growth of more radical electoral forces, which both contest and gain support at social democracy's expense. These parties rhetorically defend the remaining gains of the post-war settlement between labour and capital, whilst asserting opposition to the current conservative austerity agenda.

Under the leadership of 'Third Way' politicians, social-democratic parties came to distance themselves from their funding and organisational bases in trades unions and other social movements. But this effort to win over voters through appeals to moderation rather than radicalism, left social-democratic parties looking and sounding like – and in some cases actually being – politicians loyal to the ruling class. It became part and parcel of what Tariq Ali has dubbed 'the extreme centre'.[1]

Because these newer radical parties embraced extra-parliamentary activity and sought to give voice to concerns about the rule of elites, they were able to challenge the territory held by social-democratic parties when the established order collapsed during the financial crisis of 2007-08 and the resulting global recession.

This is a challenge that has a variety of content, from radical-socialist to nationalist-populist, but in almost every case has succeeded at social democracy's expense. Except in Britain.

PASOKIFICATION EXPLAINED

When I originally coined the phrase 'Pasokification' in September 2013, I summarised its five key features. First, despite the then-state of parliamentary politics, austerity outside parliament remained unpopular. Second, the rising support for the SNP showed that Labour – at least in Scotland – remained vulnerable to a third-party threat dressed in social-democratic rhetoric. Third, any Labour victory at the 2015 general election (which at the time of writing looked possible) would re-open, rather than seal, the division between the party and the trade unions. Fourth, amongst Labour MPs, Blairist-Brownite ideas remain dominant: Ed Miliband's modest proposals for an energy price freeze and rail renationalisation had already attracted criticism and outright opposition from many of them. Finally, while our electoral system meant that the emergence of a Syriza-style party was unlikely – notwithstanding the surge in Green Party membership and support – Labour's endorsement of austerity and neoliberalism would see both a drop in votes for the party and opportunities for other parties to emerge.[2]

Domestically, much has changed since 2013. But in Greece, where Pasokification first took root, not so much. It is against this background, as well as the rest of Europe and Sanders vs Clinton in the USA, that my thesis should be judged.

In Greece, the sister party of Labour won a general election at a time of economic crisis in October 2009 with a 43.94 per cent vote share and 160 out of 300 seats.[3] But Pasok's parliamentary leadership lacked an alternative economic programme. Consequently, Pasok ditched pre-election promises of a better way out of the crisis and suffered a loss of parliamentary support. When the Conservatives beat Pasok in two general elections in the summer of 2012, the party was reduced in size and influence (gaining 13.18 per cent of the vote and forty-one seats in May, then 12.28 per cent and thirty-three seats in June). Pasok then propped up the Greek Conservatives and their continuation of austerity.

Syriza, a coalition of anti-austerity and anti-capitalist groups with representation in the Greek Parliament, replaced Pasok as the main electoral opposition. Syriza went from only thirteen seats and a 4.6 per cent vote share in October 2009 to fifty-two seats and 16.8 per cent of the vote in May 2012, then seventy-one seats and a 26.9 per cent vote share in June 2012.

With Pasok's implosion, Syriza became a party of government in January 2015. Winning 36.3 per cent of the vote and 149 seats, Syriza formed a coalition with the nationalist-populist Independent Greeks. In that same election, Pasok won only 4.68 per cent of the vote and just thirteen seats. Now, Syriza may become the permanent replacement for Pasok; despite the former's failure to end austerity, and a split by twenty-four MPs, it won a second general election in September 2015.

These events can be seen as part of a tendency. Describing Pasok as 'an outlier rather than an anomaly', *Guardian* columnist Aditya Chakrabortty summarised my Pasokification thesis while pinpointing contradictions:

> The picture [Doran] paints is of constituency party meetings devoid of political activism or engagement, where the bulk of the members feel betrayed by their leadership and the couple of attendees under forty are either Blairite careerists or far-left agitators. Again, compare this to Syriza or Spain's Podemos, both movements where all the answers are not handed down on tablets of stone.
>
> The big difference here is obviously that Britain has the system of ballot-box protectionism otherwise known as first past the post … It is unlikely that the SNP would ever have gained the potency it has today without the incubator of the Holyrood parliament and its system of PR. But to look at the Scottish referendum, the rise of the Greens and even Ukip is to see how Labour and the Conservatives have long stopped being the centre of political excitement.
>
> Just like Pasok, Labour has spent decades under the influence of Tina: the idea that 'there is no alternative', either in how to run an economy or how to run a social democratic party. The rise of Syriza shows how that rule can be broken.[4]

PASOKIFICATION GB

The opposite tendency to Pasokification could be called 'Podemosification'. Podemos, a party founded in the wake of mass protests in Spain during 2011, is not yet a governing party; opposition to the Conservatives in Spain remains split between Podemos and the traditional social-democratic party PSOE. However, Podemos can be compared to radical-socialist formations which have emerged in most western European states in opposition to social democracy's turn towards the Third Way, often formed out of existing oppositional socialist organisations.[5]

The problem for social-democratic parties is that the Third Way programme now means governing with an austerity agenda. Whilst this can allow short-term electoral advances, it ultimately results in retreats, as 'reforms' now involve immediate attacks on the material conditions of working people.

By 2015, Labour – which had already lost its majority in the Scottish Parliament in 2007 – lost all but one of its Scottish seats in the UK Parliament. The Scottish National Party shed its 'Tartan Tory' image and presented itself to Labour voters as something akin to the Labour Party of old.

The SNP's positioning of itself as a social-democratic party allowed it, at least for a period of time, to become hegemonic in Scotland. It posed the challenge of being a potential source of parliamentary votes for a minority Labour government, or even a coalition partner at the UK level. On the eve of the 2015 general election, Labour was explicit in ruling out any post-election deal with the SNP.[6] Yet, this failed to stop the SNP gaining at Labour's expense, and did not stop the Tories using the threat of a 'coalition of chaos' between Labour and the SNP to devastating late effect, winning over swing voters in key English marginal seats.

FROM THE JAWS OF DEFEAT

Labour went from losing all but one of its seats in the Scottish heart-lands in 2015, to gaining Conservative marginals across England in the snap election of 2017. The expectation of the British establishment – and the old order in the Labour Party – had been that the Tory government would increase its majority while Labour would be wiped out as an oppositional force.

In many ways, Jeremy Corbyn's victorious 2015 leadership campaign was fought and won online before it could mobilise 'in real life'. It was Labour's first inkling of what a digital party might look like.[7] The mass availability of multi-channel communications devices presented a challenge to the organisational culture of the traditional party. Closed and hierarchical communications, nurtured by state and corporate elites, could not resist the disruptive pressures of this new, networked culture. Technology now gave members, through its potential for self-organisation, unprecedented power.

Thus, rather than viewing the recruitment of hundreds of thousands of people to the party as a source of strength, much of the Parliamentary Labour Party, alongside the party's entrenched bureaucracy, responded with wariness and distrust. Within a year, a majority of Labour's MPs had triggered another leadership contest. Despite his challenger Owen Smith adopting a more radical platform than those of his 2015 opponents, Corbyn was re-elected with an even bigger majority.

What Labour's leadership lacked before Corbyn was an approach which was centred on marshalling the resources needed to fight elections: an openness to social movements. Despite Ed Miliband's best efforts as leader, there were immediate limits to rebuilding Labour as a mass-membership party after it lost the 2010 general election, not least the fact that many Labour MPs seemed hostile towards renewal efforts. The 2015 leadership contest provided an opening for mass recruitment to be incentivised, and for members to participate in determining Labour's direction. Thus, the personality and popularity of Corbyn has the potential to crowd out any discussion of long-term strategy.

But those Labour MPs and activists who asserted their devotion to Clause One of the party's constitution (to 'maintain in parliament and the country a political Labour Party') were spectacularly missing the significance of the membership surge.[8] It was not the case that the surge represented an opposition to Labour as a party of government: Corbyn and his supporters subscribe as much to Clause One as the PLP.

Rather, events such as the abstention of the majority of Labour MPs in a parliamentary vote to cut social security payments during the 2015 leadership campaign, galvanised support for the only leadership candidate who consistently voted against the Tory government. These were proposals the Tories had not put to the electorate and which reversed reforms made by the last Labour government. Far from Corbyn looking opposed to Labour's legacy government, he appeared to be its most militant defender .[9]

PASOKIFICATION SPREADS

Compared to social-democratic and socialist parties across Europe, Jeremy Corbyn's Labour has managed to avoid becoming complicit in the failed austerity agenda. Consider the election results for some of Labour's sister parties in the years prior to the 2017 UK general election.

In March 2017, the Dutch Labour Party was dissolved at a national level, having joined the liberal-conservative party in an austerity coalition; many of its voters fled to nationalist-populist, radical-socialist, social-liberal and green parties.[10]

The Irish Labour Party joined an austerity coalition with one of the Republic of Ireland's two major parties of government, both of which were conservative. In 2016, Labour had the worst election result in its history, being overtaken by Sinn Fein and challenged by radical socialists in its heartlands.[11]

The French Socialist Party was dissolved after its leadership fell in line with the austerity economics of the European institutions. In April 2017 the party received a 6 per cent vote share in the first round of the presidential election, and then 7 per cent in the parliamentary election a couple of months later.

The French example demonstrates that Pasokification is coming from the periphery to the core of Europe: François Hollande, the sitting president at that time, was so unpopular he didn't stand again in the Socialist Party primary. Hollande's prime minister, Manuel Valls, failed to win the support of Socialist voters, who instead opted for Benoit Hamon, the anti-austerity candidate. But it was too late – in the presidential election, much of the party's vote split between candidates such as Jean Luc Mélenchon, an independent left presidential candidate, and the former Socialist finance minister Emmanuel Macron, who launched a new party and went on to win the presidency against *le Front National* candidate Marine Le Pen, in the second round.[12]

The example of Macron might be seen as proof that the Third Way could be revived in Britain. But Macron's success comes after the failure of a social-democratic party to challenge austerity and stand against the threat of a resurgent fascism. With a historically low turnout in the 2017 elections, Macron's parliamentary majority is insecure, and his continuing success is by no means certain. It is likely that the neoliberal and austerity-driven 'reforms' he intends to implement will soon face mass opposition.[13]

In Germany, the combined representation of the Social Democratic Party (SPD), the Left Party and the Greens, would have been enough to oust Angela Merkel's CDU from office after the general election in 2013. However, the leadership of the SPD was committed to continued coalition with Merkel. Despite a change of leader, the party has so far failed to break from either its 'grand coalition' or Third Way politics.[14]

The politics of the European Union – austerity, casualisation, privatisation, unemployment, wage stagnation – created the material conditions of working-class insecurity and fear, which later led to the UK vote to leave the EU. Across Europe, those social democratic parties, which failed to respond to the demand for these policies to be reversed at a national level, have faced defeat at the hands of conservative-nationalist populism and far-right populism while being outmanoeuvred on the left by more radical parties. Meanwhile in Britain, Jeremy Corbyn's Labour Party has increased its vote share, seat share and membership.

THE UNGRATEFUL DEAD

The Labour government of 1997 to 2010 was the most electorally successful in the party's history, governing for three full terms with a parliamentary majority. For advocates of the New Labour modernisation project – which involved the party dropping its constitutional aim of extending 'common ownership' and 'popular administration' – this is proof that a move towards the centre is the only way to win.

However, New Labour's tenure in government coincided with a long period of expansion in the global economy. This resulted partly from the 'great doubling' of the number of labour suppliers available to capital after the collapse of the communist regimes in Europe and the opening-up of China and India to foreign investment. It was possible in these conditions for Labour to govern for a more sustained length of time than in the past. Previously, the established pattern for Labour governments had been to end up at odds with their trade union supporters and voter base in managing a capitalist system, first losing support and then enough votes, and finding itself out of office after a single term.

After eventual defeat in 2010, despite the opportunities for change, the approach of Labour's parliamentary leadership from 2010 to 2015 was to veer between the party-union bonding of traditional social democracy (in which the funding relationship was usually accompanied by the promise and implementation of laws allowing effective trade union activity) and the party-union distancing of the Third Way (in which the funding relationship and promise of reforms coincided with a cultural gulf between the unions and the party).

In the wake of the 2010 general election defeat, the consensus amongst the PLP was that Labour should avoid being seen as too supportive of migrants or benefits claimants: both groups had been blamed by Conservatives for the drain on public finances and the imposed burden of taxation on 'hardworking families'. Instead, the Labour leadership made repeated apologies for spending too much on the welfare system, and promised cuts to benefits and tougher rules for immigrants if the party returned to government. The policy was so firmly cemented into the campaign strategy, that Labour was even selling mugs with 'controls on immigration' written on the side.[15] This obsessive submission to Conservative narratives was the framework of Labour's strategy, and while it might have appeared electorally expedient, the 2015 defeat proved it wasn't. It left behind a Labour Party that was incapable of leading a popular opposition to austerity.

TOO FAR, TOO FAST?

In preparation for an expected victory in 2015, the parliamentary leadership of the Labour Party set about accommodating the policies of austerity within a social-democratic narrative. 'Too far, too fast' was Labour's attempt to criticise Tory policies they did not intend to materially reverse in the next parliament.

The New Keynesian thinking of Ed Miliband's shadow chancellor Ed Balls actively facilitated an environment wherein Labour could not develop a critique of capitalist accumulation.[16] Primarily, this school of thought is not concerned with democratising corporate governance, or giving power to workers and consumers in determining investment priorities. Rather, New Keynesianism is interested in making capitalism work effectively for capital-owners. The half-hearted opposition of 'too far, too fast' conceded the necessity of austerity. New Keynesianism thus ended up as Non-Keynesianism: Balls accepted the Tory spending envelope for the next parliament, hoping that establishing a British Investment Bank and allowing the Green Investment Bank to operate effectively would square the circle of austerity with a human face. Rather than an anti-austerity argument, Balls played it safe. The result was that a winnable general election in 2015 was lost.

LABOUR'S DUAL POWER PROBLEM

Historically, the parliamentary leadership of the Labour Party, as Joe Guinan has pointed out, 'rejected out of hand plans for social credit, guild socialism, and other such solutions in favour of the dismal managerialism of nationalisation, and then only for industries – such as electricity, coal, gas, civil aviation, telecommunications, and railways – which were not particularly profitable at the time, and for which their owners were richly compensated.'[17]

The polarisation within the Labour Party during the late 1970s and early 1980s involved a turn by activists towards a 'resolutionary socialism': if economic democracy could not be won through the workplace or through a Labour Party which refused to implement its own programme for government, then the party itself would have to be democratised. It was a struggle which resulted in some Labour politicians breaking with the party to form the SDP.

On being elected leader, Tony Blair had the party rewrite the famous Clause Four of its constitution. Supposedly this was to correct the misconception that the party's goal of 'common ownership' and 'popular administration' meant state ownership and control of the economy. The change had the effect of defining Labour explicitly as a 'democratic socialist party' on its membership cards, but omitted any definition of what that meant in terms of the party's politics.

After the 2010 leadership contest, when Ed Miliband was elected leader, a former general secretary of the party expressed the view that 'the last thing we need is a membership drive', supposedly because members are less reflective of the priorities of voters, and membership of political parties was in terminal decline.[18] In 2014, the huge surge in SNP membership in the wake of the lost Scottish independence referendum campaign showed that this decline was not inevitable. The growth in SNP members reflected a party that, despite defeat in the referendum, had retained a sense of purpose and this would make a material difference to its 2015 electoral landslide.

What existed within Labour as soon as Jeremy Corbyn became leader has been memorably described by Ed Rooksby as 'a simultaneous and rapid process of "Pasokification" and "Syriza-ification"'.[19]

Corbyn was surrounded by a parliamentary party machinery which was suspicious of efforts to grow the party's membership. There was and is hostility on the part of the 'old order' and the party bureaucracy to increase direct membership participation in policymaking.

Corbyn did not heed the advice of those managing the decline of the party and instead encouraged the establishment of a support network, Momentum, which could both defend the platform on which he was elected and aid the continued growth in party membership and activism. This organising effort helped Corbyn's successful re-election after a leadership challenge from the old order in the party in summer 2016. It has widely been recognised, including by former critics, as playing a key role in the unprecedented scale of mass campaigning in key marginals during the 2017 general election.

What would it mean for the situation of dual power to end? Before the stunning results in the June 2017 general election, the party struggled for coherence: a leadership challenge to Corbyn was defeated, but it exposed the enduring internal divisions. Richard Seymour, author of *Corbyn: The Strange Rebirth of Radical Politics,* whilst an enthusiastic supporter of Corbynism, remains circumspect about the capacity of its support to endure because it was 'more potential than reality, its organisation is nascent, and it is roughly divided between those who lack experience and those whose experience is one of trauma'.[20] Labour was expected to lose out as a result of the forthcoming boundary review, initiated to reduce the number of MPs in parliament. In accepting the result of the referendum on Britain's membership of the EU, the Tories aimed to regain votes lost to the nationalist-populist Ukip. Labour faced challenges regarding the European question. The toxicity of the Liberal Democrats was reduced by their platform of a stronger opposition to Brexit compared to Labour. Additionally, the Brexit process was also expected to allow, after their success in the Copeland by-election, the Conservatives to build on their #WorkersParty repositioning with a particular anti-migrant spin.

But many of these challenges were overcome when the prospect of fighting to hold and gain territory for Labour had a unifying effect on the party. By accepting Brexit rather than arguing for a second referendum, Labour avoided being defined by the question of institutional arrangements and was able instead to penetrate the electorate with its message of standing 'for the many, not the few'.

TOWARDS A DIGITAL LABOUR PARTY

For the Corbyn leadership to turn Labour's membership surge and electoral advance into a hegemonic bloc capable of governing, the revival and engagement of civil society constituencies of support is required. In particular, in the digital age, Labour needs social media initiatives capable of sustaining opposition to anti-migrant and anti-claimant prejudice in order to win the battle of ideas on democratising the economy.

Aaron Bastani, co-founder of Novara Media, suggested in a prescient 2016 article that this would demand a change in how Labour conducted its campaigning:

> At the heart are these change advocates, then members, then registered supporters, then Labour voters, then potential Labour voters. If organised properly this would be a very competitive force during elections. As much as persuading strangers, activists would be mobilising pre-existing affinity groups of friends, families and colleagues to not only vote for candidates, but campaign for them as well. Additionally they would interface with extant efforts around things like food banks as well as beginning initiatives like literacy groups and breakfast clubs.

Bastani then linked this to general election campaigning:

> Until very recently, general election campaigns have been hybrids of professionalised party efforts which incorporate large numbers of volunteers. The volunteer efforts were almost entirely for offline 'ground' campaigning, while professionalised elements included public relations, media and fundraising. That has dramatically changed in recent years through the emergence of social media and crowdfunding. Additionally, the last decade has seen a move to 'personalised political communication', especially in the United States. … This kind of communication is 'personalised' in the sense that people, and not television or websites, serve as the primary media for messages. All of which means that media and mobilisation functions are now fusing into one another … [T]he Corbyn campaign found scale through the personal media networks and efforts of tens of thousands of advocates – and how this interacted

with legacy media – rather than simply the old 'one-to-many' channels. This explains, to a significant extent how Corbyn can currently enjoy a 32 per cent lead over Smith among the membership, despite little to no support from the mainstream media.

Perhaps most crucially of all, Bastani concludes with the point that such changes are much less about instrumental practice than wholesale cultural change, 'but as well as channelling this new kind of personalised campaigning through an ever-larger membership, Labour also needs to embody both collective, and connective logics of action'.[21]

Popularising the economic alternative will require these new institutions. But in addition to the development of social media campaigning strategies, a widespread and dynamic revival of the 'take back control' argument is needed, including new versions of worker co-operative movements to put any vision of an alternative into practice.[22] This would not be simply in service of the interests of a political party, but rather a commitment to a post-capitalist economy.[23] This is the scale of ambition we need after 2017; Corbyn's Labour was viewed as a portent of disaster, but rather, counter to Pasokification, it has proved to be the beginnings of a radical future.

NOTES

1. Tariq Ali, *The Extreme Centre: A Warning*, Verso: London, 2015.
2. James Doran, 'Liquidating Labour', www.novaramedia.com, 15 September 2013. For a critique of the Pasokification thesis, see Tristram Hunt, 'Neither Podemos nor Pasokification', Speech given to Policy Network at the Barrow Cadbury Trust on 15 July 2015.
3. All Greek election data is taken from the website of the Hellenic parliament: www.hellenicparliament.gr/en.
4. Aditya Chakrabortty, 'What Greek politics teaches Labour: There is an alternative', *The Guardian*, 27 January 2015.
5. Luke March, 'Beyond Syriza and Podemos, other radical left parties are threatening to break into the mainstream of European politics', *LSE Blog European*, blogs.lse.ac.uk/euroblog, 24 March 2015.
6. Patrick Wintour and Nicholas Watt, 'Ed Miliband: I won't have a government if it means deals with the SNP', *The Guardian*, 30 April 2015.
7. For commentary on this aspect of the first Corbyn leadership campaign, see Ben Sellers, '#JezWeDid: From Red Labour to Jeremy Corbyn – a tale from social media', published in Tom Unterrainer (ed.), *Corbyn's Campaign*, Spokesman Books: London, 2016.

8. Richard Angell, 'Clause One principles', www.progressonline.org.uk, 7 December 2016.

9. Alex Nunns, 'Chapter 9', *The Candidate*, OR Books: London, 2016, describes the implications of this for the 2015 Corbyn leadership campaign.

10. Pepijn Brandon, 'Defeat in victory', www.jacobinmag.com, 19 March 2017.

11. Dan MacGuill, 'Labour just had the worst election in its 104-year history', www.thejournal.ie, 3 March 2016.

12. David Broder, 'An uninspired victory', www.jacobinmag.com, 23 June 2017.

13. For background see Perry Anderson, 'The centre cannot hold', *New Left Review*, No. 105, May-June 2017, pp5-28.

14. Loren Balhorn, 'After tragedy and farce: Martin Schulz', www.jacobinmag.com, 23 April 2017.

15. For example: Toby Helm, 'Ed Miliband: we will introduce tougher rules on benefits for new migrants', *The Guardian*, 11 October 2014; Andrew Grice, 'We made mistakes on welfare, admits Ed Miliband as he pledges Labour cap on social security spending', *The Independent*, 6 June 2013.

16. Andy Morton, 'The problematic economics of Balls', *Chartist* blog, 1 November 2014.

17. Joe Guinan, 'Returns to capital: Austerity and the crisis of European social democracy' in *The Good Society*, Vol. 22 No. 1, 2013, pp46-60.

18. Peter Watt, 'The last thing we need is a membership drive', www.labour-uncut.co.uk, 29 September 2010.

19. Ed Rooksby, 'Corbyn and the left', www.jacobinmag.com, 29 September 2015.

20. Richard Seymour, *Corbyn: The Strange Rebirth of Radical Politics*, Verso: London, 2016.

21. Aaron Bastani, 'Labour can only win with Jeremy Corbyn', www.opendemocracy.net, 27 July 2016.

22. James Doran, 'Democracy at work?' *Stir*, Vol. 4, 2014; and Aditya Chakrabortty, 'How could we cope if capitalism failed? Ask 26 Greek factory workers', *The Guardian*, 18 July 2017.

23. Paul Mason, *Postcapitalism: A Guide to Our Future*, Allen Lane: London, 2015.

The Perils of Being Popular

Jack Kellam

Populism defines our current political moment. Social movements, political parties and leaders of both the left and the right are all labelled as 'populist', all variously decried or exalted because of it. Flurries of articles and comment pieces have been produced trying to explain and critique the populist phenomenon. For some it represents the 'pseudo-solution that if only politicians did exactly what the people demanded, all would be well',[1] or the dangerous belief that 'the people are always right',[2] whereas others see a populist approach as an essential measure to counter right-wing authoritarianism.[3]

Defining populism as that which rejects complexity in order to present 'simple' solutions, or as the introduction of a 'false' people vs elite dichotomy to the detriment of more 'fundamental' lines of division, is clearly already loaded with prescriptive content. Definition and critique come together. This means that exchanges frequently end up resulting in positions to the effect of 'well, if by populism you mean *that*, then I'm not against it; but I had understood that as "popular" [or some other related adjective], rather than as "populist" (which is necessarily bad!)'. This is a dynamic hardly aided by a media environment that traverses both sides of the political spectrum, one that is more frequently concerned with 'smearing' or 'catching out' an opponent, than productive discussion. Engagement with anything resembling the substantive becomes almost redundant.

Nevertheless, there is a common significance attached to populism across many centrist or liberal takes on it, even if there is not a shared 'definition' or 'meaning'. The term 'populism' is part of their attempt to make sense of the reappearance of a phenomenon many had become unfamiliar with: *politics*. Not politics in terms of the 'high political', day-to-day, Westminster lobby journalist record of events;

nor the politics of 'administration' that had long come to characterise western democracies, the politics of 'choosing' like consumers how best to manage the neoliberal economy, which is now shared across the centre-right *and* left. Instead, this is the politics of antagonism, difference and conflict. The possibility of the establishment losing control means that 'anyone who does well electorally by challenging its [the establishment's] favourite sons and daughters is dismissed as a populist'.[4]

Populism, for many of these commentators, is therefore insepa-rable from the delayed political unrest generated by the recent (and ongoing) financial crisis, which – on both the left and right – has recently taken a course away from social movementism and towards direct engagement with representative institutions and the party form. Populism has meant that those groups who had challenged neoliberal orthodoxy have reacted to the 'hollowing out' of democratic institu-tions and now question the benevolence of 'elites' and 'experts' to act in their best interests: whether this is to control immigration *or* to run an economy that supports the many.[5] The fact that many commenta-tors then go on to label populism as, paradoxically given my analysis, 'anti-political' or dangerous to the democratic political process is not, therefore, surprising.[6] Politics, for them, is synonymous with neolib-eral administration; the democratic process with 'the empty spectacle of party politics'. Being for or against populism means being for or against a politics that recognises antagonism or the genuine contesta-tion of neoliberalism. So long as such resistance is forthcoming, 'the populist question' in this form at least, will be here to stay.

HAND IN HAND WITH THE PEOPLE

For the same reason that the liberal centre has castigated populism, therefore, some on the left have heralded it as offering an effective vehicle for a successful contemporary radical politics – 'the only way to renew radical politics'.[7] Populism, from this perspective, presents an opportunity for the left to transcend both an exhausted 'Third Way' electoralism *and* a dogmatic, minoritarian leftism, condemned to remain at the margins of political discourse. The alternative on offer is instead to articulate an emancipatory politics through various populist mechanisms. Class struggle is presented through the prism of a 'people' vs. 'establishment' dichotomy, where the former term is construed in a suitably inclusive, non-reductive way, assuaging concerns about its compatibility with other progressive preoccupations such as race, gender, sexuality and so on.

Left populist thinking therefore relies on an underlying assumption, taken from the political theorist Ernesto Laclau, that by populism:

> we do not understand a *type* of movement – identifiable with either a special social base or a particular ideological orientation, but *a political logic*: the division of the social field into two antagonistic camps, the presence of vague 'empty signifiers' that serve to bind multiple groups into a common 'chain of equivalence' and the representational function of leadership.[8]

Populism is neither by definition left-wing or right-wing, progressive or reactionary. It merely represents a discursive logic that can be 'filled' with the ideological content of one's choosing. As such, advocates look towards the success of parties such as Podemos in Spain – some of whose most prominent members are former students of Laclau's – as testament to the viability of this combination, the unproblematic nature of its articulation, and as evidence of its strategic beneficence.[9] Their left-populism, supposedly successfully channels 'feelings of anger and fear', which when 'nourished by precarity are projected onto the domestic "*casta*" [the elite] rather than on immigrants'.[10] This then delivers electoral results; Podemos won 20.5 per cent of the vote in 2015 national elections, despite only being officially formed in 2014. In Greece, the recent electoral success of Syriza has also been interpreted as a 'challenge [to] neoliberal hegemony through [populist] parliamentary politics', pitting the Greek people ('us'), against the Troika ('them');[11] whilst the campaign by Bernie Sanders for the Democratic presidential nomination has also been seen as a harbinger of 'the new populism'.[12]

It might come as little surprise then, that many of those involved with or sympathetic to Jeremy Corbyn's leadership of the Labour Party think of it in terms of a left-populist experiment. For some, such a strategy had been the obvious way to frame the movement from the beginning. Others had only thought of it as such after Corbyn's office announced an explicit 'rebrand' at the end of 2016, to turn the leader of the opposition into an anti-establishment populist.[13] At the time, Aaron Bastani of Novara Media noted that 'a shift to populism is to be welcomed … [insofar as] it really is now or never for the politics of the radical left to succeed'.[14]

2017 has proved both this observation and the belief behind it to be remarkably prescient. The stunning general election campaign, the bold manifesto, the mass rallies, the social media memes – taken together, these all mean that a much wider group now think of Corbynism as a populist project *par excellence*. The incontrovertible evidence that both Jeremy Corbyn and the Labour Party are now 'popu-*lar*', makes it a lot easier for many to call this kind of politics 'popu-*list*'. But even more important than winning 41 per cent of the 8 June national vote (and in the immediate aftermath polling even higher), has been the popular 'dynamic' of the moment. On the 24 June, Corbyn addressed 200,000 people from Glastonbury Festival's Pyramid Stage, quoting Shelley's 'The Masque of Anarchy'. From the audience came both rapturous cheers, and multiple renditions of the now viral chant 'OH JE-RE-MY COR-BYN!', set to the melody of the main riff from 'Seven Nation Army' by The White Stripes. In the wake of the Grenfell Tower tragedy, as Theresa May failed to meet victims, it was Corbyn who assumed a quasi-prime ministerial role comforting the bereaved, listening to their concerns. On social media, he is referred to as 'the absolute boy', and is the subject of a vast number of supportive memes. During the electoral campaign he bene-fitted from the #Grime4Corbyn project, where prominent artists like Novelist and AJ Tracey made clear their explicit support for Corbyn's socialist politics, and in the final week marginal constituencies were flooded with unprecedented numbers of mainly young, often first-time canvassers.

After decades of a hollowed-out democratic process, this re-emer-gence of a political movement intimately suffused with 'the popular', boldly articulating a social-democratic programme, has been nothing short of enthralling. A lifelong socialist and anti-imperialist, deeply connected with movements outside of parliament, stands very close to becoming the prime minister of a Labour government, on the back of widespread popular enthusiasm. In truth, this is but the eventual realisation of a democratic moment forestalled. The 2015 leadership election was itself already a monumental achievement, a great punc-ture to the fabric of the politically possible, which promised a renewal of socialist politics in this country, powered by hundreds of thousands of ordinary members. Eighteen months of disruption, attack and sabotage though, had allowed capitalist realism to begin to reassert itself in some ways: perhaps Corbyn really could never win? Perhaps capitulation was the only route to power?

The result of 8 June, however, means that the moment subsequent to it most certainly belongs to 'the Corbyn effect'. The questions that we must ask, as we move rapidly forwards, are (fortunately) not ones of post-mortem and salvage-jobs, but rather of strategic evolution and the difficulties of government.

POPULIST ENGAGEMENT

Academic discussions of populism, particularly those oriented around the political theory of Ernesto Laclau, are plagued by a tendency to retreat into formalistic and prescriptive accounts of the concept, constructing a definition in advance of engagement with its living, historically active embodiments. Populism becomes an abstract discursive structure – 'a political logic',[15] which posits a people vs elite antagonism, relies on the vagueness of key signifiers to unite its move-ment, requires some form of leadership to embody its collective will. This suggests it is only interested in engaging with 'actually existing' populist movements to the extent that they fulfil these conditions to a greater or lesser degree.

While any sort of analysis relies on *some* form of abstraction away from concrete specificity, a central pillar of critical social theory is the maintenance of genuine 'live' engagement with the historical phenomena it sets out to study. Thinking through populism, and its potential merits for the left, therefore means thinking through what populism actually means in the here and now, as a living historical force.

Paul Mason indicates this in a recent claim that we need to think *with* populism, not necessarily for or against it:

> Trying to define populism, and even focusing on it right now [in that way], is like ... seeing a tank coming down the street and asking your-self 'what should we do about this tank? Do I need a tank?' the real issue is 'am I in a war, why, and what are we going to do about it?'[16]

Our central, guiding question should be articulating a response to trends, developments and events as they actually present themselves, as opposed to what we should make of the propositions of an idealised model – 'What does populism mean for the war we are fighting?'

This will inevitably involve some recourse to generalisations about dynamics common across different populisms, and involve taking stances on certain key, shared tenets: must we rely on the signifier 'the people'? Can there be a progressive incarnation of a friend/enemy distinction? But these must be genuinely historically situated within our current political context, so that the question becomes not 'is *the people* a good discursive tool for the left?', but 'what would it mean for the left to use *the people* as part of a rhetorical strategy, in a context of wider nationalist, xenophobic discourse?', and so on.

NAVIGATING THE NATIONAL POPULAR

An analysis of Labour's recent election campaign through the prism of left populism could start from some obvious places: the central discursive disjunction of 'for the many, not the few', the articulation of an anti-austerity chain of equivalence between different issues (public services, pay, education etc), or the central role of Corbyn as a revitalised leader addressing mass rallies. One of the most influential issues going forward, however, is the ambiguous nature of Corbyn's Labour's stance on Brexit, immigration and the free movement of people – in short, the question of the 'national popular'.

Two features of populism, highlighted by theorists such as Ernesto Laclau, are a preponderance of ambiguous political discourse, and the rhetorical deployment of 'the people' as the primary collective subject. In other words, populism involves the use of vague discourse to make simultaneous appeals to a broad spectrum of *prima facie* conflictual political identities, and to 'the people' – necessarily a bounded entity, which is almost inevitably defined in relation to the modern nation state. The popular is therefore almost always 'the national popular'.

Labour's general election campaign certainly encompassed both of these dynamics in its position on Brexit and immigration, thereby posing a number of critical questions for the radical left to address, in dealing with the viability of left-populism as a political strategy. The party articulated a position on Brexit which was – in a paradoxical sense – clear in its indeterminacy. Brexit means Britain leaving the European Union, accepting the triggering of Article 50 and foregoing membership of the single market, but nevertheless negotiating access to retain its benefits.[17] Combined with continual interventions from members of the PLP 'accenting' this in different ways (either to sound like *membership* of the single market would be retained, *or* that we would steer further clear of it than intimated), Labour was able to appeal electorally for the support of both 'remainers', who interpreted it as amounting to a 'quasi-single market' stance, *and* the 'leavers', who appreciated the clear respect of the referendum result and the clear commitment to leaving the single market. Seemingly contradictory identities could be brought together within Labour's populist 'chain of equivalence'.

Mobilising this indeterminacy as an electoral strategy proved strikingly productive – ingenious even. There were those who held that the leadership were 'confused' or 'muddled' in their Brexit strategy, insisting that this would only see the party fall through the middle as voters deserted them on either side, to the Tories and the Liberal Democrats. However, contrary to this, Corbyn and his team *knew very well what they were doing* – at the time, at least. As the specifics of negotiations crystallise, and Labour even potentially finds itself conducting them, the possibility of keeping both antagonistic groups within one 'chain of equivalence' appears more fragile. As indeterminacy turns into determinacy, when Britain *does* have to clearly leave the single market and loses access to certain 'goods', and so on, the 'emptiness' of Labour's discourse – which distinct groups had previously been able to 'fill' with their own contents – will gradually incur a far more determinate meaning. Whether Labour can keep such groups together through continued indeterminacy therefore appears doubtful. How much this will matter also remains unclear. If Labour can sufficiently rearticulate both groups into a chain of equivalence held together instead by shared commitment to an increasingly radical economic programme, through genuinely shared identity, the Brexit problem could be largely bypassed. Brexit would come to represent a historic opportunity to restructure the economy away from neoliberalism, rather than an issue defined by the specific relations of the single market. Continuing to be bold with economic policy – and the *Alternative Models of Ownership* report is a promising start – will be the principal way of articulating together divergent sections of the working class, surpassing left-populist vagueness with bold, 'popular' politics.[18]

Undoubtedly 'haunting' any such programme, however, will be the status of 'the people' appropriate for such a left populism, which crystallises one of the critical issues for Corbynite strategy moving forwards: immigration. One of Corbyn's major 'concessions' (others will read 'retreats') has been to accept that 'freedom of movement will end when we leave the European Union' to be replaced by the 'reasonable management of migration'.[19] Whilst undoubtedly utterly removed from the 'dog-whistle' politics that characterised Labour discourse on immigration for decades, Corbyn has nevertheless conceded to 'popular opinion' on either maintaining free movement of peoples between the UK and EU members, or advocating a more substantive regime of open borders.

The dilemma is whether Corbynism can maintain its status as a populist movement, appealing to notions of 'the people', whilst still fighting a longer term struggle to realise a world without borders – which I take as an at least final (if not distant) goal of the radical left. This is not so much because of doubt in the intentions of Corbyn and those around him, but rather that discourse, and the central signifiers with which this issue is concerned (i.e. 'the people'), are not so 'empty' that they can be easily imputed with the alternative 'progressive' meanings we wish they had. Instead, they are deeply 'sedimented' – imbued with centuries of connotations and allusions which cannot be easily shaken off. The national-popular signifier of 'the British people' has frequently been imperialist, exclusivist and often downright racist in its historical significance; its status as a 'progressive' identity rarely assumed.

We might therefore worry that doing 'populism' – which will always rely on *some sort* of appeal to 'the people' – might make an eventual radical revision of the stance on immigration ever more distant. Rather than challenging the hegemonic connotations of Britishness which partially feed current public opinion of issues like immigration, we could end up simply reinforcing them. Any 'left-populist' way forward must therefore acknowledge the profound difficulty of the task, and recognise that new, radical articulations of 'the people' will be products of long-term counterhegemonic struggle, rather than a short-term political campaign, and that our strategy will need to be sensitive to this fact. Britishness is not destined to be straightforwardly repurposed towards unproblematic, radical even, ends. It will also require consistent pressure from 'outside' and 'below'. There are many centrist and right-wing Labour MPs and their supporters who will not easily let the current stance on immigration go, and who have been indecently quick to attribute Labour's electoral success to its 'concession' on immigration. Corbyn's Labour Party came closer to winning a general election than almost anyone ever imagined it would without consistent racist signalling on immigration. Now Labour needs to go a step further, and win without the underlying policy.

LEADERSHIP OF THE ABSOLUTE BOY

A consistent critique of left-populist strategy has often been its alleged tendency towards hierarchical organisational structures and a prominent focus on the personality of the leadership, both of which are taken to be antagonistic to a radical left politics, denounced on both democratic and feminist grounds. In its privileging of 'the leader' – who is almost always male – the possibility of a genuinely feminist, democratic populism is forestalled. Sian Berry of the Green Party and *Guardian* writer Zoe Williams have both raised concerns in this respect pointing out the 'Big Man' saviour complex that they see pervading populist political formations.[20] Kate Shea Baird and Laura Roth have been similarly sceptical about populism's perceived fetishisation of individualised leadership, claiming that it generates a destructively antagonistic style of politics, antithetical to the 'feminisation' of the political that the authors pursue. 'Populism' in their interpretation, 'is not only incompatible with the feminization of politics; it actually reinforces patriarchy'.[21] Again, the accusation is not that left populists fail to articulate progressive policies on feminist issues, so much that the structural logic of the movements within which they reside has an inescapable hostility to a suitably *feminised* politics.

The Corbyn effect has hardly been immune from this criticism, especially over the course of the recent general election campaign. Many criticisms have of course been empty and facetious – crude portrayals of Corbynism as a 'personality cult', where the chanting of Corbyn's name is apparently reminiscent of North Korea.[22] The consistent attempts to smear Corbyn and his supporters as guilty of mass sexism and misogyny are too numerous to list. This does not mean however, that there are not genuine areas in which constructive challenge from the committed left is appropriate.

On the one hand, the continued reproduction of the Labour Party's deeply hierarchical and anti-democratic organisational structures *does* prove a challenge to the nascent populist left. Yet this is not only insofar as the party bureaucracy will be difficult to transform but rather that – in the face of this task – a temptation could arise to consolidate power *within* these structures, rather than *through* their radical transformation. This is the enticement of 'reformism' that has shaped Labourist politics for a century – to attain power, and then concede in the face of difficulty; to 'direct' reform from the top, rather than to enable change from 'below'.

The 'popular' moment around Corbyn, however, appears to be an expression of hope in a different, more substantively democratic politics than that of the Labour tradition. Rather than threatening democratic structures, the Corbyn effect appears to offer a real hope of renewing them. The temptation to take the easier road will long remain though. It is a necessity for the membership, and organisations like Momentum to push consistently for both the democratisation of internal structures *and* the spread of popular democracy *throughout* society (and beyond the narrow world of Westminster). Tom Blackburn has neatly characterised this as 'Corbynism from below'.[23]

Corbyn, therefore, neither necessarily threatens, nor easily promises the radical democratisation of the Labour Party. As an inherent expression of democratic sentiment, a reaction against the ability of ordinary people to have agency either in their own party, or within an economic system set against them, it represents an opening and a possibility – nothing more, and nothing less. This popular-democratic 'moment' could be resolved two ways: either through absorption and containment into the existent structures of the Labour Party, where 'Corbyn' is expected to resolve the difficulties on our behalf; or it can continue to be 'lived' in our radical political practice, extended both temporally, into the future, and spatially, *across* the party and wider society. Populism represents an ambiguous democratic opportunity that can be seized or conceded. Agency, however, lies with us.

WE'RE NOT ALL IN THIS TOGETHER

The Corbyn Effect needs to become a 'populism' that channels the energy that Labour in 2017 has generated, into an enduring movement animated by a desire for politics to be *more than* the mere administration of neoliberalism, and democracy to be more than the election of its managers. As such we could foresee a populism that refuses to cede to demagoguery and the fetishisation of leaders within its internal structures (even while it recognises the inescapability and importance of their role), 'practices what it preaches' democratically, and thereby conceives of a 'Corbynism beyond Corbyn'. In these circumstances then, its populist edge is essential. If this is a populism that remains open to its own contestation, that refuses to enact a total closure of its 'people' (along the lines of gender, race, nationality and so on), that recognises the internal diversity and complexity of those that – really speaking – constitute its agency, then it surely must play a central role within Corbynite strategy. So longs as it is a 'popular' populism – a populism *for* the people and *by* the people, a radical democratic, socialist movement that sets it sights upon the transformation of society; one that stresses these emancipatory dynamics over the possibilities of hierarchy and exclusivity, then such a populism is vital. One can of course say that such a populism is not a populism at all, since populism is 'by definition' *exclusive*, *demagogic* and so on, but that would be to miss the point: I am far more interested in how we can 'think with' populism to help us highlight the aspects we deem necessary within a radical political movement, and those problems that we wish to avoid. The challenge is to embed and institutionalise the democratic and radical potential promised by the popular moment that Corbyn represents. Achieving this, whether we label it 'populism' or not, lies with us.

NOTES

1. Julian Baggini, 'Jeremy Corbyn is a great populist. But that's not good for our democracy', *The Guardian*, 25 July 2016.
2. 'What is Populism?', *The Economist* Blog, 19 December 2016.
3. Owen Jones, 'The left needs a new populism fast. It's clear what will happen if it fails', *The Guardian*, 10 November 2016.
4. Yanis Varoufakis in 'What should Jeremy Corbyn's brand of leftwing populism look like?', *The Guardian*, 19 December 2016.
5. See Peter Mair, *Ruling the Void: The Hollowing of Western Democracy*, Verso: London, 2013.
6. See Mark Leonard, 'Rage against the machine: the rise of anti-politics across Europe', *New Statesman*, 5 June 2014.
7. Chantal Mouffe quoted in 'What should Jeremy Corbyn's brand of leftwing populism look like?', *The Guardian*, 19 December 2016.
8. Ernesto Laclau, *On Populist Reason*, Verso: London, 2005, p117.
9. On the directness of the relationship between Ernesto Laclau, his long-time collaborator Chantal Mouffe and Podemos, see both Dan Hancox,

'Why Ernesto Laclau is the intellectual figurehead for Syriza and Podemos', *The Guardian*, 9 February 2015, and the recent volume co-authored by Mouffe and Íñigo Errejon (the political secretary of Podemos), entitled *Podemos: In the Name of the People*, Lawrence & Wishart: London, 2016.

10. Alexandros Kioupkiolis, 'Podemos: The ambiguous promises of left-wing populism in contemporary Spain', *Journal of Political Ideologies*, Vol. 21 No. 2, pp99-120, p103.

11. Chantal Mouffe, 'In defence of left-wing populism', www.theconversation.com, 29 April 2016.

12. John Cassidy, 'Bernie Sanders and the New Populism', *The New Yorker*, 3 February 2016.

13. See Heather Stewart and Jessica Elgot, 'Labour plans Jeremy Corbyn relaunch to ride anti-establishment wave', *The Guardian*, 15 December 2016.

14. Aaron Bastani, 'What would a populist Jeremy Corbyn look like?', opendemocracy.net, 22 December 2016.

15. Ernesto Laclau, *op. cit.*, p117.

16. This quotation, is taken from a live event organised by *Novara Media*, entitled 'Choose Life, Choose Populism'.

17. *For the Many Not the Few: The Labour Party Manifesto 2017*, pp23-33.

18. *Alternative Models of Ownership*, Labour Party, 2016.

19. *Labour Party Manifesto*.

20. Both made these comments at 'Choose Life, Choose Populism', *ibid*.

21. Kate Shea Baird and Laura Roth, 'Left-wing populism and the feminization of politics', *ROAR Magazine*, 13 January 2017.

22. Ian Dunt, 'Ooooh Jeremy Corbyn: Never chant a politician's name', www.politics.co.uk, 28 June 2017.

23. Tom Blackburn, 'Corbynism from below?', www.newsocialist.org.uk, 12 June 2017.

Marginal Gains

Paula Surridge

The 2017 general election revealed a changed political land-scape, where previously it seemed Labour was doomed to finish in third place in Scotland and be an increasingly ineffective polit-ical force in the south of England (outside of London). Results showed that Labour, under Jeremy Corbyn, had made significant gains in places the party had not won in decades. Victories in Canterbury and Kensington were the most obvious of these, but gains in Stroud and Bristol North West were also symptomatic of this change. The effect of the 'Corbyn surge' was also to bring into play seats where Labour seemed out of the running after the 2015 election.

In 2015, there were ninety-three seats where the majority (the difference in votes between the winning candidate and second place) was under 3500 votes; and just thirty where the majority was less than 1000 votes. With Labour's starting position a hundred seats adrift of the Tories, this appeared an impossible mountain to climb. After 2017 the number of marginals has risen to 135; with fifty-one of those having majorities of less than 1000 votes. The mountain, whilst not quite shrunken to a mole hill, has certainly become more of a mound. Table 1 breaks down all seats (excluding Northern Ireland) by their marginality and by the type of battle-ground they represent.

Of the most marginal seats after 2017, the largest group (fifteen seats) are currently held by the Conservatives of which Labour are in second place in thirteen. This is an optimistic outlook but there is no room for complacency, a further ten of these most marginal seats in 2017 were Labour gains from the Conservatives with five more being Labour holds. In setting out an electoral strategy looking to make new gains from the Conservatives, it will also be critical to ensure those new gains and existing Labour marginals are held.

A substantial number of the most marginal seats are in Scotland; partially reflecting increased inter-party competition here where three party (and even four party) competition is the norm; unlike in England where all but the major parties have been significantly squeezed. This will be important for party strategies; failure to capture or hold on to marginal seats in Scotland means that more would have to be won in England, extending the target list further into places with stronger Conservative majorities such as Shipley and Lewes.

Others have offered accounts of the strategies Labour could follow to secure a majority at the next election, that is not the main aim here.[1] In this piece, the most 'winnable' seats are compared with the most vulnerable in terms of people living in them; to look at the types of places Labour needs to win to secure power and those where a further loss of ground to the Conservatives would be electorally costly.

DEFINING THE LABOUR BATTLEGROUND

In British politics, the mathematics of parliamentary majorities have become increasingly complicated: hung parliaments, coalitions or confidence and supply arrangements seem to be becoming more and more likely rather than the simple winner-takes-all that the first past the post system is known for. The magic number for a majority government is 326 seats of the 650 contested. The speaker and deputies do not participate in votes and so the number of seats 'in play' is 646; this is further complicated by elected members for Sinn Fein not taking up their seats. In 2017, this was seven seats and so further reduced the 'in play' seats to 639, making the number for a working majority 320 seats.

	Less than 1000	1000 to 3500	Over 3500
Conservative			
Hold	15	28	254
Gain from Labour	1	5	
Gain from LibDems		1	
Gain from SNP	1	4	7
Gain from UKIP			1
Labour			
Hold	5	10	211
Gain from Conservatives	10	9	9
Gain from LibDems		1	1
Gain from SNP	4	2	
LibDem			
Hold	1	1	2
Gain from Conservatives	1	1	3
Gain from SNP		2	1
SNP			
Hold	9	15	11
PC			
Hold	1		2
Gain from LD	1		
Green			
Hold			1

Table 1. After 2017: Marginal seats and type of battleground.

The current position in the Commons suggests that it would be considerably easier for Labour to form a working coalition, with the potential to draw on support from the SNP, PC, the Greens and the Liberal Democrats (the so-called 'progressive alliance') than for the Conservatives, whose only obvious allies remain the DUP. But coalitions are not currently popular with the electorate. Just 21 per cent of the electorate believe that 'coalitions are more effective than single party governments', while 62 per cent believed 'parties can't deliver on their promises' when in a coalition.[2] The experience of the

2010-15 Conservative/Liberal Democrat coalition suggests that the smaller partners are often those who suffer the most, but in a situation where the secondary partner was the SNP it is unclear how this might work out. Voters in England would be unable to 'punish' the smaller partner for unpopular compromises. Given the complexities of parliamentary competition, Labour's strategy must be to win outright (whilst recognising that there are several plausible paths to power that do not require all the target seats identified here to turn red on election night).

Analysis immediately following the election suggested that Labour need only win thirty-four (or if taken directly from the Conservatives twenty-nine) more seats to 'win' the next election.[3] Here I define the target seats as those needed for a workable parliamentary majority to avoid the analyses relying on the results of other constituency competitions (for example those in Scotland between the SNP and the Conservatives). This puts the fate of Labour in its own hands, and would ensure the kind of majority needed to implement radical policy propositions. A little like the England football team in the group stages of international competition (with apologies to Scottish, Welsh and Northern Irish readers for the analogy), it is much better to win all your own matches than rely on the results of others.

The 'target seats' are all marginals where the majority was less than 3500 votes and the Labour Party were in second place. This gives sixty-six target seats, two more than required to just pass the winning line and has the benefit of allowing one or two 'near misses' on the night. These sixty-six are compared with the thirty-six gains made in 2017; the fifteen seats where Labour is defending a majority of less than 3500 and all other Labour seats. Data is taken from official electoral returns and the 2011 Census of Population.

For analysis, the target seats are separated into seats in England and Wales and those in Scotland. Party competition in Scotland is different (Labour's target seats here are in competition with the SNP rather than the Conservatives) and as a result socio-demographics, political values and identity are connected to voting in different ways. The Scottish target seats are presented in a separate section, as despite this different character they are nonetheless crucial to the overall strategy.

There are two important caveats to this analysis. First, it is possible that the next election may occur under new constituency boundaries. Initial suggestions were that the new boundaries would be considerably less favourable to Labour,[4] but the changed political landscape after 2017 has also changed the potential impact of boundary changes with more recent assessments suggesting net losses of twenty seats for the Conservatives and seventeen for Labour (though also suggesting losses for the SNP, PC and the Liberal Democrats),[5] the net effect of which would change the position for the Conservatives from being eight seats short of a majority to being three seats short. Whilst the mathematics of victory would be different it is unlikely that overall the types of places needed for victory would change dramatically. It is also possible that the next election will occur before boundary changes are implemented.

Second, an assumption is made here about marginality of seats: seats where the margin of victory in 2017 was 3500 or under. As shown in Scotland in 2015 with the SNP's sweeping gains, in an era of rapidly changing political circumstances, with an electorate more volatile than ever, there is increasingly no such thing as a 'safe' seat. What this analysis does is give a sense of the types of places where Labour must win, and conversely must not lose, to have a workable majority to implement its vision 'for the many not the few'.

THE POLITICAL CHARACTERISTICS

Turning first to the political characteristics of these seats, figure 1 shows the average estimated leave vote across each group of constituencies.[6] This highlights the challenge facing the Labour party on perhaps the defining issue of our time; an issue which reflects not only attitudes to the EU but also deeper divides on a wider set of values too. In those seats in England and Wales that Labour gained in 2017, the average vote to leave is 47.5 per cent (thus overall these seats were in favour of remaining in the EU); this compares with 54.9 per cent for the target seats in England and Wales (Scottish target seats, shown in figure 6, are more pro-remain with an estimated leave vote of 35.4 percent) and especially starkly with the seats the party needs to defend where the average estimated leave vote was 63.5 per cent.

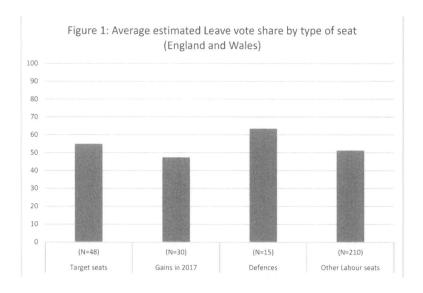

Figure 1: Average estimated Leave vote share by type of seat (England and Wales)

Matthew Goodwin, Maria Sobolewska and Rob Ford have argued that Jeremy Corbyn found a 'Third Way' on Brexit – 'Brexit Blairism' – which enabled Labour to gain in both remain and leave areas.[7] But it is unclear whether this can be sustained as the Brexit negotiations gather pace and divisions within the Parliamentary Labour Party are exposed. The 2017 gains were places where the remain vote was stronger and so may be vulnerable to a hardening of the party's Brexit position; but at the same time, there are seats which Labour held with small majorities where a softening of the Brexit position may lead to losses.

A similar picture emerges with the Ukip share of the vote in 2015 in these seats. As with the estimated leave vote, target seats and non-marginal Labour seats are similar but recent gains and marginal defences are quite different. Among the 2017 Labour gains, the average Ukip vote in 2015 was 10.1 per cent; in marginals Labour must defend it was 17.9 per cent. Whilst currently Ukip appears as something of a spent force in British politics, its core mission fulfilled, there remains a contradiction in some areas where the former Ukip voters are both in favour of left-wing economic policy and remain significantly socially conservative.[8] There remains space on the political landscape for a party appealing to these voters and this could be to the detriment of Labour in some areas.

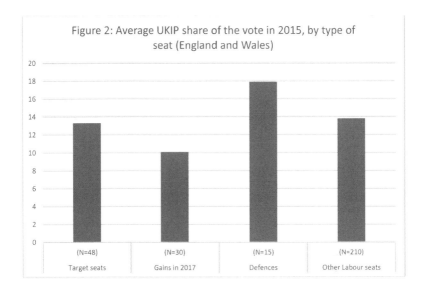

Figure 2: Average UKIP share of the vote in 2015, by type of seat (England and Wales)

A PARTY FOR THE YOUNG?

According to most reports, one of the defining characteristics of the 2017 election was the 'youthquake' and the suggestion often made is that this was the single biggest factor behind Labour's unexpectedly good performance.[9] Turnout rose among young voters with overwhelming support for Labour in the youngest age groups. Is it the case that the places Labour needs to win at the next election are 'young' places?

As Figure 3 shows, the seats Labour must win next time have the lowest proportion of 18-24 year-olds, whilst those it gained in 2017 have the highest. The marginal seats Labour must defend are similar to those they must win; both have lower proportions of young people than the other seats Labour already hold. This is also reflected at the other end of the age spectrum. The existing Labour seats have the lowest proportion of those aged sixty-five and over; while the targets and the defences both have higher proportions of these older voters.

These age profiles suggest that 'more of the same' may not be the best way forward in aiming to win sufficient seats for a working majority. To continue appealing to young voters may not be enough on its own, the seats with larger proportions of over-65s are likely to have been more affected by the presentation of social care issues during the campaign, Labour can't rely on the Conservatives failing to appeal to these voters again next time.

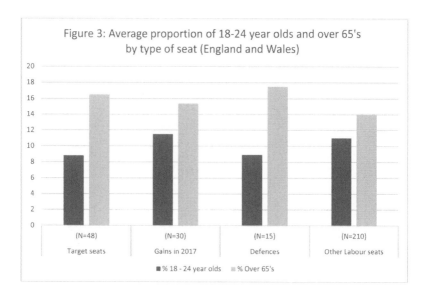

Figure 3: Average proportion of 18-24 year olds and over 65's by type of seat (England and Wales)

LABOUR AND THE WORKING CLASS

If Labour in 2017 gained more ground in the south than in its traditional northern heartlands this leads to questions about whether the party is 'losing' the working class, or perhaps leaving them behind as it tries to broaden its electoral appeal.

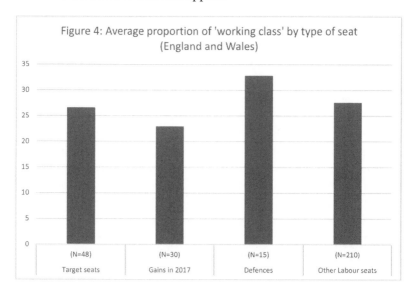

Figure 4: Average proportion of 'working class' by type of seat (England and Wales)

Figure 4 shows the proportion in 'working class' occupations (defined as the proportion in 'semi-routine' or 'routine' occupations in the ns-sec occupational classification) in each group of seats. Whereas in terms of age profile, target and defence seats appeared quite similar, they are more distinct when looking at the class profile. The new gains in 2017 are the least 'working class' areas here, with 22.9 per cent in routine or semi-routine occupations. Target seats are similar to existing Labour seats, with a little over a quarter in working-class occupations. Meanwhile, those Labour must defend have almost one in three in working class occupations.

This underscores the arguments already made that there are signs that the Labour Party is falling behind in previous areas of strength. This also poses a problem for an electoral strategy focussed on target seats. It is usually assumed that a party doing well enough to capture seats on its target list will also be doing well enough not to lose seats elsewhere. But the days of uniform swing are long since gone and there is a danger in any strategy that appeals to certain types of seats that it may be costly elsewhere.

NEW DIVIDES? EDUCATION AND DIVERSITY

Since the EU referendum, there has been much debate about the extent of 'new divides' in the electorate. Apart from values, which are not dealt with by the demographic data being used here, these new divisions are focused on education levels and ethnic diversity. Whilst there is a long history of ethnic minority groups voting Labour in Britain; the education divide is relatively new. In 2017, the Conservatives lost support in areas with higher proportions of people with degree level qualifications and appeared to also fall back from any gains made among ethnic minority voters in 2015.

Figure 5 highlights how different the seats Labour must defend are from other types of seats on these two measures. The average proportion of people holding a degree in these constituencies is just 10 per cent, compared with over 20 per cent in the new gains. This is a stark reflection of educational change and political values in the 'cosmopolitan' areas where students and graduates are more likely to be concentrated, compared with areas that have benefited only marginally from a rapidly expanding higher education sector. These places are also much less ethnically diverse than other Labour seats, new gains and target seats. Taking this with the class profiles in Figure 4, the seats Labour must defend in England and Wales are very much the 'white, working-class' places that were drivers of the vote to leave in the EU referendum.

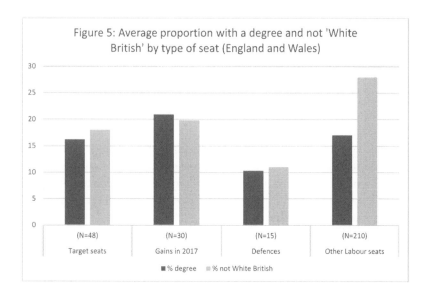

Figure 5: Average proportion with a degree and not 'White British' by type of seat (England and Wales)

The gains made in 2017 are in places with a higher proportion of those with degrees than the new targets, and the existing Labour seats, and both types of seat are also less ethnically diverse than current Labour seats; once again suggesting that simply looking for 'more of the same' types of gains as in 2017, will not be sufficient to win the next election. A broader appeal beyond places of high diversity and the university towns will be necessary to secure power.

SCOTLAND

The picture from Scotland is a little different. Figure 6 shows the key demographics broken down by target seats and 2017 gains.

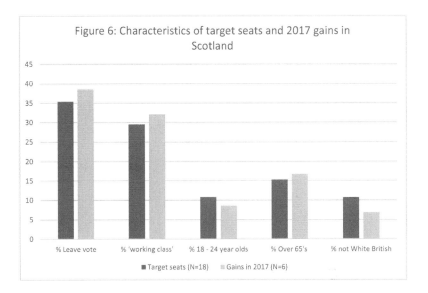

Figure 6: Characteristics of target seats and 2017 gains in Scotland

Whilst in England and Wales newly gained seats are likely to be younger and less 'working class' than the target seats, the new gains in Scotland are slightly older and have a slightly higher proportion of 'working class' occupations than the target seats there. They also have a higher estimated number of leave voters than the target seats there; though this is still notably below the proportion of leave voters in English and Welsh target seats and overall suggests these areas are pro-remain. This is a further reminder that the political landscape in Scotland is different, and whilst those target seats and new gains are central to a successful electoral strategy this would be best served by a distinctive Scottish Labour campaign.

A WINNING STRATEGY?

Writing for Policy Network, and based on a similar analysis of marginal constituencies, Patrick Diamond and Charlie Cadywould have suggested two strategies to take Labour forward into the next election.[10] There is the 'Bernie Sanders' strategy, of bringing together an electoral coalition of: the professional middle class; economically precarious younger voters; and the poorest groups on the very lowest incomes. This is as opposed to the 'Clem Atlee' strategy which seeks to build a stronger cross-class alliance for 'national renewal'.[11] The analysis presented here suggests the latter of these is more likely to produce a workable majority Labour government, though the former could well produce electoral gains sufficient to form a minority Labour government with the support of other parties. Exactly which groups of voters are needed to produce that broader coalition is contested and further complicated by problematic definitions of 'class', but a good starting point is to look not only at the places Labour needs to win but also those where the Conservatives are snapping at the heels of sitting Labour MPs.[12]

The seats Labour needs to win the next election are clearly not 'more of the same' types of seats that it gained in 2017; 'one more heave' is unlikely to be sufficient as after the gains in 2017, Labour already holds most of the places with well-educated and diverse populations. However, the seats needed are not too dissimilar to the types of constituencies Labour already holds, suggesting that an electoral strategy to appeal to these places need not alienate all other areas of Labour support.[13] But there is another danger. The places where Labour is most vulnerable (those with the smallest majorities) *are* distinctive from both seats gained in 2017 and the target seats. They have more older voters, with a higher than average proportion of white British residents, fewer voters at, or who have been to, university and more 'working-class' people.[14] Almost the definition of the 'left behind', these places are also at risk of being left behind by the Labour Party in its quest for electoral success. From a narrow electoral viewpoint, it is possible to take the perspective that this might be a price worth paying for eventual victory in the polls. But for a Labour Party led by Jeremy Corbyn with its 'for the many not the few' message to sacrifice the strong presence and force for hope it once had in these communities, surely the strategy must be more inclusive? Labour's road to power may have become easier after the June 2017 election but the politics of any such achievement remain unsettled.

NOTES

1. See for example Patrick Diamond and Charlie Cadywould 'Don't forget the middle', Policy Network, 3 July 2017; Craig Dawson 'Return to a two-horse race', Fabian Society, 21 June 2017.
2. Source: British Election Survey, 2015.

3. See George Eaton, 'Why a Labour majority at the next election has become far easier', *New Statesman*, 10 June 2017.

4. Stephen Bush, 'Why are boundary changes bad for Labour?', *New Statesman*, 12 February 2016.

5. New Constituency Boundaries, www.electoralcalculus.co.uk, 12 June 2017.

6. As estimated in Chris Hanretty, 'A real interpolation and the UK's referendum on EU membership', *Journal of Elections, Public Opinion and Parties*, 17 March 2017.

7. Matthew Goodwin, Maria Sobolewska and Rob Ford 'Corbyn's Brexit strategy may have paid off after all in 2017 election', www.theconversation.com, 26 June 2017.

8. See Paula Surridge 'Who's left?', www. medium.com, 24 June 2017.

9. Alan Travis and Caelinn Barr, 'Youthquake behind Labour election surge divides generations', *The Guardian*, 20 June 2017.

10. Patrick Diamond and Charlie Cadywould, 'Don't forget the middle', Policy Network, 3 July 2017. See also Charlie Cadywould 'Why Labour will need more than just "one more heave" to take power', *New Statesman*, 3 July 2017.

11. *Ibid.*, p3.

12. Owen Jones 'Armageddon hasn't happened', *The Guardian,* 6 July 2017.

13. A similar point is made by Owen Jones*, ibid.*

14. Based on the Office for National Statistics Ns-Sec classification of occupations.

Labour's Battleground Seats:
A Smart Campaign Guide

The next general election will be in 2022 under the Fixed Term Parliaments Act, unless an early election is called. To win an outright majority Labour needs to win an extra sixty-six seats plus hold on to all its existing seats. To win all sixty-six would require a 3.6 per cent swing to Labour, taking the 2017 vote as a baseline. A swing away from Labour to the Tories and SNP on the other hand, of just 0.98 per cent, would see Labour lose nineteen seats which currently have a majority of under 1000.[1]

Labour has committed itself to a 'Permanent Election' with Jeremy Corbyn and his shadow cabinet visiting all sixty-six marginals, to build Labour's support and the party has launched an appeal to fund such an initiative. The journalist and activist Owen Jones (@owenjones84) is also organising mass canvasses with huge support in key vulnerable Tory constituencies, including the seats currently held by Iain Duncan Smith and Boris Johnson. He will release information on Twitter about the next seats he is intending to visit.

Of course, the electoral terrain changes, but we have to start from somewhere.[2] Listed opposite and overleaf are the locations where a 'smart campaign' is necessary, one which prioritises both Labour's most winnable seats and those that could be lost with the smallest of swings against the party. These targets and defences are listed in rank order of swing required to win or save. For readers who would like to join in this 'smart campaign' also included are the local contact details for the Labour campaign in each target and each defence constituency.

TARGETS: THE MARGINAL SEATS LABOUR NEEDS TO WIN

Constituency	Held by	Majority	% Swing for Labour to Win	Local Labour Contact
1. Southampton Itchen	C	31	0.03%	@soton_labour
2. Glasgow South West	SNP	60	0.08%	@GlasgowLabour
3. Glasgow East	SNP	75	0.10%	@GlasgowLabour
4. Arfon	PC	92	0.16%	@WelshLabour
5. Airdrie & Shotts	SNP	195	0.26%	@AirdrieShottsLP
6. Pudsey	C	331	0.31%	@PudseyLabour
7. Hastings & Rye	C	346	0.32%	@HastingsRyeLab
8. Chipping Barnet	C	353	0.32%	@ChippingLabour
9. Thurrock	C	345	0.34%	@thurrocklabour
10. Lanark & Hamilton East	SNP	360	0.36%	@scottishlabour
11. Preseli Pembrokeshire	C	314	0.37%	@PembsLabour
12. Motherwell & Wishaw	SNP	318	0.38%	facebook.com/ LabourMotherwell
13. Inverclyde	SNP	364	0.49%	@InverclydeCLP
14. Calder Valley	C	609	0.52%	facebook.com/ CalderValleyLabour
15. Norwich North	C	507	0.55%	@NorwichLabour
16. Broxtowe	C	863	0.78%	@broxtowelabour
17. Stoke-on-Trent South	S	663	0.80%	@SouthPottsBLP
18. Telford	C	720	0.81%	@TelfordLabour
19. Dunfermline & Fife West	SNP	844	0.83%	@ScottishLabour
20. Bolton West	C	936	0.92%	@LabBoltonWest
21. Aberconwy	C	635	0.99%	@AberconwyLabour
22. Northampton North	C	807	1.00%	@Npton_Labour
23. Hendon	C	1072	1.03%	@HendonLabour
24. Mansfield	C	1057	1.05%	@mansfieldlabour
25. Middlesbrough South & Cleveland East	C	1020	1.07%	@borolabour
26. Milton Keynes South	C	725	1.34%	@MKLabourParty
27. Northampton South	C	1159	1.41%	@Npton_Labour
28. Pendle	C	1279	1.43%	@PendleLabour
29. Edinburgh North & Leith	SNP	1625	1.44%	edinburghlabour northernandleith.org.uk

Constituency	Held by	Majority	% Swing for Labour to Win	Local Labour Contact
30. Milton Keynes North	C	1915	1.50%	@MKLabourParty
31. Morecambe & Lunesdale	C	1399	1.53%	@LabourMorecambe
32. Finchley & Golders Green	C	1657	1.58%	@FGGLabour
33. Glasgow North	SNP	1060	1.58%	@ScottishLabour
34. Camborne & Redruth	C	1577	1.63%	@CRHLabour
35. Putney	C	1554	1.66%	@PutneyLabour
36. Harrow East	C	1757	1.73%	@HarrowLabour
37. Watford	C	2092	1.78%	@WatfordLabour
38. Copeland	C	1695	1.95%	@LabourCopeland
39. Morley & Outwood	C	2104	2.01%	@MorleyClp
40. Vale of Glamorgan	C	2190	2.04%	facebook.com/valeofglamorganlabour
41. Corby	C	2690	2.24%	corbyenclp1@gmail.com
42. Glasgow South	SNP	2027	2.27%	@ScottishLabour
43. Swindon South	C	2464	2.40%	@LabSouthSwindon
44. Worcester	C	2490	2.42 %	@WorcesterLabour
45. Crawley	C	2457	2.44 %	@crawleylabour
46. Blackpool North & Cleveleys	C	2023	2.47 %	@BNandCLabour
47. Dunbartonshire West	SNP	2288	2.60%	@ScottishLabour
48. Chingford & Woodford Green	C	2438	2.60%	@cwg_labour
49. Linlithgow & Falkirk East	SNP	2919	2.60 %	@ScottishLabour
50. Reading West	C	2876	2.78 %	@ReadingLabour
51. Paisley & Renfrewshire North	SNP	2613	2.80%	facebook.com/paisleylabour
52. Derbyshire North East	C	2861	2.84%	@DerbysLabour
53. Carlisle	C	2599	3.01%	@Labour_Carlisle
54. Southport	C	2914	3.04%	@SouthportLabour
55. Paisley & Renfrewshire South	SNP	2541	3.05%	facebook.com/paisleylabour
56. Glasgow Central	SNP	2267	3.15%	@ScottishLabour
57. Rossendale & Darwen	C	3216	3.21%	@LabourRossendale
58. Glasgow North West	SNP	2561	3.30%	@ScottishLabour
59. Truro & Falmouth	C	3792	3.35%	@TruroFalLabour

Constituency	Held by	Majority	% Swing for Labour to Win	Local Labour Contact
60. Na-H-Eileanan An Iar	SNP	1007	3.4%	facebook.com/ naheileanananiar labourparty
61. Scarborough & Whitby	C	3435	3.4%	www.labour4scarborough andwhitby.net
62. Walsall North	C	2601	3.41%	@WMLabour
63. Stevenage	C	3384	3.43%	@StevenageLabour
64. East Kilbride, Strathaven & Lesmahagow	SNP	3866	3.57%	@eklabour
65. Camarthen West & Pembrokeshire South	C	3110	3.68%	facebook.com/ cwasplabour
66. Livingston	SNP	3878	3.69%	@scottishlabour

DEFENCES: THE MARGINAL SEATS LABOUR NEEDS TO SAVE

Constituency	Labour Majority	% Swing against for Labour loss	Local Labour Contact
1. Kensington	20	0.03%	@KensingtonCLP
2. Dudley North	22	0.03%	facebook.com/ DudleyNorthLabour
3. Newcastle-under-Lyme	30	0.03%	@NUL_Labour
4. Crewe & Nantwich	48	0.04%	@CreweLabour
5. Canterbury	187	0.16%	@Labour4C
6. Barrow & Furness	209	0.22%	@Barrowclp
7. Keighley	249	0.24%	@KeighleyLabour
8. Rutherglen & Hamilton	265	0.26%	facebook.com/rutherglenclp West
9. Kirkcaldy & Cowdenbeath	25	0.28%	@LesleyLaird
10. Glasgow North East	242	0.38%	@PaulJSweeney
11. Ashfield	441	0.44%	@AshfieldLabour
12. Stroud	687	0.54%	@Stroud_Labour
13. Bishop Auckland	502	0.58%	@HelenGoodmanMP

Constituency	Labour Majority	% Swing against for Labour loss	Local Labour Contact
14. Peterborough	607	0.64%	@Labour4Pboro
15. Colne Valley	915	0.76%	@labourcv
16. Ipswich	831	0.81%	@IpswichLabour
17. Bedford	789	0.81%	@BedfordLabour
18. Stockton South	888	0.82%	@PaulWilliamsMP
19. Midlothian	885	0.98%	@DaniRowley

NOTES

1. All electoral data is from 'Battleground 2022', www.electionpolling.co.uk.
2. For full constituency profile details see 'UK election 2017: Full results', www.theguardian.com, 9 June 2017.

Corbyn's Effects, Further Reading and Other Resources of Hope

The best two existing introductions to Corbynism are *The Candidate: Jeremy Corbyn's Improbable Path to Power* by Alex Nunns and Richard Seymour's *Corbyn: The Strange Rebirth of Radical Politics*. Another good place to start is the free ebook, *Corbyn and the Future of Labour* available to download from www.versobooks.com. This was published immediately after Jeremy Corbyn was re-elected Labour leader in 2016, beating Owen Smith.

Reclaim Modernity: Beyond Markets Beyond Machines by Mark Fisher and Jeremy Gilbert brilliantly explains the potential of the post-neoliberal moment, and is available for free from www.compassonline.org.uk. A digest of Jeremy Gilbert's current and recent writing, mainly though not exclusively on Corbynism, can be found at www.jeremygilbertwriting.wordpress.com.

Many of the chapters in *The Corbyn Effect* suggest that the neoliberal consensus inherited from Thatcherism was never sufficiently challenged by Thatcher's Labour successors, Tony Blair and Gordon Brown. An understanding of Thatcherism's break with the post-war 1945-79 settlement is therefore vital. For the original *Marxism Today* debates on this, read *The Politics of Thatcherism* edited by Stuart Hall and Martin Jacques alongside Andrew Gamble's *The Free Economy and the Strong State*. A good update on the post-Thatcher Conservative Party is provided by Tim Bale's *The Conservative Party from Thatcher to Cameron*. Painful though it is, a daily visit to www.conservativehome.com provides insights into how the Tories are coping with the 2017 landslide-that-never-was.

Setting the post-2015 extraordinary growth of Labour Party membership in some kind of broader context, there is Peter Mair's *Ruling the Void: The Hollowing of Western Democracy* and Colin Crouch's *Post-Democracy*. New ideas on how to organise politically, arising from the Bernie Sanders' campaign are recorded in *Rules for Revolutionaries: How Big Organising Can Change Everything* by Becky Bond and Zack Exley. *Is the Party Over?* by Andra Adnan, published as another Compass free download at www.compasson-line.org.uk explores what a twenty-first century party might look like. The quarterly journal *Renewal*, www.renewal.org.uk, contains some of the brightest and boldest thinking on how the Labour Party should function, written in a way that could attract support from across the party.

Labour MP Jess Phillips is one of many from the Corbyn critical wing who needs to be involved in any such dialogue; her book, *Everywoman*, is full to bursting point with bold and imaginative thinking towards a feminised Labour Party. For an earlier indication of what such a party might look like, read *Beyond the Fragments: Feminism and the Making of Socialism* co-authored by Sheila Rowbotham, Lynne Segal and Hilary Wainwright; it is now out in an updated edition for a new generation, who are still undertaking the task of changing the left's organisational culture. From a social movement perspective, Paul Mason's *Why It's Still Kicking Off Everywhere* is an invaluable analysis of how social, economic and generational change now demands that we organise our politics in different ways, including within the Labour Party.

Gerry Hassan's website www.gerryhassan.com is a good place to start for coverage of Scottish politics. *A Nation Changed: The SNP and Scotland Ten Years On* edited by Hassan and Simon Barrow explain both the SNP's 2015 'Tartan Landslide' and their 2017 setback too. Mixing Scottish cultural politics with left-leaning nationalism, www.bellacaledonia.org.uk is both lively and thought-provoking. For a Scottish left perspective try Cat Boyd's weekly column in *The National*, which can be found, with much else, on Boyd's Twitter feed @kittycatboyd. *Scottish Left Review* describes itself as 'a journal of the left in Scotland' and is rightly pluralist in its definition of what that means from Labour to the SNP left, and inside and outside of both parties too: www.scottishleftreview.org.

For an introduction to the work of Ralph Miliband, read the collection *Class War Conservatism and Other Essays*, and Miliband's classic work on the Labour Party, *Parliamentary Socialism*. Hilary Wainwright's *Labour: A Tale of Two Parties* was at least in part a sort of update, published at the high point of 1980s Bennism. Her new book, due out February 2018, *New Politics from the Left* has been written to deepen our understanding of the contradictions and possibilities in Labourism. *Socialist Register* is published annually and remains another key source of current new left thinking.

Naomi Klein's *No Logo* was one of the first books to explore the meaning and impact of branding. *Get Real: How To See Through the Hype, Spin and Lies of Modern Life* by Eliane Glaser connects this kind of analysis to current everyday examples and experiences, but also draws the necessary conclusions about how the way in which politics is conducted and consumed is affected too.

Walls Come Tumbling Down: The Music and Politics of Rock against Racism, 2-Tone and Red Wedge is author Daniel Rachel's wonderful history of three vital collisions of the political with the musical. Co-founders of Rock Against Racism Roger Huddle and Red Saunders in their book *Reminiscences of RAR: Rocking Against Racism 1976-79* have done a fine job recording the story of one of those collisions. Dave Randall's *Sound System: The Political Power of Music* combines the use of these and other examples to make an argument for an ongoing all-embracing musical movement of resistance. All of this gained contemporary relevance in 2017 with #Grime4Corbyn, and Dan Hancox's vivid interpretation of grime, *Stand Up Tall: Dizzee Rascal and the Birth of Grime*, helps make sense of the music for both those familiar and unfamiliar with it. *New Ethicities and Urban Culture* by Les Back offers a sociological study of the kinds of communities out of which grime has emerged.

Sue Goss's *Open Tribe* makes a powerful case for pluralism as an essential value in the unfolding development of Corbynism. The outright rejection of any sort of 'Progressive Alliance' by Corbyn and his allies was for some a limiting factor in Corbynism's potential. Making the case for it was Jeremy Gilbert's *The Progressive Alliance: Why Labour Needs It*, still available, free from www.compassonline.org.uk.

Coupled with pluralism, any seriously radical project must be futurist too. The left is very good at looking to the past: 1945, 1917, the Suffragettes, Chartists, Tolpuddle, Levellers, Diggers and more. But it struggles to look to the future. Paul Mason's *Postcapitalism: A Guide to the Future* is an excellent reversal of that bad habit, while *Inventing the Future: Postcapitalism and a World Without Work* by Nick Srnicek and Alex Williams offers a similar analysis. Sophie Raworth's *Doughnut Economics: Seven Ways to Think Like a Twenty-First Century Economist* is likewise direct with its injunctions to rethink the present, for the future.

An earlier effort to address the future was the 'New Times' debate from the magazine *Marxism Today*. This was collected together as *New Times: The Changing Face of Politics in the 1990s*, edited by Stuart Hall and Martin Jacques. More recent work on this is *After Neoliberalism: The Kilburn Manifesto*, edited by Stuart Hall, Doreen Massey and Michael Rustin.

The best single body of work on the changes in production and class relations at the turn of the twentieth century, and what this means for a next left, is the trilogy of books written by Michael Hardt and Antonio Negri, beginning with *Empire*, then *Multitude* and concluding with *Commonwealth*. For regular insights into Labour politics originating from broadly this kind of perspective read Phil Burton-Cartledge's blog www.averypublicsociologist.blogspot.co.uk.

Paul Gilroy's *After Empire: Melancholia or Convivial Culture?* remains not only a classic but also an unsettling account of race and Britishness. Satnam Virdee's *Racism, Class and the Racialized Outsider* frames this intersection in terms of the political outcomes around immigration on the left and the right. *The End of Tolerance* by Arun Kundnani and by the same author *The Muslims are Coming!* trace how these outcomes have been decisively shaped post-9/11 by the ill-fated 'war on terror' and the resultant growth of Islamophobia. Conversations about this have also been dominated in recent years by the unfolding horrors of an international refugee crisis on an unprecedented scale, which has provoked both the most generous of humanitarian solidarity and the ugliest forms of right-wing racist reaction. Patrick Kingsley's *The New Odyssey* tells this story very well. The Institute of Race Relations, www.irr.org.uk, has for years been – and continues to be – a hugely important resource on all matters of race and racism. New, younger initiatives have also developed in its wake, and sometimes under its influence. One of the best is Media Diversified at www.mediadiversified.org with a rich mix of culture, politics and campaigning.

Syriza: Inside the Labyrinth is Kevin Ovenden's excellent introduction both to the politics of Syriza today and the political contexts which led to its emergence and eventual replacement of Pasok as Greece's dominant left party.

Against Meritocracy: Culture, Power and Myths of Mobility by Jo Littler is the definitive work on one of the abiding myths of the neoliberal era, which has afflicted both Tory and Labour policy-making. It deserves to be read alongside *The Spirit Level* by Richard Wilkinson and Kate Pickett, which was one of the first books to puncture that particular myth. Probably the most prolific author on this key subject is Danny Dorling: www.dannydorling.org has information about all of his latest books, publications and articles.

Chantal Mouffe and Íñigo Errejón's *Podeomos: In the Name of the People* is a conversation between them about how one of the most exciting of Europe's political parties was formed and how it has come so close, in such a short time, to taking power. *Politics in a Time of Crisis: Podemos and the Future of a Democratic Europe* by the leader of Podemos, Pablo Iglesias, makes a compelling case for the broader relevance for the European left of all that Podemos has achieved. Edited by Catarína Principe and Bhaskar Sunkara, *Europe in Revolt* consists of a wide range of articles detailing the state of these varied parties and movements of Europe's outside left.

The beginnings of Ernesto Laclau and Chantal Mouffe's theoretical work on populism can be found in their book *Hegemony and Socialist Strategy: Towards a Radical Democratic Politics*. A theory of populism was further developed by Laclau in his book *On Populist Reason* and by Mouffe both in her book *On the Political* and her widely-circulated writings, which make the case for a left-wing populism. Jan-Werner Müller's *What is Populism?* and *The Populist Explosion* by John B. Judis each feature an international perspective on this political label that appears to be applied to everyone from Trump and Farage to Tsipras and Corbyn.

A Friday morning visit to @BritainElects provides weekly updates on how Labour is doing in council by-elections and all other polls. Paula Sturridge is an academic who does the hard work of analysing all the data to provide an honest appraisal (see @p_surridge). A decent modelling site which aggregates all the data to predict seat-by-seat results is www.electoralcalculus.co.uk. Momentum ran a hugely successful 'My Nearest Marginal' initiative during the 2017 general election twinning activists with their nearest winnable Labour seat: www.mynearestmarginal.com.

Mark Perryman's keynote essay in this volume adapts the title of Stuart Hall's classic essay on the eve of Thatcherism 'The Great Moving Right Show'. The best single volume of Stuart Hall's work is *Selected Political Writings: The Great Moving Right Show and Other Essays* edited by Sally Davison, David Featherstone, Michael Rustin and Bill Schwarz. For a similar insight into Stuart Hall's huge impact on cultural studies a companion volume of his lectures *Cultural Studies 1983: A Theoretical Perspective*, edited by Jennifer Daryl Slack and Lawrence Grossberg is also recommended. *Without Guarantees: Essays in Honour of Stuart Hall* edited by Paul Gilroy, Lawrence Grossberg and Angela McRobbie is a wide-ranging collection from a great variety of authors detailing Hall's huge influence on their work and subjects. Following his death in 2014 the Stuart Hall Foundation, was established by his colleagues and friends. Their website www.stuarthallfoundation.org is a source for a superb range of ideas and work which continue to be inspired by Stuart Hall.

To sustain interest in, and maintain the momentum (*sic*) of the Corbyn effect, a daily Twitter update is an essential treat. Richard Seymour's Twitter feed @leninology is an excellent digest of news and analysis from a broadly Corbynite perspective. Also useful in this context are @owenjones84, @misselliemae and @paulmasonnews. The website www.newsocialist.org.uk publishes strategic thinking on how to take the Corbynite agenda forward. To keep up with the activities of the Labour centre-right: a daily dose, if you can stand it, of @LukeAkehurst for Labour First and @RichardAngell for Progress.

Turning Corbyn's effect into reality will take ideas matched by initiative. Plenty of both are provided by the campaigning thinktank Compass which grew originally out of the best of Labour's soft left, but has developed into something much broader and no less radical as a result, see www.compassonline.org.uk.

'A new kind of politics' is what Momentum promises, and has begun to deliver; find out more via www.peoplesmomentum.com and follow @peoplesmomentum. Initiated by Momentum, The World Transformed is a fantastically ambitious festival of ideas both run alongside Labour Conference and sometimes on tour too, www.theworldtransformed.org and @TWT_NOW.

Notes on Contributors

Mark Perryman has edited a wide range of books on left politics. He is a regular contributor to a range of publications including the *Morning Star*, the Labour left website *Left Futures*, *Open Democracy*, Compass, and *Counterfire*. Mark is also the co-founder of self-styled 'sporting outfitters of intellectual distinction' aka Philosophy Football. In the 1980s he worked for, wrote for and was on the editorial board of *Marxism Today*. Mark is a member of Lewes Constituency Labour Party and of Momentum. **@phil_football**

Jeremy Gilbert is Professor of Political and Cultural Theory at the University of East London. He is editor of *New Formations: A Journal of Culture, Theory, Politics*, and over the past two years has written regularly on the shaping of Corbynism for *The Guardian* as well as *Open Democracy*, the *Fabian Review* and elsewhere. He is a member of Walthamstow CLP, was on the founding committee of Momentum and remains a member, as well as also being on the Compass Management Committee. **@jemgilbert**

Andrew Gamble is Professor of Politics at the University of Sheffield and Emeritus Professor of Politics at the University of Cambridge. His most recent books are *Crisis Without End? The Unravelling of Western Prosperity* and *Can the Welfare State Survive?* During the 1980s, Andrew was one of the pioneers of understanding Thatcherism in the magazine *Marxism Today*.

Jessica Garland was formerly a senior political advisor with several years' experience working in the Westminster Parliament. She is currently a doctoral researcher at the University of Sussex working on political party organisation and membership. She has written on this subject for both *The Political Quarterly* and *Renewal: A Journal of Social Democracy*. Jessica is a member of Hove and Portslade Constituency Labour Party. **@jessicajgarland**

Gerry Hassan is a writer, commentator and researcher on Scottish and UK politics, and on issues of power, democracy and social change. He is editor, co-author and author of over two dozen books including the bestselling *Caledonian Dreaming: The Quest for a Different Scotland* and *Scotland the Bold: How Our Nation Has Changed and Why There is No Going Back* – the last of which examines Scotland and the UK after the independence referendum and Brexit. Gerry's latest book, co-edited with Simon Barrow is *A Nation Changed? The SNP and Scotland Ten Years On*. He is currently writing a history of the Labour Party and Britishness. **@gerryhassan**

Des Freedman is Professor of Media and Communications at Goldsmiths, University of London. An active trade unionist, he is secretary of Goldsmiths UCU as well as a founding member of the Media Reform Coalition. Des writes widely on media activism and media power, including for *The Conversation*, *Open Democracy* and *Counterfire*. His most recent book on the subject is *The Contradictions of Media Power*. **@lazebnic**

Hilary Wainwright is a longstanding socialist-feminist activist and author. Her books include, co-authored with Lynne Segal and Sheila Rowbotham, *Beyond The Fragments: Feminism and the Making of Socialism*, as well as *Labour: A Tale of Two Parties* and *Reclaim the State: Experiments in Popular Democracy*, Hilary's latest book *A New Politics from the Left* will be published in early 2018. Founder and co-editor of the magazine *Red Pepper*, Hilary is a member of Hackney South and Shoreditch Constituency Labour Party, and Momentum. **@hilarypepper**

Eliane Glaser is both a Senior Lecturer in the College of Liberal Arts at Bath Spa University and an Associate Research Fellow in the Department of English and Humanities at Birkbeck College, University of London. A Compass Associate, Eliane has also written for the New Economics Foundation and the Institute for Public Policy Research. Author of *Get Real: How to See Through the Hype, Spin and Lies of Modern Life*, Eliane's new book on 'anti-politics' is a defence of ideology, authority and the state, which will be published in 2018. **@elianeglaser**

Monique Charles completed her PhD at Warwick University focusing on race, spirituality, class, gender and music as it relates to #grime. Her book chapter entitled 'Grime Central! Subterranean Ground-In Grit Engulfing Manicured Mainstream Spaces' in Kehinde Andrews and Lisa Amanda Palmer (eds), *Blackness in Britain* was one of the first academic articles to focus specifically on grime music and culture. Monique has also written on #Grime4Corbyn for both *The Conversation* and the *New Statesman*. **@Neake81**

Sue Goss works as a strategic advisor, coach and systems leadership consultant for a not-for-profit employee-owned organisation. She is a member of the Compass management committee, and of the editorial group of *Renewal: A Journal of Social Democracy*. Her books on politics include *Open Tribe* and with Hetan Shah, *Democracy and the Public Realm*. Sue writes and speaks widely on the subject of public service reform and local government. She has been a member of the Labour Party since the 1980s. **@suegossthoughts**

Phil Burton-Cartledge is a Lecturer in Sociology at the University of Derby. His research interests include social theory, social movements and the critique of political economy. He is an active member of Stoke-on-Trent Central Constituency Labour Party and a regular contributor to the *Left Futures* website. **@philbc3.**

Maya Goodfellow is a freelance writer focussing mostly on UK politics, race, migration and gender. As well as being a columnist for *Media Diversified*, Maya's writing appears regularly in *The Guardian*, the *New Statesman* and *LabourList*. She is also a PhD candidate researching race and racism in the UK at SOAS, University of London. Maya is a member of West Ham Constituency Labour Party. **@mayagoodfellow**

Marina Prentoulis is a Senior Lecturer in Politics and Media at the University of East Anglia. As a UK spokesperson for Syriza, Marina has given numerous interviews for broadcast media on Greek politics including on *Newsnight*, *The Andrew Marr Show* and *Daily Politics*. A regular writer on Syriza and issues around left populism for *Open Democracy*, *The Guardian* and *Soundings*, Marina is a member of the Labour Party. **@prentoulis**

Jo Littler is the author of *Against Meritocracy, Culture, Power and Myths of Mobility*. She is Reader in the Centre for Culture and Creative Industries in the Department of Sociology at City, University of London and in the Editorial Collective of *Soundings*. Jo is a member of Walthamstow Constituency Labour Party and Momentum. **@littler_jo**

James Doran first coined the term 'Pasokification' in 2013, a concept that has been widely-debated ever since. He has written on this and other Labour Party-related subjects for *Novara Media*, *LabourList*, *Counterfire* and *The Pileus*. An active campaigner for co-operatives and workplace democracy, James is a Labour and Co-operative Party member in Darlington Constituency Labour Party, formerly a Labour Party branch secretary and a member of Momentum. **@doran_j**

Jack Kellam is a postgraduate student at Mansfield College, University of Oxford, working on the contemporary relevance of hegemony theory. He has written on populism and other subjects for *Novara Media*. Jack is a member of both Oxford East Constituency Labour Party and Momentum. **@KellamJack**

Paula Surridge is Senior Lecturer in the School of Sociology, Politics and International Studies, University of Bristol. Paula's research includes the application of advanced analysis techniques, including multi-level modelling and confirmatory factor analysis, using large-scale secondary data sources. She has been applying all of this to the 2017 general election results. Based on this work, her analysis of increased voter turnout in 2017 was widely cited including in *The Guardian*, the *New Statesman* and the *Huffington Post*. **@p_surridge**

Acknowledgements

The Corbyn Effect began life in the immediate aftermath of Jeremy Corbyn's re-election as Labour leader in 2016. When the February 2017 Copeland and Stoke Central by-elections were called, fearing the worst, the book was put on hold. One win and one defeat meant we continued but with the word 'crisis' inserted (temporarily, thank goodness) into a new subtitle. Then an early general election was called; so, once again fearing the worst and anticipating another Labour leadership election, the book was not only put on hold but also earmarked for likely cancellation. The 8 June election, and the campaign leading up to it, changed all that. I owe many thanks to all contributors who turned around rewritten and in some cases entirely new chapters so quickly. And special thanks to those authors whose original chapters, after all these changes, I wasn't able to include in this final version: Glen O'Hara, David Rosenberg, Matt Bolton and Harry Pitts.

Lawrence and Wishart, as a politically committed publisher, small in scale but large in ambition, are a joy to publish with. Katharine Harris, Kirsty Capes, Lynda Dyson and Sally Davison have helped see this book through from beginning to end. Peter Brawne and Sophie Gibson are two of the most imaginative designers I have ever had the pleasure to work with, and thanks go to them for the superb cover design. Thanks to Jason Bye and Geoff Dexter for the cover photos too.

Jane Foot, Adam Geaery, Paul Jonson and Heather Wakefield provided invaluable feedback as advance readers for my chapter 'The Great Moving Left Show' and hugely helped with the writing of its final version.

In the summer of 2016, the #LewesJeremyforLabour group was formed for the leadrship re-election campaign. Those who came together for this inspired my belief in the 'Corbyn effect' and have sustained it too through any bouts of pessimism. Thanks to Tony Adams, Toby Aisbitt, Belinda Chapman, Judith Colquhoun, Emilia Bolin-Ransom, Nicky Bryant, Charlie Dobres, Karen Dobres, Peter Faulkner-Murphy, Angela Fisher, Newell Fisher, Jamie Freeman,

Stevie Freeman, Matthew Geraghty, Lin Heyworth, Keane, Maggie Lambert, Liz McVicar, Andrea Peters, Jon Redford, Naomi Salaman, Zuky Serper, Jane Thomas, Sean Tunney, Lily Waugh, Chris Smith and Ellie Woodruff-Bryant in particular.

The Lewes branch of the Labour Party has pioneered a culture of open discussion meetings which, for a small market town in East Sussex, has in a remarkably short space of time established both a large audience and a significant impact for free-thinking ideas from the left. This has been another stage in convincing me of the power of the 'Corbyn effect'. Thanks to convenor Gill Short and the organising group Denzil Jones, Sue Davies, Joy Mercer, Maggie Symons and Sheila O'Sullivan, who have all been kind enough to welcome my involvement and tolerate my occasional disagreements. Thanks also to Ann Pettifor, James Meadway, Andrew Simms, Steve Bell, Josh Sutton, Denis Campbell, Daniel Rachel, Stewart Lansley and others who joined us for these discussions and aided considerably my own thinking on Corbynism.

The Lewes branch, like many other Labour Party branches and CLPs, has had to accommodate rapid growth ever since the Corbyn surge. The experience of coping with this (and sometimes not coping with it) has been a learning curve towards where the Corbyn effect might end up. Richard Baskott, Nick Belcher, Emily Clarke, Linda Drabble, Arthur Hammond, Vincent Tickner, Pam Lewis, Will Perry, Philippa Thompson, Sheila Massey, and Gaby Weiner have done more than most, sometimes with reservations and misgivings admittedly, to turn that curve upwards towards positive outcomes rather than downwards towards negatives ones. Again, thanks.

For much of May, I helped organise charabancs and convoys to the Brighton constituencies of Hove and Portslade, and Kemptown in the vain hope of saving one seat and winning the other. The energy and imagination of both campaigns, the enthusiasm of those who joined in from Lewes, the welcome provided by Labour Party members of every background and viewpoint, the eventual triumphant re-election of Peter Kyle and election of Lloyd Russell-Moyle, without that great lot this book wouldn't have been worth writing. Huge thanks. All of this was an early indicator of the potential too for what I call 'smart campaigning'. Next time we'll head to Hastings and Rye; Amber Rudd has no idea what's coming her way.

A range of places have been generous enough to provide the space for me to air my views on all things Corbyn since 2015. Special thanks to the *Morning Star* newspaper, the websites *Open Democracy*, *Left Futures* and *Counterfire* and the can-do thinktank Compass.

My ideas and whatever abilities I might have as an author and editor of books on left politics owe a huge debt of early influence to the magazine *Marxism Today* in my twentysomething and thirtysomethings. These were ideals and experiences I never forgot, although they took a bit of a knocking under the sorry experience of New Labour. Thanks in particular to Martin Jacques, Beatrix Campbell, Ros Brunt and Eric Hobsbawm for the education and inspiration you provided me, and I'm sure none of them will mind me saying that the very biggest thanks of all go to Stuart Hall.

Since Jeremy Corbyn was elected Labour leader, he has had to face a tidal wave of criticism, more than enough to plant the seeds of doubt in the minds of even his most convinced supporters. Thanks therefore to Owen Jones, John Harris, Neal Lawson, Ellie Mae O'Hagan and Richard Seymour; while they do not always agree with Corbyn, blind faith is not what is required, they are always committed to the possibility of change. Other commentators have had an unquestioning belief that everything and everyone connected with Corbyn is absolutely useless and that they are dragging Labour towards certain defeat and disintegration; this has been much less appreciated. It was all topped off by Nick Cohen's pre-election advice Corbyn's supporters: 'In my respectful opinion, your only honourable response will be to stop being a fucking fool by changing your fucking mind'.[1] I give no thanks to Nick and his sorry lot of co-thinkers.

Closer to home I have appreciated, if sometimes been rankled by, Anne Coddington's suspicion and cynicism towards the Corbyn effect. Choosing to disagree isn't always easy, but we can all learn something from that experience. Thank you for this, and everything. Edgar Coddington-Perryman sometimes confuses Jeremy Corbyn with Michael Rosen, both have got beards and are a similar age, after all, and seeing both in the same room would quite possibly be Edgar's worst nightmare. Nevertheless, he joined me on 8 June in Kemptown, to do the last evening's round of getting out the vote. This was without doubt for me the best and happiest experience of the 2017 general election. To top it all off, he reliably informed me after canvassing that he'd just eaten 'the best cheese toastie in the world, Daddy' at The Bevenden, a community-owned pub in the heart of the constituency. Bliss.

But the final word of thanks must be, of course, for Jeremy Corbyn. It is not personality cultist to say that without Corbyn, none of this would be possible. Thank you, and I hope to see you outside Number Ten with the flag-waving crowds, prime minister Corbyn, sometime soon.

Mark Perryman, September 2017.

NOTES

1. Nick Cohen, 'Don't tell me you weren't warned about Corbyn', *The Guardian*, 19 March 2017.

Index